CW00864672

THE UNITED STATES CONSTITUTION AND THE BIBLE CONFLICT OR COMPROMISE

Exercise Your "Rights"
as a Citizen Christian
Pursuing the
American Dream

MORGAN CHAWAWA

WestBow Press books may be ordered through booksellers or by contacting:

WestBow Press
A Division of Thomas Nelson & Zondervan
1663 Liberty Drive
Bloomington, IN 47403
www.westbowpress.com
1 (866) 928-1240

ISBN: 978-1-9736-5382-0 (sc)
ISBN: 978-1-9736-5381-3 (hc)
ISBN: 978-1-9736-5383-7 (e)

Library of Congress Control Number: 2019901794

Print information available on the last page.

WestBow Press rev. date: 2/20/2019

DEDICATION

To my God almighty, whose grace gave me opportunity, passion, and enthusiasm to write this book and share with the world the kingdom perspective on issues addressed by the US Constitution.

As I wrote this book, so many generously gave their time to help me.

I thank my wife, Tine Chawawa, and our children, Elizabeth, Vimbai, and Jonathan for the moral and spiritual support that was critical for the success of this project.

I thank Dr. Stewart, chancellor of Immanuel Baptist Theological College, in Georgia, for giving me the opportunity to realize this book and for his support and many helpful suggestions and discussions.

Special thanks to Dr. Musin, president of Atlanta School of Biblical Studies, for his advice, supervision, guidance, and encouragement. Without those, this book would not have been possible. In particular, I thank him for numerous discussions we had and on his expertise in biblical matters.

Further thanks go to Larry, Billy, Gorkem, Anette and Mr. Khan for their help and suggestions regarding some of the issues covered by the book.

Pastor Abass, I am grateful for the sleepless nights you spent typing the manuscript.

CONTENTS

PREFACE

Fifty years ago, Dr. Martin Luther King Jr. addressed a crowd of 250,000 people gathered in Washington, DC, and called on the people of the United States and the government to live up to the principles espoused in the Declaration of Independence.

Dr. King was not a champion of civil rights as much as he was a champion of God-given rights. He made clear in his famous address that the liberty and equality before the law that he was demanding did not originate in human government. The right to equality before the law is not only a civil right but also a right ordained by God and therefore a right civil government has a duty to protect and defend.

Dr. King quoted the Old Testament books of Amos and Isaiah. He also made subtle references to Psalm 30 and the New Testament book of Galatians. When he said he hoped his children would be judged not by the "color of their skin but by the content of their character," he was applying God's fixed, eternal standard, not a malleable man-made one.

Unlike many modern-day welfare-state proponents, Dr. King's demands were right because they were based on a righteous pretense. In debate about private and public policy, we must remember that God created only one race—the human race. Therefore, all elevation or denigration of individuals or groups based on skin color is immoral and shameful because it violates the law of nature and of nature's God.

Many Christians face the dilemma of choosing between their rights as citizens of America and as citizens of God's kingdom in their daily decisions and interaction with others. The two are intertwined in many ways, but the choices we make may determine how we live our lives as citizens of the United States and as children of the Living God because a lot hinges on this knowledge. The Constitution provides civil and political rights to all citizens of the United States. These are rights that protect individuals' freedom from infringement by the government, social organizations, and individuals. They ensure one's ability to participate in the civil and political life of the United States without discrimination or repression. There is no need to challenge the Constitution but to help Christians live a full and active life as citizens of the United States and as citizens of God's kingdom: "I will behave myself wisely" (Psalm 101:2).

The Bible or The Word demonstrates that Christians are citizens of two realms—earthly and spiritual—and they have rights and responsibilities in both spheres. As citizens of heaven (Philippians 3:20), Christians are commanded to be obedient to the Lord Jesus (Exodus 20:1–5). Our Lord's instruction to "render therefore unto Caesar the things which be Caesar's and unto God the things which be God's" (Luke 20:25) means giving ultimate allegiance only to God. It means paying our taxes, but it means much more. The apostle Paul instructs us that as Christians, we have the responsibility to be good citizens of the state "for conscience sake" because God has ordained government to punish and restrict evildoers and to reward and protect moral behavior (Romans 13:1–7). Christians are to support civil government unless the authorities require them to support or do evil in direct contradiction to their ultimate allegiance to their heavenly Father.

Christians are also commanded by Jesus to be the salt of the earth and the light of the world (Matthew 5:13–16). This involves citizen Christians in active engagement with the world persevering as salt and light. Thus, the responsibilities of citizen Christians include not just obedience to the state but also involvement in society.

The Baptist Faith and Message confession of faith affirms this call to involvement with the world.

> "All Christians are under obligation to seek to make the will of Christ supreme in our own lives and in human society ... In the spirit of Christ, Christians should oppose ... every form of greed, selfishness, and vice ... seek to bring industry, government, and society as a whole under the sway of the principles of righteousness, truth, and brotherly love." The 2000 Baptist Faith & Message

This statement clarifies our responsibilities as Christians and our rights as citizens. When we bring our religious and moral convictions into the marketplace of ideas and involve ourselves in the political arena, we are standing solidly in the best of our traditions as Americans and Baptists. Far too often in recent decades, we have allowed ourselves to be driven from the arena of debate by false understandings and misleading applications of church-state separation and religious liberty.

Jesus Christ is the King and Lord of the Kingdom of God: "And he hath on his vesture and on his thigh a name written, King Of Kings, And Lord Of Lords" (Revelation. 19:16). The Word says that when you receive Christ into your life as Savior and Lord, you are born again, born into the family of God, a chosen people. As such, you are a citizen of the Kingdom of God a holy nation. "In reply Jesus declared, 'Verily verily, I say unto thee, except a man be born again, he cannot see the Kingdom'" (John 3:3).

The Bible represents a real kingdom with privileges for its citizens, a constitution of sorts, statutes, and laws and is a monarchy. This government, led by the return of Christ the King and His true disciples (those who obey Christ) will rule over all the nations on earth for a thousand years: "The kingdoms of this world are become the kingdoms of our Lord, and of his Christ" (Revelation 11:15).

As a follower of Christ, you are expected to learn how to live on earth in a manner consistent with your royal status, and you are expected to obey your King and His teachings.

> If ye continue in my word, then are ye my disciples indeed. (John 8:31)
>
> If ye love me, keep my commandments. (John 14:15).
>
> If a man love me, he will keep my words. (John 14:23)
>
> Abide in me and I in you. (John 15:4).
>
> If ye keep my commandments, ye shall abide in my love. (John 15:10)
>
> And this is his command, that we should believe on the name of his Son Jesus Christ, and love one another, as he gave us His commandment. And he that keepeth his commandments dwelleth in him, and he in them. And

> hereby we know that he abideth in us, by the Spirit which he hath given us. (1 John 3:23–24)

The Bible is God's handbook for humans that defines reality—principles of truth concerning the ways things really are. The gospel of Christ was His teaching on how we can be reconciled with God and restored to humanity's original nature and the Kingdom/heaven, the government that rules heaven and all God's creation. "And Jesus went about all Galilee, teaching in their synagogues, and preaching the gospel of the kingdom, and healing all manner of sickness and all manner of disease among the people" (Matthew 4:23). "For unto us a child is born, unto us a son is given, and the government shall be upon his shoulder" (Isaiah 9:6). God's Government rests on Jesus Christ who is our Lord and Savior, who is the Head of all on earth and heaven!

The Bible also says those who make Christ both Savior and Lord become God's children, so one would think it wise to understand the kingdom, its culture, and its government because in a kingdom, one's rewards are tied to obedience to the King, Jesus Christ, who said, "If ye continue in my word, then are ye my disciples indeed; And ye shall know the truth, and the truth shall make you free" (John 8:31–32). "Jesus answered and said unto him, If a man love me, he will keep my words: and my Father will love him, and we will come unto him, and make our abode with him" (John 14:23). This is the first issue of a new series on

Citizenship in the Kingdom of God

This book will shed light on key principles of truth in the Kingdom and share practical insights on some incredible implications of this reality on those who are citizens of the United States, believe Christ is the Son of God, and have put their trust in Him as Savior and Lord. Does that sound strange? That's because Americans do not understand the kingdom form of government and most churches are not teaching their congregations about the Bible as Christ instructed them to do.

Differences between a Representative Democracy and the Bible

America is a Representative democracy, but God's government is a monarchy. In the United States, we have come to believe that representative democracy is the best form of government. This is true only because we live in a world where most people are controlled by their sinful nature and create an environment of greed, self-dealing, and corruption; Representative Democracy creates checks and balances to mitigate those evils. However, a kingdom form of government is much superior if it is led by a righteous king or queen. Let's look at some reasons.

- The kingdom form of government is the natural order of things and is how the universe is governed.
- The primary focus of a righteous king is the well-being of the people under his authority.
- As a citizen of the kingdom, you are under the protection of the king and his kingdom.
- Decisions are based on truth and what is right, not on what is politically or personally in the best interest of a person or party.
- It is more efficient and nimble.
- It creates order, focus, and consistency.
- You have freedom and rewards if you obey the king and adhere to his culture.

> For by him were all things created, that are in heaven, and that are in earth, visible and invisible, whether they be thrones, or dominions, or principalities, or powers: all things were created by him, and for him. And he is before all things, and by him all things consist. And he is the head of the body, the church: who is the beginning, the firstborn from the dead: that in all things he might have preeminence. (Colossians 1:16–18)

> And Jesus came and spake unto them, saying, "All power is given unto me in heaven and in earth." (Matthew 28:18)

> "For He 'thou hast put all things under his feet.'" (Ephesians 1:22)

> Now when it says that 'everything' has been put under him, it is clear that this does not include God himself, who put everything under Christ. (1 Corinthians 15:27)

> Jesus answered, "My kingdom is not of this world: if my kingdom were of this world, then would my servants fight, that I should not be delivered to the Jews: but now is my kingdom not from hence." "Art thou a king then?" Jesus answered, "Thou sayest that I am a king. To this end was I born, and for this cause came I into the world, that I should bear witness unto the truth. Every one that is of the truth heareth my voice." (John 18:36–37)

Jesus was saying His kingdom was not an earthly kingdom yet.

Following are some key characteristics of a kingdom form of government. As you read them, consider the many verses in scripture that deal with these topics and I believe the Bible will start to make more practical sense as you understand your citizenship in God's kingdom.

A king is never voted into power or takes it by force; he is born into power. Kingship is a birthright. the Bible says Jesus is the Son of God, a king: "And lo a voice from heaven, saying, This is my beloved Son, in whom I am well pleased" (Matthew 3:17).

Accordingly, a king cannot be voted out of power and serves for life. Christ will never die; the Bible says Christ "will reign forever and ever" (Revelation 11:15).

In a kingdom, the king determines who will be its citizens and the standards for becoming a citizen. Jesus said, "For many are called, but few are chosen" (Matthew 22:14).

In a righteous kingdom, the welfare of the citizens is the personal responsibility of the king. "I am come that they might have life, and that they might have it more abundantly" (John 10:10).

Those who submit to a king come under his welfare.

> If thou shalt hearken diligently unto the voice of the Lord thy God, to observe and to do all his commandments which I command thee this day, that the Lord thy God will set thee on high above all nations of the earth: And all these blessings shall come on thee, and overtake thee, if thou shalt hearken unto the voice of the Lord thy God. (Deuteronomy 28:1–2)

The word of a king is law, and he is bound by it. His word cannot be challenged, changed, or countermanded. "Concerning thy testimonies, I have known of old that thou hast founded them for ever" (Psalm 119:152). "Let us hold fast the profession of our faith without wavering; (for he is faithful that promised)" (Hebrews 10:23–24).

The authority of a king is unconditional. It can't be changed by anyone or any governing body such as a congress or parliament.

> For when God made his promise to Abraham, because he could not swear by no greater, he sware by himself, saying, surely blessing I will bless thee, and multiplying I will multiply thee ... Wherein God, willing more abundantly to shew unto the heirs of promise the immutability of his counsel, confirmed it by an oath: That by two immutable things, in which it was impossible for God to lie, we might have a strong consolation, who have fled for refuge to lay hold upon the hope set before us: Which hope we have as an anchor of the soul, both sure and stedfast, and which entereth into that within the veil. (Hebrews 6:13–19)

In a kingdom the king is the government. He doesn't represent the government; he is the government. He does not represent the authority; he is the authority. Wherever he goes, the government and all its power and authority are present. "The time is fulfilled, and the Kingdom is at hand: repent ye, and believe the gospel" (Mark 1:15). Jesus was announcing as King that since He was on earth, the Kingdom was there as well.

The king's authority is delegated through his name, and he can delegate authority to others to act in his name or on his behalf. This includes the authority to set up kings and kingdoms under his kingdom. "Then I came to the governors beyond the river, and gave them the king's letters. Now the king had sent captains of the army and horsemen with me" (Nehemiah 2:9). Note that God the father gave such authority to Jesus: "And Jesus came and spake unto them, saying, All power is given unto me in heaven and in earth" (Matthew 28:18–19). Christ the King has also delegated certain authority to His disciples—those who obey him.

> Verily, verily, I say unto you, He that believeth on me, the works that I do shall he do also; and greater works than these shall he do; because I go unto my Father. And whatsoever ye shall ask in my name, that will I do, that the

> Father may be glorified in the Son. If ye shall ask any thing in my name, I will do it. (John 14:12–14)

In a kingdom, the king owns everything; there is no personal ownership, only stewardship over the king's property. "The earth is the LORD's, and the fullness thereof; the world, and they that dwell therein. For he hath founded it upon the seas, and established it upon the floods" (Psalm 24:1–2).

A king's status is measured by his prosperity and that of his citizens and their quality of life.

> So king Solomon exceeded all the kings of the earth for riches and for wisdom. And all the earth sought to Solomon, to hear his wisdom, which God had put in his heart. (1 Kings 10:23–24)

> Bring ye all the tithes into the storehouse, that there may be meat in mine house, and prove me now herewith, saith the LORD of hosts, if I will not open you the windows of heaven, and pour you out a blessing, that there shall not be room enough to receive it. And I will rebuke the devourer for your sakes, and he shall not destroy the fruits of your ground; neither shall your vine cast her fruit before the time in the field, saith the LORD of hosts. And all nations shall call you blessed: for ye shall be a delightsome land, saith the LORD of hosts. (Malachi 3:10–12)

In a kingdom, the king has a realm and a reign. His realm is the territory or geographical boundaries over which he reigns. His reign is his rule, power, or authority. In the Bible, the term *kingdom* is thought to generally mean wherever the reign of God is manifested. Because He is the creator of "the heavens and the earth" (Genesis 1:1), He owns it all and it is all part of His realm. He also has a realm in heaven (the realm we can't see) where His throne is: "Your kingdom come, thy will be done in earth as it is in heaven" (Matthew 6:10). Here, Jesus refers to both God's reign and the part of His realm where the throne of God is. This is specifically referred to in Matthew 23:22: "And he that shall swears by heaven sweareth by the throne of God, and by him that sitteth thereon." Note here that Christ says we are not to swear by God's name because God is King and Christ is the only one who represents God. By using

His name, we would be representing all that God has given us, His authority to use His name in our testimony. We have been given authority to use the name of Jesus only, who is the Head of God's Kingdom. Most authors seem to agree that in the Bible, the terms *Kingdom Of Heaven* and *Bible* generally refer to the same thing (compare Matthew 4:17 with Mark 1:14–15, Matthew 5:3 with Luke 6:20, and Matthew 13:31 with Mark 4:30–31).

The Bible and Christ's Ministry

"Thou sayest that I am a king. To this end was I born, and for this cause came I into the world, that I should bear witness unto the truth. Every one that is of the truth heareth my voice." (John 18:36–37). Christ did not come to earth to establish a religion; He came to define reality, to execute a plan of restoration of humankind and His creation and to reestablish the Kingdom on earth.

God gave humans authority to rule earth when He created them, but they lost that authority when they disobeyed God, and Satan assumed dominion over the earth (Genesis 1–3). Satan demonstrated that dominion when tempting Jesus.

> Again, the devil taketh him (Jesus) up into an exceeding high mountain, and sheweth him all the kingdoms of the world, and the glory of them. "And saith unto him, All these things will I give thee, if thou wilt fall down and worship me." (Matthew 4:8–9)

> For this purpose the Son of God was manifested, that he might destroy the works of the devil. (1 John 3:8)

The focus of Christ's teaching on earth was twofold: the restoration of humankind and all creation, and teaching about the gospel of the kingdom.

"From there he went all over Galilee. He used synagogues for meeting places and taught people the truth of God. God's kingdom was his theme – that beginning right now they were under God's government, a good government! He also healed people of their diseases and of the bad effects of their bad lives" (Matthew 4:23 Message). Christ made it clear that His followers were also to teach about restoration and the Kingdom represented by The Bible.

> And this gospel of the kingdom shall be preached in all the world for a witness unto all nations; and then shall the end come. (Matthew 24:14)

> And Jesus came and spake unto them, saying, All power is given unto me in heaven and in earth. Go ye therefore, and teach all nations, baptizing them in the name of the Father, and of the Son, and of the Holy Ghost: teaching them to observe all things whatsoever I have commanded you: and, lo, I am with you always, even unto the end of the world. Amen. (Matthew 28:18–20)

This has become known as the Great Commission. This is why I highly recommend you take time to understand The Bible and the rights responsibilities and rewards of being a people belonging to God.

You can exercise your rights under the US Constitution and your rights as a child of God in God's kingdom if you have The Bible first in all your decisions and make it the standard for your life. Any decision that goes against the Word of God is contrary to the will of God for your life and is therefore not permissible for Christians.

As Christians, we must know that everything in life has a specific spiritual right. God created us to occupy particular positions to accomplish His purposes predicated on our rights. By exercising our rights, we experience true meaning to life and enjoy a sense of direction in what we do. Without a clearly defined understanding of our rights, everything appears to be transitory, experimental, and life may turn out to be dangerous, disappointing, and sometimes a total disaster. We become victims of environmental conditions and other extraneous factors. Time loses its meaning. Energy may be lost in doing irrelevant things. There are no precision is our lives. How would you feel if your company phased out your position and your rights as company director? If your wife and children told you they did not respect your rights as head of your family? If your football coach took back your rights as captain of your team? If a board of elders revoked your rights as pastor?

We find significance and relevance in our rights; that search for relevance is our prime mover. Some of us find relevance based on our education, political offices we hold, or our military ranks. But many times, a search relevance and rights frustrates people and leads to such tragic conclusions as suicide and premature death. Many positions do not turn out to offer what they seemed to have promised, and people can feel victimized if their rights are lost or disappear.

Therefore, we must know our position and rights in the US and God's kingdom because many of our promises are tied to them. Our future depends on it. God created specific positions for His children to receive their promises. The same is true with the Constitution. We must find our positions and promises and know them; then, we will experience productive, rewarding, joyful, and exciting lives.

We can learn to make correct decisions that please God without disobeying our government. This book will help us understand The Bible with us and our position and promises in it. I will analyze the Constitution for the same reason as we can compare and contrast some of the principles of the kingdom and the Constitution. We need to have a thorough knowledge of God's government and its eternal place in our lives. We are pilgrims in this world; we are in this world but not for this world; our destination is heaven. However, while we journey through this world, we need a basic understanding of our human government that was placed over us and relate to it appropriately without compromising our eternal destiny in God's plan.

Christians are under obligation to obey God's will in the most secular of their daily activities as much as they are in their prayer closets or at the communion table. They have no right to separate their lives into two realms and acknowledge different moral codes in each. The Bible is a good rule for Sunday, but it should be the rule throughout the week. It is a good rule for religion, but it is also a good rule for business and politics.

God reigns over all everywhere. His will is the supreme law in all relations and actions. His inspired word, loyally read, will inform his is of His will in every relation and act of life, secular as well as religious; and the man is a traitor who refuses to walk therein with scrupulous care. The Bible includes all sides of human life, and it is a kingdom of absolute righteousness. You are either a loyal subject or a traitor. When the King comes, how will he find you doing? (Charles Hodge 1972) "The Church is Everywhere Represented As One." Jonathan Lockwood Huie: *www.funny-quotes-life.com/quote/church-everywhere-represented-one...*

Abraham Lincoln wrote on March 30, 1863,

> It is the duty of nations as well as of men to own their dependence upon the overruling power of God; to confess

> their sins and transgressions in humble sorrow, yet with assured hope that genuine repentance will lead to mercy and pardon; and to recognize the sublime truth, announced in the Holy Scriptures and proven by all history, that those nations only are blessed whose God is the Lord … We have forgotten the gracious hand which preserved us in peace, and multiplied and enriched and strengthened us; and we have vainly imagined, in the deceitfulness of our hearts, that all these blessings were produced by some superior wisdom and virtue of our own. Intoxicated with unbroken success, we have become too self-sufficient to feel the necessity of redeeming and preserving grace, too proud to pray to God that made us … Let us rest humbly in the hope authorize by the divine teachings, that the united cry of the nation will be heard on high, and answered with blessings no less than the pardon of our national sins, and the restoration of our now divided and suffering country and its former happy condition of unity and peace" Abraham Lincoln, Speech, March30, 1863 "Proclamation Appointing A National Fast day" Washington D, C.

The cry of the president was essentially for the restoration of God as the head of our nation.

First, God must head your personal life in all things you do and think. If this is not the case, you need to review the status of your relationship with Him. God has made your position in Christ secure for eternity. In it, you're entitled to God's eternal promises for your life.

INTRODUCTION

There is no authority except from God, and that which exists was established by God (Romans 13:11). No one has any rightful power over other human beings that is not derived from God. All human power is delegated and ministerial. God has ordained us to live in this world for him. The Bible states clearly our role and mission and how God intends to accomplish them.

We have The Bible with God who created a specific position and rights for each of us within the overall scheme of His plan by which we can ultimately receive our promises. The Old and New Testaments are clear on the dictates of His plan. We need to know the details of this plan so we can be approved as workers not ashamed of their work and rightly dividing the word of truth.

The Constitution is a legal agreement between people to form a union and live under laws that derive from it. It also specifies their position and promises in it. Our rights and privileges are also derived from it by explicit and implicit interpretations. When we know our position and promises under the Constitution, we are happy to be called Americans. Our position is designed to provide security, assurance, and confidence in our future in the United States.

The violation of our rights and position in The Bible goes back to Adam and Eve, which resulted in death. Even today, death is still our companion. The Bible clearly states that death came out of sin (Romans 5:12). We could not live in God's divine, predestined positions and promises. We were separated from God eternally. However, God in His infinite wisdom planned to restore us to our original position so we could appropriate His promises as originally intended.

God produced life out of death through His faithful Son, Jesus Christ, who came not only to restore our rights and position before God but also to fulfill His promises. We cannot live happily without knowing the position God designed for us in our eternal relationship with Him. His position is always the best; there is no substitute. Jesus left His heavenly throne to ensure our return to God's position for us. His work at Calvary is all that was needed for us to rediscover God's position and promises for our lives, which are eternal and immutable. The promises that come from our position in Christ are in scripture; we must take time to know and possess them. The Bible contains all essential details. Our duty is to dig and appropriate them. How many times in the past have we failed to take advantage of our promises because we didn't understand our position? The same is true with the Constitution. We cannot enjoy our position and promises as US citizens until we know them.

These two legal agreements can help us know where we are going and how we should relate to them. We are looking for a life of fulfillment, peace, joy, and purpose. We should not confuse the Bible with the Constitution because the two provide different positions and promises and are based on accomplishing different purposes. Many times, we experience a conflict in our relationships with the Bible and the Constitution. Where do you get your final authority to make the best decision? Benjamin Franklin wrote,

> I believe in one God, the Creator of the universe. That he governs it by His Providence. That he ought to be worshipped. That the most acceptable service we render to him is in doing good to his children. That the soul of man is immortal and will be treated with justice in another life respecting its conduct in this. (The writings of Benjamin Franklin, Boston and |London 1722-1726)

CHAPTER 1

Christian Citizenship in America

Christianity is the most adhered to religion in the United States; 75 percent of polled American adults identified themselves as Christian in 2015.[1, 2] This is down from 85 percent in 1990, lower than 81.6 percent in 2001, [3] and slightly lower than 78 percent in 2012.[4] About 62 percent of those polled claimed to be members of a church congregation.[5] The United States has the largest Christian population in the world with nearly 280 million Christians though other countries have higher percentages of Christians. The official motto of the United States as established by a 1956 law signed by President Dwight D. Eisenhower is "In God We Trust."[6, 7, 8] The phrase first appeared on US coins in 1864.[7]

On October 22, 2016, Davenant president Dr. Bradford Littlejohn[13] spoke at St. Matthew's Episcopal Church in Richmond, Virginia, on "What Does It Mean to Be a Christian Citizen?" The lecture focused on questions such as, Should I be focused on building the church or reforming the state—or both? How should and shouldn't the Bible guide/govern/regulate/inform my political discipleship?

Excerpts from his lecture have helped me greatly in understanding my rights as a Christian citizen. In his great treatise *On the Freedom of a Christian*, which served as a manifesto for the great reforming effort he had just undertaken, Martin Luther famously declared, "A Christian man is the most free lord of all, and subject to none; a Christian man is the most dutiful servant of all, and subject to everyone." (Bradford Littlejohn, What does it mean to be a Christian, 2016?) This paradox echoes the statement of St. Paul in 1 Corinthians 9:19: "For though I be free from all men, yet have I made myself servant unto all," and his injunction in Romans 13:8: "Owe no one anything, but to love one another."

Christians' dual citizenship can be best understood in the terms of this paradox. In the following, I want to pursue two main objectives. First, I want to distinguish between Christians' two citizenships to show that Christian life should be characterized as a dualism though not the kind of dualism many Christians carelessly assume or critique. Second, I want to unite these two citizenships to show that Christians' earthly citizenship is still a form of distinctively Christian citizenship; it is not as if the Christian is different on the inside because of a different spiritual state. It looks exactly the same on the outside as they pursue life in society and politics the same way as their non-Christian neighbors do.

I will do this by looking at the Christian motivation for politics, the Christian content of political ideals, and the Christian method of political engagement. So first, let's distinguish those two citizenships.

Distinguishing Two Citizenships

Free Lord of All

What does it mean for a Christian to be the "free lord of all"? Freedom is of course the dominant theme of American political discourse, even if we rarely know quite what we mean by it. This theme also dominates not merely Luther's writings but the New Testament as well. Galatians 5:1 proclaims, "Stand fast therefore in the liberty wherewith Christ hath made us free, and be not entangled again with the yoke of bondage."

In Romans 6:13–14, Paul admonishes us,

Neither yield ye your members as instruments of unrighteousness unto sin: but yield yourselves unto God, as those that are alive from the dead, and your members as instruments of righteousness unto God. For sin shall not have dominion over you: for ye are not under the law, but under grace.

And in the next chapter, Romans 7:4, 6 (KJV), he says,

Wherefore, my brethren, ye also are become dead to the law by the body of Christ … But now we are delivered from the law, that being dead wherein we were held; that we should serve in newness of spirit, and not in the oldness of the letter.

And then just a bit later, in one of the most famous chapters of scripture, we read,

What shall we then say to these things? If God be for us, who can be against us? He that spared not his own Son, but delivered him up for us all, how shall he not with him also freely give us all things? Who shall lay any thing to the charge of God's elect? It is God that justifieth. Who is he that condemneth? It is Christ that died, yea rather, that is risen again, who is even at the right hand of God, who also maketh intercession for us. Who shall separate us from the love of Christ? Shall tribulation, or distress, or persecution, or famine, or nakedness, or peril, or sword?

Nay, in all things we are more than conquerors through him who loved us. For I am persuaded, that neither death, nor life, nor angels, nor principalities, nor powers, nor things present, nor things to come, nor height nor depth, nor any other creature, shall be able to separate us from the love of God, which in Christ Jesus our Lord. (Romans 8:31–39)

What is this message of freedom? It is a proclamation of freedom from sin, from death, and from the law, the three masters that have enslaved fallen man since Adam. We know too well that we are *not* free from any of these three things in the sense of having them wholly removed from us. We all still sin daily, hourly, sometimes grievously. We are all still under the authorities of laws of all sorts—not just the civil laws that we are so fond of complaining and bickering about but also the moral law of scripture and nature that governs all our conduct and reveals the fact that we sin daily and hourly. And of course, we are all subject to death, the ever-present reality of futility, grief, and separation that we in the modern world have sought to hide ourselves from but which has a way of thrusting itself into our lives when we least expect it.

So in what does our freedom consist? It is that nothing will be able to separate us from the love of God in Christ Jesus, our Lord. Death is not a separation for the faithful but a reunion. Sin is a separation only if harbored and clung to. Therefore, the law draws us toward God rather than highlighting how far short of him we fall.

The freedom of a Christian is the freedom from fear. Hebrews 2:14–15 says,

He also himself likewise took part of the same; that through death he might destroy him that had the power of death, that is, the devil; and deliver them who through fear of death were all their lifetime subject to bondage.

And 1 John 4:16–20 says,

And we have known and believed the love that God hath to us. God is love; and he that dwelleth in love dwelleth in God, and God in him. Herein is our love made perfect, that we may have boldness in the day of judgment: because as he is, so are we in this world. There is no fear in love; but perfect love casteth out fear: because fear hath torment. He that feareth is not made perfect in love. We love him, because he first loved us.

What does all this have to do with a Christian's citizenship? Everything. Consider how much of our lives of earthly citizenship are dominated by fear. Fear of enemies abroad drives our defense policy. Perhaps even more intensely in recent years, fear of our political foes at home drives our partisanship and our voting. Consider the 2016 US presidential election. Most voters hated both Hillary and Donald at least when they felt they had other options. So why were they voting for them? Because they were terrified of the alternative.

By stoking and channeling fear of Hillary, Trump has managed to sustain a strong coalition through every misstep and humiliation. And likewise for Hillary with Trump.

Fear of persecution, fear of loss of influence, or simply fear of regulation and taxation hits our pocketbooks, which drives most of American politics. And of course, when you put it this way, you should see that the Christian's earthly citizenship includes an awful lot more than politics strictly speaking. Our social lives, beginning with kindergarten and continuing right through our careers, are dominated by the kind of jostling for position driven by fear of being an outsider and fear of being unpopular, unloved, or insignificant. Fear of change that might destabilize things I hold dear, or leave me marginalized, is another dynamic that drives our social lives. The same dynamics underlie so much of church politics. Such fear is to some extent inevitable whenever we try to find meaning or rest our identities in our social lives, for we are restlessly seeking something that our souls can rest secure in—and nothing finite and fallible can possibly provide such security.

When those around us fail, even when we turn to religion to sustain us, we seek security in our own actions and merits, hoping to impress God somehow so that He will give us his stamp of approval. It is to all this that the New Testament, and later the Protestant Reformation, pronounces a firm no. In Christ alone we find our rest, we find our safety, we find our security, and in Christ as grasped by faith alone, not earned by any works or status. In him alone we are to find meaning, in him alone we are to root our identity, and having done so, we find that this identity is unshakeable *whatever* the world may throw against us. Our families may fail us, our churches may blow apart in an ugly scandal, our governments may turn godless or crumble altogether, or we may fall to invading hordes, yet the Christian need not and should not fear or lose heart. This is what it means for Paul to say that "our citizenship is in heaven," that "our lives are hid with Christ in God."

The primacy of this citizenship serves to radically qualify all earthly loyalties and sources of identity, to establish a radical detachment from all earthly attachments. By this means the Christian learns to walk by faith and not by sight, clinging not to the things that pass away, but to the source of resurrection life.

Dutiful Servant of All

Does this mean, then, that the Christian is to float heedlessly above the troubles and travails of the world? "This world is not my home, I'm just a-passing through"—we've heard this sort of line from many Christians in many eras. Is this faithful Christianity? No, for while we must not cling to earthly loyalties and attachments out of fear, as we so often do, we can and must cling to them out of love. Let's look at the flipside of many of the passages we've quoted.

Galatians 5:13–14 says, "For, brethren, ye have been called unto liberty; only use not liberty for an occasion to the flesh, but by love serve one another. For all the law is fulfilled in one word, even in this; Thou shalt love thy neighbor as thyself."

Romans 6 and 7 say, "But God be thanked, that ye were the servants of sin, but ye have obeyed from the heart that form of doctrine which was delivered you. Being then made free from sin, ye became the servants of righteousness." (6:17–18) "Likewise, my brothers, you also have died to the law through the body of Christ, so that you may belong to another, to him who has been raised from the dead, in order that we may bear fruit for God."

And of course, 1 John 4:7–8 "Beloved, let us love one another: for love is of God; and every one that loveth is born of God, and knoweth God. He that loveth not knoweth not God; for God is love."

This is the second half of Luther's paradox: Christians are dutiful servants of all. Luther is worth quoting extensively on this point.

Although, as I have said, inwardly, and according to the spirit, a man is amply enough justified by faith, having all that life requires to have, except that this very faith and abundance ought to increase from day to day, even till the future life; still he remains in this mortal life upon earth, in which it is necessary that he should rule his own body, and have relations with men.

For man does not live for himself alone in this mortal body, in order to work on its account, but also for all men on earth; nay, he lives only for others and not for himself. For it is to this end that he brings his own body into subjection, that lie may be able to serve others more sincerely and more freely; as Paul says: "None of us liveth to himself, and no man dieth to himself. For whether we live, we live unto the Lord; and whether we die, we die unto the Lord." (Romans 14: 7–8) Thus it is impossible that he should take his ease in this life, and not work for the good of his neighbors; since he must needs speak, act, and converse among men; just is Christ was made in the likeness of men, and found in fashion as a man, and had His conversation among men."

For this reason, law, which has no power to condemn the one who clings to Christ by faith, retains relevance and a certain kind of authority in the Christian life. Freed from slavery to sin to become slaves of God, we should each desire to present ourselves as sacrifices of thanksgiving to God, cleansed of sin that defiles us and harms our neighbor. And the second great commandment, to love our neighbor as yourself, flows out of the first, to love God with all our heart, mind, soul, and strength. Accordingly, no sooner must the Christian turn inward and upward, turning his gaze away from the things of earth that entice and intimidate, claiming a loyalty and significance that they do not deserve, than the Christian must turn back to the things of this world, the people around him, and the social and political structures in which he finds himself. The law of God directs the believer in how he can serve his neighbor in love, but civil law and earthly authorities also have a role to play, and this is particularly significant given our topic today, so let's pause and make sure we understand this role.

Clearly, from the standpoint of our heavenly citizenship, our identity hidden in Christ, the laws of princes and parliaments can be laughed at. For law gains its power by fear, fear of the consequences if we should disobey. to be sure, law also has an instructive component, which we shall come back to in a moment, but the thing that makes it law specifically, rather than mere instruction, is its capacity to impose penalties for disobedience. Since the Christian knows that none of these penalties can separate her from the love of Christ, such laws in themselves have no power over her. And even as mere instruction, human laws can claim authority only inasmuch as they correspond to Christ's authority, only inasmuch as they instruct us to value the things that he tells us to value. It would seem, then, that the conscience bound to Christ has no need of human laws; the Christian can ignore them and focus simply on serving Christ and doing his will.

But we know that it is not so. Paul himself, not long after proclaiming the Christian's freedom from earthly powers, admonishes us, "Let every soul be subject unto the higher powers. For there is no power that be are ordained of God." (Rom. 13:1) Why would he do this? Well, let's begin with the call to love one another, the principle that governs the Christian's earthly citizenship. We are called to love one another as *human beings*, not as disembodied souls. For this reason, loving one another as human beings means seeking to ensure that we each have education, as much as our short time and scant resources permit, and are blessed with arts and culture. And it means of course drawing each of us to the highest blessings offered by religion, and specifically the true religion of Jesus Christ.

So while our citizenship is heaven, our vocation is lived out on earth, and our vocation means trying to achieve all these things for our neighbors. It might possibly be that each of us is meant to pursue these goods alone, but we know that is not the case, for God said from the beginning, "It is not good for man to be alone." We were made to live with one another; we were made to live in community. And that quickly gets complicated. And of course, we will make mistakes. Even assuming the best political process, we will have fallible leaders framing our laws and these laws will not always be best for the purpose at hand. Sometimes the mistakes will be glaring. Sometimes we'll be convinced we know better. But here's the thing. We will still be obliged, more often than not, to obey. Not, mind you, because of what human authority is in itself—as we've already noted, it is nothing in itself, but only as a channel of God's authority, and to the extent that it directs us badly, it cannot be channeling God's authority. Nor, mind you, because of the power it has to compel us with penalties if we disobey, for we've seen already that for the Christian, such penalties ought not to be able to instill any fear. Rather, because of humility and love of neighbor. Humility should lead us to constantly question our own judgment; when we dissent from the laws established and think we know how to do better, we should think twice, and even thrice. There are few arts in human life that demand more skill. Love of neighbor should lead us to ask, "Even if I am convinced that this law is making my neighbor's life worse, do I think that my unilaterally disobeying it would actually make his life better?" Indeed, if everyone is allowed to unilaterally disobey whenever they think they have a better plan, our laws will crumble altogether and our common life be reduced to chaos. Thus it is that the Christian, while a bondservant of Christ alone, is obliged to be in his earthly citizenship a dutiful servant of all, and especially of those to whom God has granted political authority.

Uniting the Two Citizenships

Now, we have established that the Christian's earthly citizenship, his vocation to serve his neighbor, is distinct from his heavenly citizenship, his hidden identity in Christ. And indeed it would seem that even though the Christian might be (certainly should be!) more concerned with serving his neighbor than the average Joe, that there is nothing particularly Christian about his vocation in this realm. Simply by virtue of our creation as human beings, we are obligated to try to see to it that one another are fed, clothed, sheltered, and all the rest. If this is the business of the Christian's earthly citizenship, in what sense is it a *Christian* citizenship? Are all the things that make us distinctively Christian inward and spiritual things, so that when it comes to our earthly life together, we are mere Americans or Canadians or Frenchmen, called to the same kind of conduct regardless of creed? Well in some respects, yes, but there are several important ways in which ours is a distinctively Christian citizenship and these include:

Motivation

Whereas the majority of earthly politics proceeds on the basis of fear, the Christian are political engagement ought to be characterized by a profound freedom from fear. Yes, bad politics can do a great deal of evil, and we should not be apathetic or complacent. But bad politics, even at its worst, cannot do as much evil as we often fear—it cannot bring the world to an end, it cannot overthrow the kingship of Christ or frustrate God's purposes in the world, it cannot even succeed in separating a single saint from his Lord. But a tendency to invest politics with too much significance, and accordingly to respond in fear every time it doesn't seem to go our way, is a natural human temptation that can be tamed only with the recognition that there is a king above all earthly thrones, "who has measured the waters in the hollow of his hand, and marked off the heavens with a span, enclosed the dust of the earth in a measure, and weighed the mountains in scales, and the hills in a balance," before whom "the nations are like a drop from a bucket, and are accounted as the dust on the scales" (Is. 40:12, 15)

Since the Christian is not motivated by fear, as the world so often is, she is motivated instead by love, love of God and love of neighbor. Earthly politics, on the other hand, is too often driven by various forms of self-love. This is evident of course in the naked ambition of politicians determined to rise to the top, or the economic self-interest of corporations and their lobbyists, the "special interests" that have crippled American politics, as they have crippled so many commonwealths in the past. It is evident in the "don't tread on me" mentality that drives much American conservatism, particularly clear in the recent Tea Party movement and the embrace of tax evasion that has appeared among some on the Christian Right. It is evident also in the preoccupation with national self-interest when it comes to foreign policy, irrespective of our responsibilities among the global family of nations.

Limited Aims and Aspirations

A Christian politics recognizes the limits of politics. We have already seen that the Christian's dual citizenship serves as a warning against investing too much hope and meaning in political identity, expecting too much what good politics may achieve or fearing too much what evil it may bring about. A Christian politics recognizes that the true fruition of our human life together lies outside the bounds of history as we know it and beyond any human power to bring about; it also recognizes that God will bring about this fruition *no matter how much* we might make errors along the way. It might seem like an obvious and banal point to say that politics can only achieve so much, but in fact, it is something of a uniquely Christian contribution, since the natural human tendency is to look to earthly powers for our redemption and fulfillment, investing nations and rulers with a religious significance rather than recognizing that their authority is derivative and limited.

Mindfulness of human sin and frailty

Following from the previous point, a Christian politics is mindful of the depth of human sin and frailty. As Richard Hooker says, "Laws politic, ordained for external order and regiment amongst men, are never framed as they should be, unless presuming the will of man to be inwardly obstinate, rebellious, and averse from all obedience unto the sacred laws of his nature; in a word, unless presuming man to be in regard of his depraved mind little better than a wild beast, they do accordingly provide notwithstanding so to frame his outward actions, that they be no hindrance unto the common good for which societies are instituted: unless they do this, they are not perfect." This also means that Christians have tended to be hesitant about investing too much authority in any particular ruler, insisting that rulers too must be limited by laws and that authority should be well-dispersed in a society. These principles were famously operative in the American Constitution, reflecting the Christian intellectual heritage of the Founders.

Charity and forbearance

One of the most important freedoms of all is freedom of conscience, and although Christians cannot accept the modern secular rationale for such freedom—that is, that ultimate truth cannot be known and so every private creed is as good as any other—they can and should still defend this freedom. Why?

Because of the first point about the limited aims and aspirations of human political life. It is beyond the ability of politics to make everyone believe rightly, and the attempt to do so usually brings more harm than good to the cause of truth. A Christian politics, then, while reserving the right to openly name and oppose error, and indeed to restrain certain forms of error from being carried out in action, seeks to exercise as much charity and forbearance as possible to those of other creeds, putting its trust in patient witness and persuasion rather than legal force.

Respect for human life

While recognition of the value of human life tends to be natural to us regardless of creed, Christians are particularly mindful of it given our knowledge that God has created each of us in his image and endowed human beings with a unique dignity above other creatures. Christians thus rightly prize human life as a priority of public policy, with a particular emphasis on the lives of the innocent and the vulnerable. This means an urgent concern for the lives of the unborn; an issue on which Christians have been particularly vocal in recent politics, but we must remember that it should translate into a concern for life across the board. Christians should be the first to confess that black lives matter (and that white lives matter), and to insist that not just American lives matter, but the lives of those abroad as well, who are often the victims of our callous pursuit of national interest.

> In short, the Christian life is one in which we are summoned, in James Davison Hunter's words, to a "faithful presence" in all spheres of life and culture, learning to live as free people who do not fear the bondage of sin or death or law, and who are determined to let the love of Christ shine through in our dealings with our neighbors day by day. Recognizing that we were made for one another, we know that we cannot escape life in community, and thus our faithful presence must be a presence as citizens in the commonwealth. Recognizing that ours is a commonwealth defined by diversity, we must patiently, strategically, and winsomely seek to show, through our motivations, our method, and the content of our political witness, the difference that the kingship of Christ makes, knowing all the while that we will not see that kingship properly revealed until the Lord returns. (https://davenantinstitute.org/mean-christian-citizen/)

CHAPTER 2

The Bible, God's Plan for Humanity, and the US Constitution

This book is designed to help you gain knowledge of your basic rights and promises in the Bible and the Constitution as you interact with other people and the government so you can live your life as a Christian in a manner that pleases God and humanity. Your purpose for existence comes from God, but He has placed your purpose in Christ Jesus and given you a geographical location so you can fulfill your assignment to both humanity and God. Jesus came that you might have life and have it more abundantly. It is not wise for you to put all your faith in the Constitution because it cannot live for eternity and its inherent shortcomings for you as a child of God.

The Constitution was written by men who were constrained by the political and social circumstances of their time and had to think about all the details of power sharing, citizenship, legal system, the Bill of Rights, and many other things they felt were likely to affect the Union. They had to specify requirements for citizenship based on what they felt were suitable and ideal standards for the people who occupied the colonies at that time. Only those who qualified for citizenship could take advantage of their position and promises as specified by the Constitution. God did not have to think about our position and promises; He planned it all in His Son, Jesus Christ.

Without Jesus Christ, you cannot find your God-ordained rights, position, and promises. All things are predetermined. In your predetermined position, you will find adequate provision for your life. Let us walk through the Bible, which is our Constitution with God, and the US Constitution, and come to know what has been prepared for us. Scriptures reveal that

God takes seriously the issue of position. He ordained in creation to have its position. The principle of position states that every purpose must be accomplished in a particular position. Position determines our relationship to everything else in God's universe.

God has made it clear that our rights and promises cannot be found outside His universal plan revealed in His Son, Jesus Christ. We cannot work our way into that position; we cannot attain it otherwise. Once in it, we are promised eternal life. There are rights we have as citizens of this great country, but whatever they are, they cannot be compared to our benefits in Jesus Christ, which are good for eternity.

How then are we going to find out our rights and promises in these important Constitutions so we can exercise them fully and live full, abundant lives? What I am recommending here are God's commands to us for now and eternity. Decisions we make now affects our eternity. Our age-old ideas about the world will be challenged, our principles will be put to test, our options will be shaken, our preconceived ideas will come under fire, and our lives will be changed forever.

What We Need to Know

> And it shall be with him, and he shall read therein all the days of his life: that he may learn to fear the LORD his God, to keep all the words of this law and these statutes, to do them. (Deuteronomy 17:19)

> For Ezra had prepared his heart to seek the law of the LORD, and to do it, and to teach in Israel statutes and judgments. (Ezra 7:10)

> Seek ye out of the book of the LORD, and read: no one of these shall fail … for my mouth it hath commanded. (Isaiah 34:16)

> And Jesus answering said unto them, Do ye not therefore err, because ye know not the scriptures, neither the power of God? (Mark 12:24)

These were more noble than those in Thessalonica, in that they received the word with all readiness of mind, and searched the scriptures daily, whether those things were so. (Acts 17:11)

For whatsoever things were written aforetime, were written for our learning, that we through patience and comfort of the scripture might have hope. (Romans 15:4)

Study to shew thyself approved unto God, a workman that needeth not to be ashamed, rightly dividing the word of truth. (2 Timothy 2:15)

And that from a child thou hast known the holy scriptures, which are able to make thee wise unto salvation through faith which is in Christ Jesus. (2 Timothy 3:15)

Blessed is he that readth, and they that hear the words of his prophecy, and keep those things which are written therein: for the time is at hand. (Revelation 1:3)

Ye are the light of the world. A city that is set on a hill cannot be hid. (Matthew 5:14)

For what does it profit a man, if he shall gain the whole world and lose his own soul? (Mark 5:14)

In the world you shall have tribulation: but be of good cheer, I have overcome the world. (John 16:33)

I pray thee, if I have found grace in thy sight; show me thy way that I may know thee, that I may find grace in thy sight. (Exodus 33:13)

Lead me in thy truth, and teach me: for thou art God of my salvation. (Psalm 25:5)

Principles

- God has an everlasting Constitution with you.
- God's Constitution is supreme for His children.
- You need to know your position and promises in the US Constitution and God's Constitution.
- Only God's Constitution will give you abundant life.
- God's Constitution was made before the foundation of this world.
- You must choose life in the name of Jesus.

CHAPTER 3

The Constitution, the Bible, and Humanity

The US Constitution has a dynamic meaning; it has the properties of an animate being in the sense that it changes. The idea is associated with views that contemporaneous society should be taken into account when interpreting key constitutional phrases. Over the past couple of decades, it has become popular to refer to the Constitution as a living document. The term comes from the title of a book published in 1937. By living document, liberal humanists mean that the Constitution has no fixed meaning. They say that language and people change, the needs of people change, and our interpretations must adapt to present circumstances. Ultimately this means that the original document has no direct usefulness and can be ignored. My conclusion then is that the term *living document* really means *dead document* in a classic example of liberal newspeak. I suspect that if the original living document the apostle said was "living and active and sharper than any two-edged sword" had been given a higher place in the church than the Constitution would have retained in the courts.

While arguments for the living constitution vary, they can generally be broken into two categories. First, the pragmatist view contends that interpreting the Constitution in accordance with its original meaning or intent is sometimes unacceptable as a policy matter and thus that an evolving interpretation is necessary. The second, relating to intent, contends that the constitutional framers specifically wrote the Constitution in broad and flexible terms to create such a dynamic, living document. Opponents of the idea often argue that the Constitution should be changed through the amendment process and that allowing judges to determine an ever-changing meaning of the constitution undermines democracy, etc. The main alternative to the living constitution is most commonly described as originalism.

The Constitution has been called a living because it has managed over the last 200 years to serve both as a symbol of national unity and a somewhat adaptable and changing instrument of government. The secret is an in the principle separation of powers and a system of checks and balances that checks power with power.

Is the Bible a Living Document?

The Bible is a living document able to guide, instruct, comfort, and console. It gives strength to the weak, hope for the hopeless, freedom to the captives, and eternal life to a dead man. Many have tried to silence the Word of God, but despite burnings, bans, and laws against, Bible endures, reaching back into the past, and forward into the future, teaching all who will hear about God's love, mercy, kindness, and revealing His plan for salvation.

God's Kingdom represented by the Bible, is a living document. It's able to affect and enlighten all men; as powerful and relevant today as when it was written centuries ago. How do I know The Bible is alive? No matter what I am facing, The Bible speaks to me. I have never looked into its pages with an open heart and mind that it failed to move me, and in times of need, its words flood my mind, calming and instructing me. The Bible is a living document, able to change and save those who are still in bondage to sin, choosing unbeknownst to them the path to Hell. It is the single most important document that has ever been or ever will be written, preserved as it has been by God almighty so that all might know Him and His unfailing love.

All Decisions in Life Are Critical

There are no neutral choices in life. All decisions we make are either promoting God's agenda or the devil's. We must be aware that God's commands take precedence over our personal desires. We cannot have our cake and eat it too. The Bible is His Living Word. His promises to us are based on His stability and credibility. Unlike many manufacturers, He will never declare bankruptcy. He is capable of keeping His promises forever because they were made before the foundation of the world.

We occupy a predetermined position. Conditions in our lives do not affect His plans for us. Conditions in our nation affect many of our constitutional rights and privileges. We must know the fundamental differences between these Constitutions as Christians and understand why we live under The Bible and the Constitution. This knowledge will permit us to possess what is rightfully our position and promises.

US Constitution	REPUBLIC OF THE U SA	God's Constitution- The Bible, KINGDOM
Article 1	Legislative Branch	
	Congress	God the Father
Article 2	Executive Branch	God the Son
	President	Jesus Christ
Article 3	The Judiciary	
	The Supreme Court	Holy Spirit
Article 4	Interstate relations	Relationship between diety and the human race
	Full faith and credit	
	Privileges and Immunities	
Article 5	Constitution can be amended Congress	Bible cannot be amended It is inerrant and infallible
Article 6	Supremacy Act – The US Constitution	The Bible
Article 7	Ratification of the US Constitution needed 9 nine states	Old Testament – The Bible ratified by the blood animals New. Testament- The Bible ratified by the bold of Jesus Christ
	SUMMARY OF AMENDMENTS TO THE US CONSTITUTION	
1st Amendment	Separation of church and State	God is the Head of our Nation

US Constitution	REPUBLIC OF THE U SA	God's Constitution- The Bible, KINGDOM
	Freedom of speech	No corrupt and ungodly speech
	Freedom of the press	The Bible is our press
	Freedom to petition the Government	Freedom to petition God through Jesus Christ
	Freedom of |Association	Freedom to assemble as believers
2nd Amendment	A well regulated militia	God is our banner in battle
	The right to bear arms	Put on the whole armor of God
3RD Amendment	No quartering of soldiers in homes without consent of owners	Holy Spirit lives in us when we are born again
4th Amendment	The right to privacy	Nothing from God in our lives
5th, 6th Amendments	Rights of defendants below the law	We are all guilty before God
7th, 8th Amendments	Defendants are innocent until proven guilty	All men are guilty and must repent
9th Amendment	Rights retained by the people	Rights of God's children
10th Amendment	Rights reserved by the people	Jesus has all authority
11TH Amendment	No power over foreign suits	Jesus has all the powers
12th Amendment	Representatives are elected	God appoints all representatives

US Constitution	REPUBLIC OF THE U SA	God's Constitution-The Bible, KINGDOM
13th Amendment	Freedom of slaves	All people are slaves to sin and can only be freed by Jests Christ (Romans6:6-7)
16th Amendments	Power to levy taxes and Congressional pay	Jesus said, "Render to Caesar what belongs to Caesar
18th 2st Amendment	Consumption of alcohol	Be filled with the Holy Spirit
20th Amendment, 22nd Amendment	Limits on presidential terms	Eternal authority of Jesus Christ
25th Amendment	Replacing the President	Christ lives forever

While we have three separate branches of government in the Constitution, in the Bible, we speak of the Trinity—God the Father, God the Son, and God the Holy Spirit—as being one performing all legislative, executive, and judicial functions.

The Doctrine of the Trinity - www.biblestudytools.com/bible-study/topical-studies/the-doctrine-of-the-trinity-11626770.html

> The doctrine of the Trinity is foundational to the Christian faith. It is crucial for properly understanding what God is like, how he relates to us, and how we should relate to him. But it also raises many difficult questions. How can God be both one and three? Is the Trinity a contradiction? If Jesus is God, why do the Gospels record instances where he prayed to God?
>
> While we cannot fully understand everything about the Trinity (or anything else), it is possible to answer questions like these and come to a solid grasp of what it means for God to be three in one. (https://www.desiringgod.org/articles/what-is-the-doctrine-of-the-trinity)

One God, Three Persons

The doctrine of the Trinity means that there is one God who eternally exists as three distinct Persons—the Father, Son, and Holy Spirit. Stated differently, God is one in essence and three in person. These definitions express three crucial truths: The Father, Son, and Holy Spirit are distinct persons. Each Person is fully God. There is only one God.

The Father, Son, and Holy Spirit are distinct Persons. (https://www.desiringgod.org/articles/what-is-the-doctrine-of-the-trinity)

The Bible, which is God's Covenant with man speaks of the Father as God (Philippians 1:2), Jesus as God (Titus 2:13), and the Holy Spirit as God (Acts 5:3–4). Are these just three different ways of looking at God, or simply ways of referring to three different roles God plays? The answer must be no because the Bible also indicates that the Father, Son, and Holy Spirit are distinct. Since the Father sent the Son into the world (John 3:16), He cannot be the same person as the Son. Likewise, after the Son returned to the Father (John 16:10), the Father and the Son sent the Holy Spirit into the world (John 14:26; Acts 2:33). Therefore, the Holy Spirit must be distinct from the Father and the Son.

In the baptism of Jesus, we see the Father speaking from heaven and the Spirit descending from heaven in the form of a dove as Jesus comes out of the water (Mark 1:10–11). John 1:1 affirms that Jesus is God and at the same time that he was with God, thereby indicating that Jesus was a distinct person from God the Father (see also John 1:18). And in John 16:13–15, we see that although there is a close unity between the three persons, the Holy Spirit is also distinct from the Father and the Son.

The fact that the Father, Son, and Holy Spirit are distinct persons means that the Father is not the Son, the Son is not the Holy Spirit, and the Holy Spirit is not the Father. Jesus is God, but he is not the Father or the Holy Spirit. The Holy Spirit is God, but he is not the Son or the Father. They are different Persons, not three different ways of looking at God. The personhood of each member of the Trinity means that each Person has a distinct centre of consciousness. Thus, they relate to each other personally—the Father regards himself as "I" while he regards the Son and Holy Spirit as "you." Likewise, the Son regards himself as "I," but the Father and the Holy Spirit as "you."

Often it is objected, "If Jesus is God, and then he must have prayed to himself while he was on earth." But the answer to this objection lies in simply applying what we have already seen. While Jesus and the Father are both God, they are different Persons. Thus, Jesus prayed to God the Father without praying to himself. In fact, it is precisely the continuing dialogue between the Father and the Son (Matthew 3:17; 17:5; John 5:19; 11:41–42; 17:1ff) that furnishes the best evidence that they are distinct Persons with distinct centers of consciousness.

Sometimes the Personhood of the Father and Son is appreciated, but the Personhood of the Holy Spirit is neglected. Sometimes the Spirit is treated more like a "force" than a Person. But the Holy Spirit is not an "it," but a "he" (see John 14:26; 16:7–15; Acts 8:16). The fact that the Holy Spirit is a Person, not an impersonal force (like gravity), is also shown by the fact that he speaks (Hebrews 3:7), reasons (Acts 15:28), thinks and understands (1 Corinthians 2:10–11), wills (1 Corinthians 12:11), feels (Ephesians 4:30), and gives personal fellowship (2 Corinthians 13:14). These are all qualities of personhood.

In addition to these texts, the others we mentioned above make clear that the Personhood of the Holy Spirit is distinct from the Personhood of the Son and the Father. They are three real persons, not three roles God plays.

Another serious error people have made is to think that the Father became the Son, who then became the Holy Spirit. Contrary to this, the passages we have seen imply that God always was and always will be three Persons. There was never a time when one of the Persons of the Godhead did not exist. They are all eternal.

While the three members of the Trinity are distinct, this does not mean that any is inferior to the other. Instead, they are all identical in attributes. They are equal in power, love, mercy, justice, holiness, knowledge, and all other qualities.

Each Person is fully God. If God is three Persons, does this mean that each Person is "one third" of God?

The doctrine of the Trinity does not divide God into three parts. The Bible is clear that all three Persons are each one-hundred-percent God. The Father, Son, and Holy Spirit are each fully God. For example, Colossians 2:9 says of Christ, "in him dwelleth all the fullness of the Godhead bodily." We should not think of God as a "pie" cut into three pieces, each piece representing a Person. This would make each Person less than fully God and thus not God at all. Rather, "the being of each Person is equal to the whole being of God" (Grudem, Systematic Theology, 1994, page 255). The divine essence is not something that is divided between the three persons, but is fully in all three persons without being divided into "parts."

Thus, the Son is not one-third of the being of God; he is all of the being of God. The Father is not one-third of the being of God; he is all of the being of God. And likewise with the Holy Spirit. when we speak of the Father, Son, and Holy Spirit together we are not speaking of any greater being than when we speak of the Father alone, the Son alone, or the Holy Spirit alone.

> There is only one God. If each Person of the Trinity is distinct and yet fully God, then should we conclude that there is more than one God? Obviously we cannot, for Scripture is clear that there is only one God: " …and there is no God else beside me, a just God and a Savior; there is none beside me. Look unto me, and be ye saved, all the ends of the earth: for I am God, and there is none else" (Isaiah 45:21–22; see also Isaiah 44:6–8; Exodus 15:11; Deuteronomy 4:35; 6:4–5; 32:39; 1 Samuel 2:2; 1 Kings 8:60).
>
> Having seen that the Father, the Son, and the Holy Spirit are distinct Persons, that they are each fully God, and that there is nonetheless only one God, we must conclude that all three Persons are the same God. In other words, there is one God who exists as three distinct Persons.
>
> If there is one passage which most clearly brings all of this together, it is Matthew 28:19: "Go ye therefore, and teach all nations, baptising them in the name of the Father, and of the Son, and of the Holy Ghost." First, notice that the Father, Son, and Holy Spirit are distinguished as distinct Persons. We baptize into the name of the Father and the Son and the Holy Spirit. Second, notice that each Person must be deity because they are all placed on the same level. In fact, would Jesus have us baptize in the name of a mere creature? Surely not. Therefore each of the Persons into whose name we are to be baptized must be deity. Third, notice that although the three divine Persons are distinct, we are baptized into their name (singular), not names (plural). The three Persons are distinct, yet only constitute one name. This can only be if they share one essence. (https://www.desiringgod.org/articles/what-is-the-doctrine-of-the-trinity)

Not one God in three phases. Not three different gods coexisting. <u>One divine being, three offices</u>.

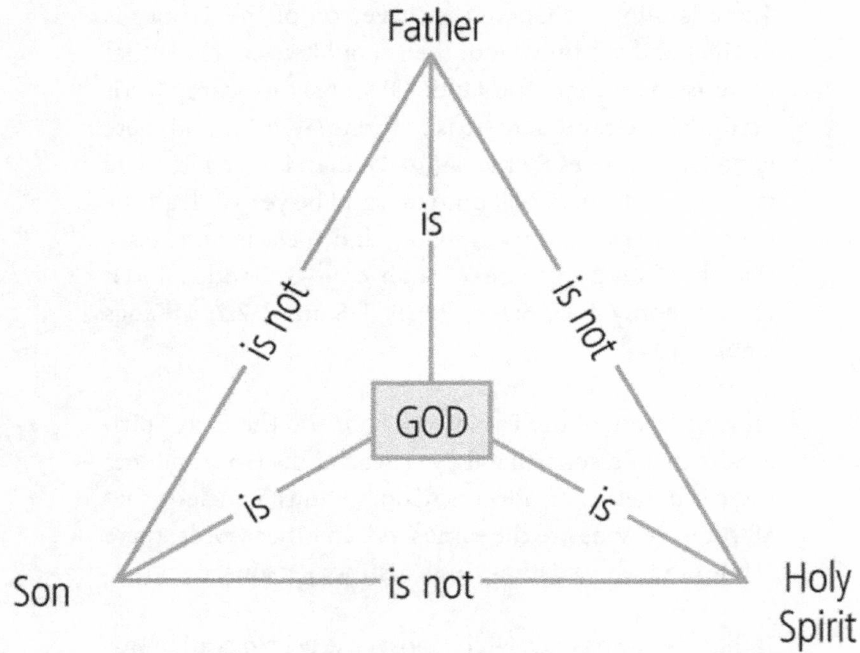

Credit: Crossway Bibles. The ESV Study Bible. Wheaton, IL: Crossway Bibles, 2008.

What the Bible Says about the Trinity

> And Jesus, when he was baptized, went up straightway out of the water: and lo, the heavens were opened unto him, and he saw the Spirit of God descending like a dove, and lighting upon him. (Matthew 3:16)

> Go ye therefore, and teach all nations, baptizing them in the name of the Father, and of the Son, and of the Holy Spirit. (Matthew 28:19)

> And the Holy Ghost descended in bodily shape like a dove upon Him [Jesus], and a voice came from heaven, which said, Thou are my beloved Son; in thee I am well pleased. (Luke 3:22)

> But the Comforter, which is the Holy Ghost, whom the Father will send in my [Jesus'] name, he shall teach you

all things, and bring all things to your remembrance, whosoever I have said unto you. (John 14:26)

But when the Comforter is come, whom I [Jesus] will send unto you from the Father, even the Spirit of truth, which proceedeth from the Father, he shall testify about Me. (John 15:26)

And, being assembled together with them, commanded them that they should depart from Jerusalem, but wait for the promise of the Father, which, saith he, ye have heard of Me." (Acts 1:4)

Therefore being by the right hand of God exalted, and having received of the Father the promise of the Holy Ghost, he hath shed forth this, which ye now see and hear. (Acts 2:33)

How God anointed Jesus of Nazareth with the Holy Ghost and with power: who went about doing good, and healing all that were oppressed of the devil; for God was with him. (Acts 9. 10:38)

And declared to be the Son of God with power, according to the spirit of holiness, by the resurrection from the dead. (Romans 1:4)

But ye are not in the flesh, but in the Spirit, if so be that the Spirit of God dwell in you. Now if any man have not the Spirit of Christ, he is none of his. (Romans 8:9)

And such were some of you; but ye are washed, but ye are sanctified, but ye are justified in the name of the Lord Jesus, and by the Spirit of our God. (1 Corinthians 6:11)

The grace of the Lord Jesus Christ, and the love of God, and the communion of the Holy Ghost, be with you all. (2 Corinthians 13:14)

And because ye are sons, God hath sent forth the Spirit of his Son into your hearts, crying, Abba Father. (Galatians 4:6)

That the God of our Lord Jesus Christ, the Father of glory, may give unto you the spirit of wisdom and revelation in the knowledge of him. (Ephesians 1:17)

For through Him we both have access by one Spirit unto the Father. (Ephesians 2:18)

In whom [Jesus] ye also are builded together for an habitation of God through the Spirit. (Ephesians 2:22)

Which he [the Holy Spirit] shed on us abundantly through Jesus Christ our Savior (Titus 3:6)

How much more shall the blood of Christ, who through the eternal Spirit offered himself without spot to God, purge your conscience from dead works to serve the living God? (Hebrews 9:14)

Elect according to the foreknowledge of God the Father, through sanctification of the Spirit, unto obedience and sprinkling of the blood of Jesus Christ: Grace unto you, and peace, be multiplied. (1 Peter 1:2)

(https://overviewbible.com/trinity-bible-verses/)

Principles

- God is the source and author of all truth.
- We must seek His truth and live by it.
- We must exercise God's truth to live a full life.
- Truth allows us to make correct decisions in life.
- God has promised us His truth for eternity.
- We are never correct without God's truth.

CHAPTER 4

What Does God Expect of Us as Christians in His Kingdom?

- to make God our priority
- to minister the gospel correctly
- to magnify the truth
- to move in the flow of the Holy Spirit
- to monitor our minds and thoughts
- to manifest faithfulness in our ministry
- to maintain a deep commitment to the Word
- to master our position, power, prospects and promises in the Bible

Who Controls Your Life?

Every day as a Christian, you face the demands and requirements of the laws in the Constitution and the Bible representing God's Covenant with man. You are living under spiritual as well as spiritual laws. You have rights under the US Constitution, but God has prepared for you a special Covenant that entitles you to special privileges, position, power, prospects, and promises in His eternal kingdom.

We must respect and honor the US Constitution while adhering reverently to God's Word. We face issues everyday arising out of our relationship to God almighty. He cares about us, and through the Holy Spirit, He is constantly teaching and encouraging us to stay faithful to his Word. There is no way God could have merely made us and placed us on earth but then left us alone to our own devices and uncontrolled guidance. His decree is just as comprehensive as His government. His government extends over all His creation and all events. He is concerned about our lives and deaths, about our state in time, and about our state in eternity. God works all things from His own counsel.

What God's The Bible Says

> But seek ye first the Kingdom, and his righteousness; and all these things shall be added unto you. (Matthew 6:33)
>
> Ask (for wisdom), and it shall be given; seek, and ye shall find; knock, and it shall be opened unto you. (Matthew 7:7)
>
> But if from thence thou seek the Lord thy God, thou shalt find him, if thou seek him with all thy heart, and with all thy soul. (Deuteronomy 4:29)
>
> Seek the Lord and his strength, seek his face continually. (1 Chronicles 16:11; Psalm 105:4)
>
> The humble shall see this, and be glad: and your heart shall live that seek God. (Psalm 69:32)
>
> Blessed are they that keep his testimonies, and that seek him with the whole heart? (Psalm 119:2)
>
> I love them that love me; and those that seek me early shall find me. (Proverbs 8:17)
>
> Seek ye the Lord while he may be found, call ye upon him while he is near. (Isaiah 55:6)
>
> Yet they seek me daily, and delight to know my ways, as a nation that did righteousness, and forsook not the ordinance of their God: they ask of me the ordinances of justice; they take delight to approaching to God. (Isaiah 58:2)
>
> For the pastors are become brutish, and have not sought the LORD: therefore they shall not prosper, and all their flocks shall be scattered. (Jeremiah 10:21)

> And ye shall seek me, and find me, when ye shall search for me with all your heart. (Jeremiah 29:13)
>
> The Lord is good unto them that wait for him, to the soul that seeketh him. (Lamentations 3:25)
>
> And I set my face unto the God, to seek by prayer and supplications, with fasting, and sackcloth, and ashes. (Daniel 9:3)
>
> For he that cometh to God must believe that he is, and that He is a rewarder of them that diligently seek him. (Hebrews 11:6)

Jesus Christ Is Coming Back

As followers of Christ, we cannot forget that all things on this planet shall pass away. Christ is coming back to receive us into His kingdom. We cannot forget that eternity is our goal. We shall live in the presence of the Lord forever. The price we must pay is present comfort and conveniences of this world. We cannot conform to this world because the Bible says it is enmity with Him. We therefore live to please God knowing that he holds our destiny in the palm of his hand. The Old Testament scriptures on His coming to earth to die for the world were all fulfilled.

Prophecies on his second coming abound in the Bible, and this means our hope in Him is substantial.

What God's The Bible Says

- That He will come Himself. (1 Thessalonians 4:16)
- That He will shout. (1 Thessalonians 4:16)
- That the dead will hear His voice. (John 5:28)
- That the raised and changed believers will be caught up to meet Him in the air. (1 Thessalonians 4:17)
- That He will receive them unto Himself. (John 14:3)
- That He will minister unto His watching servants. (Luke 12:37)
- That He will come to the earth again. (Acts 1:11)

- That He will come to the same Mount Olive from which He ascended. (Zechariah 14:4)
- That He will come in flaming fire. (2 Thessalonians 1:8)
- That He will come in the clouds of heaven with power and with glory. (Matthew 24:30; 1 Peter 1:7, 4:13)
- That He will stand upon the earth. (Job 19:25)
- That His saints (the church) will come with Him. (Deuteronomy 33:2; 1 Thessalonians 3:13; Jude 14)
- That every eye will see Him. (Revelation 1:7)
- That he will destroy the Antichrist. (2 Thessalonians 2:8)
- That He will sit on the throne. (Matthew 25:31; Revelation 5:13)
- That the nations will be gathered before Him, and He will judge them. (Matthew 25:32)
- That He will have the throne of David. (Isaiah 9:6–7; Luke 1:32)
- That it will be on earth. (Jeremiah 23:5–6)
- That He will have a kingdom. (Daniel 7:13–14)
- That He shall rule over it with His saints. (Revelation 5:10)
- That all kings and nations will serve Him. (Isaiah 49:6–7; Revelation 15:4)
- That the kingdoms of this world will become His kingdom. (Zechariah 9:10; Revelation 11:15)
- That the people will gather unto Him. (Genesis 49:10)
- That every knee will bow to Him. (Isaiah 45:23)
- That they will come and worship the King. (Zechariah 14:16)
- That He will build up Zion. (Psalm 102:16)
- That His throne will be in Jerusalem. (Isaiah 33:20–21)
- That the apostles will sit upon twelve thrones judging the twelve tribes of Israel. (Matthew 19:28; Luke 22:28–30)
- That He will rule all nations. (Psalm 2:8–9; Revelation 2:27)
- That He will rule with judgment and justice. (Isaiah 9:7)
- That the temple in Jerusalem will be rebuilt and the glory of the Lord will come into it. (Ezekiel 40:48, 43:2–5, 44:4)
- That the glory of the Lord will be revealed. (Isaiah 40:5)
- That the wilderness will bear fruit. (Isaiah 32:15)
- That the desert will blossom as the rose. (Isaiah 35:1–2)
- That His rest will be glorious. (Isaiah 11:10)

Principles

- We have a sacred duty to give our first allegiance to God almighty.
- Our duty is to live to please Him in all things.
- God's authority extends to all creation.
- We are to remember that Jesus is coming back.
- God is working to accomplish His will in us.
- We are to maintain unwavering allegiance to God's Constitution.

CHAPTER 5

Why Should We Know Our Rights as Christians?

The Center for Constitutional Studies helps us to understand why we need to know our rights in the Constitution summarized in the excerpts below.

> Sept. 17, 2009, marks the 222nd anniversary of the day that delegates to the United States Constitutional Convention met for the last time to sign one of the best-known American historical documents. It's a significant moment in the history of our country, one that's worth noting on this day—now called Constitution Day—since 2004 when Congress mandated that all publicly funded educational institutions provide a lesson on the Constitution on the day in history that it was adopted. In every school and college that receives public money across the country today, students are learning about this remarkable document.
>
> Many do not realize that this document guarantees our civil liberties, as outlined by the Bill of Rights, limits government power and establishes checks and balances to ensure that the people are protected. Some people feel that the Constitution goes too far in the rights it guarantees. What they fail to realize is that these rights don't belong to a select few, government officials, the press or the media or some nebulous establishment.
>
> The power to govern was vested, ultimately and irrevocably, in the hands of the people 222 years ago when 39 delegates signed the Constitution we celebrate today. The rights set

> forth in this document belong to every American citizen. These fundamental freedoms are guaranteed under law. We can't protect our democracy by repressing the very freedoms that nurture it. This is, after all, a government of the people, by the people, for the people. And that places the responsibility for governance directly on the people. So they need to pay attention to what's going on, exercise their rights, be active participants in their own governance and hold their elected officials accountable. And they can start today by learning more about the Constitution. (https://www.mlive.com/opinion/kalamazoo/index.ssf/2009/09/editorial_why_should_we_learn.html)

The answer to the question, "Why should we study the Constitution?" is below.

> The American Constitution is the document by which our country operates. Along with the Bill of Rights, the Constitution dictates the laws of our land and the rights of its residents. Thus, in order to help our country progress properly in the ever-shifting present, we must study the Constitution to familiarize ourselves with this country's roots, the source from which change can emerge. Here are some additional reasons why studying the constitution is useful.
>
> Know Your Rights: As an American, it is crucial to know your rights. The fastest way to learn these rights is to study the Constitution. Written during the revolutionary times, and revised as progress demanded, the Constitution dictates what is legal and illegal for all United States citizens. Protect yourself against fines and arrests by learning this country's rules.
>
> Understand the Legislative Process: Do you ever wonder how the government imparts new laws? The Legislative branch of the United States government, consisting of the Senate and House of Representatives, create new laws by

reevaluating, questioning, and defending the Constitution daily. Thus, studying the Constitution is a great way to familiarize oneself with America's current governing laws, to help one better follow the moves made in contemporary politics to change these laws.

Justice System Knowledge: Have you ever found yourself in legal trouble? If you have, you know that the entire legal process can be incredibly confusing, stressful, and expensive. Instead of simply relying on your lawyer's legal knowledge, educate yourself about how the judicial system works. Study the Constitution and Bill of Rights to better understand where your case's facts really fall in the eye of the court.

Participate in Change: Would you like to help rewrite our country's laws or participate in preserving the judicial system? To change the rules, you have to know those rules. Studying the Constitution is the best way to learn how the American government operates. From there, you can decide which laws you agree or disagree with, further directing you toward what kind of bills you would like to draft. This knowledge opens doors through which you can make your mark on this nation and truly impart change." (https://nccsid.wordpress.com/2014/07/15/why-should-we-study-the-constitution/)

Why Should We Know God's The Bible?

1. Reading the Bible daily helps us to live life better.

    But he answered and said, it is written, Man shall not live by bread alone, but by every word that proceedeth out of the mouth of God. (Matthew 4:4)

    For this commandment is a lamp, and the law is light; and reproofs of instruction are the way to life. (Proverbs 6:23)

Receive I pray thee, the law from his mouth, and lay up his words in thine heart. (Job 22:22)

1. It helps us do God's will, obey Him, and not sin.

   Wherewithal shall a young man cleanse his way? by taking heed thereto according to thy word. With my whole heart have I sought thee: O let me not wander from thy commandments. Thy word have I hid in mine heart, that I might not sin against thee. Blessed art thou, O LORD: teach me thy statutes. (Psalm 119:9–12)

   The law of his God is in his heart, none of his steps shall slide. (Psalm 37:31)

   Then said I, Lo, I come in the volume of the book it is written of me, I delight to do thy will, O my God: yea, they law is within my heart. (Psalm 40:7–8)

2. It guards us from false teachings and false teachers.

   Beloved, believe not every spirit, but try the spirits whether they are of God: because many false prophets are gone out into the world. (1 John 4:1)

   For there shall arise false Christs, and false prophets, and shall shew great signs and wonders; insomuch that, if it were possible, they shall deceive the very elect and perform great signs and wonders to deceive, if possible, even the elect. Behold, I have told you before. Wherefore if they shall say unto you, behold, he is in the desert; go not forth: behold, he is in the secret chambers; believe it not. (Matthew 24:24–26)

3. It helps us spend time with the Lord.

   For the LORD giveth wisdom; out of his mouth cometh knowledge and understanding. He layeth up sound wisdom for the righteous: he is a buckler to them that walk uprightly. (Proverbs 2:6–7)

All scripture is given by inspiration of God, and is profitable for doctrine, for reproof, for correction, for instruction in righteousness. (2 Timothy 3:16)

4. It helps us be more convicted of our sin.

For the word of God is quick, and powerful, and sharper than any two-edged sword, piercing even to the dividing asunder of soul and spirit, and of the joints and marrow, and is a discerner of the thoughts and intents of the heart. (Hebrews 4:12)

5. It helps us know more about our beloved Savior, Jesus, the cross, the gospel, etc.

Jesus saith unto him, I am the way, the truth, and the life: no man cometh unto the Father but by me. (John 14:6)

And ye have not his word abiding in you: for whom he hath sent, him ye believe not. Search the scriptures; for in them ye have eternal life: and they are they which testify of me. And ye will not come to me, that might have life. I receive not honor from men. (John 5:38–41)

In the beginning was the Word, and the Word was with God, and the Word was God. The same was with God in the beginning with God. All things were made by him; and without him was not any thing made that was made. In him was life; and the life was the light of men. (John 1:1–4)

Moreover, brethren, I declare unto you the gospel which I preached unto you, which also ye have received, and wherein ye stand; By which also ye are saved, if ye keep in memory what I preached unto you, unless ye have believed

> in vain. For I delivered unto you first of all that which I also received, how that Christ died for our sins according to the scriptures; And that he was buried, and that he rose again the third day according to the scriptures. (1 Corinthians 15:1–4)

6. It encourages us.

> For whatsoever things were written aforetime were written for our learning, that we through patience and comfort of the scriptures might have hope. Now the God of patience and consolation grant you to be likeminded one toward another according to Christ Jesus. (Romans 15:4–5)

> This is my comfort in my affliction: for thy word hath quickened me. (Psalm 119:50)

> Have not I have commanded thee? Be strong and a good courage; be not afraid, neither be thou dismayed: for the LORD thy God is with thee whithersoever thou goest. (Joshua 1:9)

> And Jesus looking upon them saith, with men it is impossible, but not with God: for with God all things are possible. (Mark 10:27)

7. It helps us to not start getting comfortable. We should make sure Christ is always first in our lives; we don't want to drift from Him.

> Nevertheless I have somewhat against thee, because thou hast left thy first love. (Revelation 2:4)

> Not slothful in business, fervent in spirit, serving the Lord. (Romans 12:11)

> He that turneth away his ear from hearing the law, even his prayer shall be abomination. (Proverbs 28:9)

8. It's exciting, and it makes us want to praise the Lord more.

> Bless the LORD, ye his angels, that excel in strength, that do his commandments, hearkening unto the voice of his word. Bless ye the LORD, all ye his hosts; ye ministers of his, that do his pleasure. (Psalm 103:20–21)
>
> In God I praise his word: in the LORD will I praise his word. In God have I put my trust: I will not be afraid what man can do unto me. (Psalm 56:10–11)
>
> Praise ye the LORD. O give thanks unto the LORD; for he is good: for his mercy endureth for ever. Who can utter the mighty acts of the LORD? Who can shew forth all his praise? (Psalm 106:1–2)

9. We will get to know God better.

> So then faith cometh by hearing, and hearing by the word of God. (Romans 10:17)
>
> As newborn babes, desire the sincere milk of the word, that ye may grow thereby: if so be ye have tasted that the Lord is gracious. (1 Peter 2:2–3)

10. We will have better fellowship with other believers. With scripture, we can teach, bear each other's burdens, give biblical advice, and so on.

> All scripture is given by inspiration of God, and is profitable for doctrine, for reproof, for correction, for instruction in righteousness. (2 Timothy 3:16)
>
> Wherefore comfort yourselves together, and edify one another, even as also ye do. (1 Thessalonians 5:11)

11. We will be able to defend the faith.

> But if ye suffer for the righteousness' sake, happy are ye: and be not afraid of their terror, neither be troubled; but sanctify the Lord God in your hearts: and be ready always to give an answer to every man that asketh you a reason of the hope that is in you with meekness and fear: having a good conscience; that, whereas they speak evil of you, as of evildoers, they may be ashamed that falsely accuse your good conversation in Christ. (1 Peter 3:14–16)

> Casting down imaginations, and every high thing that exalteth itself against the knowledge of God, and bringing into captivity every thought to the obedience of Christ. (2 Corinthians 10:5)

12. We will defend ourselves against Satan.

> Put on the whole armor of God, that ye may be able to stand against the wiles of the devil. (Ephesians 6:11)

> Above all, taking the shield of faith, wherewith ye shall be able to quench all the fiery darts of the wicked. And take the helmet of salvation, and the sword of the Spirit, which is the word of God. (Ephesians 6:16–17)

13. God's Word is eternal while the earth is not.

> Heaven and earth shall pass away, but my words shall not pass away. (Matthew 24:35)

> For ever, O LORD, thy word is settled in the heavens. (Psalm 119:89)

> Thou art near, O LORD; and all thy commandments are truth. Concerning thy testimonies, I have known of old that thou hast founded them for ever. Consider mine

affliction, and deliver me: for I do not forget thy law. (Psalm 119:151–53)

14. God's voice will give us direction.

Thy word is a lamp unto my feet, and a light unto path. (Psalm 119:105)

My sheep hear my voice, and I know them, and they follow me. (John 10:27)

15. The Bible helps us to grow as believers.

Blessed is the man that walketh not in the counsel of the ungodly, nor standeth in the way of sinners, nor sitteth in the seat of the scornful. But his delight is in the law of the LORD; and in his law doth he meditate day and night. And he shall be like a tree planted by the rivers of water, that bringeth forth his fruit in his season; his leaf also shall not wither; and whatsoever he doeth shall prosper. The ungodly are not so: but are like the chaff which the wind driveth away. (Psalm 1:1–4)

For this cause we also, since the day we heard it, do not cease to pray for you, and to desire that ye might be filled with the knowledge of his will in all wisdom and spiritual understanding; That ye might walk worthy of the Lord unto all pleasing, being fruitful in every good work, and increasing in the knowledge of God. (Colossians 1:9–10)

Sanctify them through thy truth; thy word is truth. (John 17:17)

16. Scripture helps us serve God better.

That the man of God may be perfect, thoroughly furnished unto all good works. (2 Timothy 3:17)

17. It will teach us to use our time wisely instead of turning our minds into mush.

    See then that ye walk circumspectly, not as fools, but as wise, redeeming the time, because the days are evil. (Ephesians 5:15–16)

18. It teaches us spiritual discipline.

    Now no chastening for the present seemeth to be joyous, but grievous: nevertheless afterward it yieldeth the peaceable fruit of righteousness unto them which are exercised thereby. (Hebrews 12:11)

    But I keep under my body, and bring it into subjection: lest that by any means, when I have preached to others, I myself should be a castaway. (1 Corinthians 9:27)

19. We will learn more about history.

    Which we have heard and known, and our fathers have told us. We will not hide them from their children, shewing to the generation to come the praises of the LORD, and his strength, and his wonderful works that he hath done. (Psalm 78:3–4)

    Through faith we understand that the worlds were framed by the word of God, so that things which are seen were not made of things which do appear. By faith Abel offered unto God a more excellent sacrifice than Cain, by which he obtained witness that he was righteous, God testifying of his gifts: and by it he being dead yet speaketh. (Hebrews 11:3–4)

Reminder: before you read The Bible, tell God to speak to you through His Word.[39]

The Meaning of "Rights"

> Rights are legal, social, or ethical principles of freedom or entitlement; that is, rights are the fundamental normative rules about what is allowed of people or owed to people, according to some legal system, social convention, or ethical theory. (https://en.wikipedia.org/wiki/Rights)

Rights are divided into two main categories.

> General: (1) Justified, recognized, and protected (violation of which is unlawful) claim on, or interest in, specific tangible or intangible property.
>
> (2) Freedom, immunity, power, or privilege, due to one by agreement, birth, claim, guaranty, or by the application of legal, moral, or natural principles.
>
> (A) Liberty: right to something a right-holder cannot be prevented from, such as to speak freely or follow a particular belief, and
>
> (B) License: right to do something which is otherwise illegal, such as to sell liquor or drive a powered vehicle.
>
> Other categories of rights include: Alienable: rights that can be taken away or transferred, such a property rights. (http://www.businessdictionary.com/definition/right.html)

Summary of Rights

- our entitlements
- our appropriate possessions
- what we are authorized to have and do
- what is legally permitted
- areas in which we are responsible

Christians cannot give the rights they enjoy under the Constitution and in God's Kingdom the same precedence, the same weight, or the same priority. America is a great democracy. It offers freedoms that are admired and envied by many nations; America's rights draw many people to this country. American Christians and missionaries have given the world Christianity through television missionaries and the radio. They have done a great deal for Christianity, but there is a danger of missing their own rights and promises in Christ Jesus if they put the Constitution on the same plane and pedestal as God's Word.

God is a jealous God. He cannot share the glory with the Constitution. Christians are advised to reconsider this issue in light of the facts revealed in this book for the sake of their position in Christ and His promises for His children. There is no conflict between the two, but there is a potential area of compromise if Christians are not walking in the Spirit and give glory to human institutions to the detriment of their fellowship, rights, position, and promises in Christ Jesus.

The Constitution is a legal document on which the US government is based. It is the system of fundamental laws and principles that prescribe the nature, functions, and limits of the US government. It was adopted in 1787 and put into effect in 1789.

Principles of the Constitution

- to protect people in the enjoyment of their civil rights
- to define those rights relating to all questions of property and person
- to provide for their vindication
- to regulate interstate relations
- to provide all means necessary for its own preservation

God does not deal with humanity in terms of rights because His relationship with humanity is based on the Bible, not a constitution. The Bible contains His Covenant with us, which can be summarized as follows.

- a conditional promise made by almighty God to Adam, a free agent
- a formal sealed agreement or contract
- God's promises to humanity as recorded in the Old and New Testaments

An absolute complete The Bible is a voluntary convention, pact, or agreement between distinct persons, about the ordering and dispensing of things in their power, unto their mutual concern and advantage. (John Owen, *The Works of John Owen* (Edinburgh, Scotland: The Banner of Truth Trust, 1991), XXII: 78, 80, 81, 89, 142)

Conventions, which are usually clauses of agreement contained in a deed, whereby either party may stipulate for the truth of certain facts, or may bind Himself to perform, or give something on the other." Sir William Blackstone, "Codifying Conventions and Royal Prerogatives Essay. 816 Words Oct 19th, 2013)

God made an eternal contract with humanity that was ratified by the death of Jesus Christ and His resurrection to enforce it.

God did not make an ordinary constitution with humanity; it was a Covenant represented by the Bible, which cannot be broken. The Bible cannot ever be altered; it remains forever for all the parties involved, and we must honor the letter and the spirit of The Bible. God's Covenant with humanity was the only one made. No one else is capable of making a Covenant with us.

The Word of God gives us a brief account of creation, the making of humanity, and humanity's fall. We have no difficulty in ascertaining that the trial to which Adam and Eve were subjected in Eden had been divinely foreseen: "The Lamb slain (in the purpose of God) from the foundation of the world" (Revelation 13:8). This makes it clear that in view of the fall, God provided for the recovery of His people who had apostatized; the means of that recovery were consistent with the claims of His divine holiness and justice.

He had arranged all the details and results of His plan of mercy from the beginning. In Genesis 1:26, we learn of God's plan to make us.

> And God said, Let us make man in our own image, after our likeness- and let them have dominion over the fish of the sea, and over the fowl of the air, and over the cattle, and over all the earth, and over every creeping thing that creepeth upon the earth.

The plan was executed in Genesis 1:27–30.

> So God created man in his own image, in the image of God created he him; male and female created he them.

> And God blessed them, and God said unto them, Be fruitful, and multiply, and replenish the earth, and subdue and have dominion over the fish of the sea, and over the fowl of the air, and over every living thing that moveth upon the earth.

God made a Covenant with humanity in Genesis 1:29–30.

> And God said, Behold, I have given you every herb bearing seed, which is upon the face of all the earth, and every tree, in the which is the fruit of a tree yielding seed; to you it shall be for meat.
>
> And to every beast of the earth, and to every fowl of the air, and to everything that creepeth upon the earth, wherein there is life, I have given every green herb for meat: and it was so.

That defined humanity's rights and promises. God instructed humanity on its obligations in Genesis 2:16–17.

> And God commanded the man, saying, Of every tree of the garden thou mayest freely eat: But of the tree of knowledge and evil, thou shalt not eat of it: for in that day that thou eatest thereof thou shalt surely die.

The Bible demonstrates that God never made a constitution with humanity because He is omnipotent, omnipresent, and omniscient. Constitutions involve equals. In this case, God voluntarily gave up some of His authority to Adam, but He set a few conditions for this new relationship. God promised not to break His Covenant with Adam, and even today, the Bible stands.

What The Bible Says

In the first the Bible, the parties involved were God and Adam. Adam was promised life and favor. The conditions for fulfillment were perfect obedience to the law: "Abstain from the fruit of the tree of knowledge." The penalty for not doing that was this.

In the day thou eatest thereof thou shalt surely die. (Genesis 3:16–17)

But with thee will I establish my Covenant; and thou shalt come into the ark, thou and thy sons, and thy wife, and thy sons' wives with thee. (Genesis 6:18)

And I will remember my Covenant, which is between me and you and every living creature of all flesh; and the waters shall no more become a flood to destroy all flesh. (Genesis 9:13)

God made a Covenant with the Israelites. Now therefore if ye will obey my voice deed, and keep my Covenant, then ye shall be a peculiar treasure unto me above 11 people: for all the earth is mine. And ye shall be unto me a kingdom of priests, and a holy nation. (Exodus 19:5–6)

And Moses took half of the blood, and put is in basins; and half of the blood he wrinkled on the altar. And he took the book of The Law and read in the audience of the people: and said, All that the Lord hath said will we do be obedient. (Exodus 24:6–7)

And the LORD God commanded the man, saying, of every tree of the garden mayest freely eat. But of the tree of knowledge of good and evil, thou shalt eat of it: for in that thou eatest thereof thou shalt surely die. (Genesis 2:16–17)

But with thee will I establish my Covenant; and thou shalt come into the ark, thou rid thy sons, and thy wife, and thy sons' wives with thee. (Genesis 6:18)

And hath confirmed the same to Jacob for a law, and to Israel for an everlasting The Bible, saying, unto thee will I give the land of Canaan, the lot of your inherit wee. He suffered no man to do them wrong: yea, he reproved kings for their Lakes. (Chronicles 16:16–18, 21)

According as he hath chosen us in him before the foundation of the world, that we should be holy and without blame before him in love: having predestinated us unto the adoption of children by Jesus Christ to himself to the good pleasure of his will. (Ephesians 1:4–5)

And the Scripture, foreseeing that God would justify the heathen through faith, preached before the gospel unto Abraham, saying in thee shall all nations be blessed. So then they which be of faith are blessed with faithful Abraham. (Galatians 3:8–9)

Christ has redeemed us from the curse of the law, being made a curse for us: for it is written, Cursed is every one that hangeth on a tree. That the blessing of Abraham might come Gentiles through Jesus Christ; that we might receive the promise of the Spirit through faith. (Galatians 3:13–14, 17)

This I will make with them after those days, saith the LORD, I will put my laws into their hearts, and in their minds will I write them. (Hebrews 10:16)

In the same day made a Covenant with Abram, saying, Unto thy seed have I given this river of Egypt unto the great river, the river of Euphrates: The Kenites, and the Kenizzites, and the Kadmonites. And the Hittites, :Perizzites, and the Rephaims. And the Morites, the Canaanites, and the Girgashites, and the Jebusites. (Genesis 15:18–21)

And the Lord appeared unto him, and said, Go not down into Egypt; dwell in the land which I shall tell thee of Sojourn in this land, and I will be with thee, and will bless thee; for unto thee and unto thy seed, I will give all these countries, and I will perform the oath which I swore unto Abraham thy father. (Genesis 26:2–3)

And he declared unto you his Covenant, which he commanded you to perform, even ten commandments;

and he wrote them upon two tables of stone. (Deuteronomy 4:1–3)

The Lord our God made a Covenant with us in Horeb. (Deuteronomy 5:2)

Keep therefore the words of this Covenant, and do them, that ye may prosper in all that ye do. (Deuteronomy 29:9)

And the angel of the Lord came up from the Gigal to Bachim, and said, I made you to go up out of Egypt, and have brought you unto the land which I swore unto your fathers; and I said, I will never break my Covenant with you. (Judges 2:1)

I have made a Covenant with my chosen, I have sworn unto David my servant. Thy seed will I establish forever, and build up thy throne to all generations. Selah. (Psalm 89:3–4)

And I will make an everlasting Covenant with them, that I will not turn away from them, to do them good; but I will put my fear in their hearts, that they shall not depart from me. (Jeremiah 32:40)

Behold, the days come, saith the Lord, that I will make a new Covenant with the house of Israel, and with the house of Judah. (Jeremiah 31:31)

Exercising Your Civil Rights

You should exercise your rights for a number of reasons.

- to get to a point of enjoying your rights
- to be certain of what belongs to you
- to regard or accept as true or beyond doubt your rights
- to be capable of appropriating what belongs to you
- to have practical knowledge of a subject matter

- to have a thorough experience of a thing
- to know and access your portion of inheritance

The Bible has been emphatic about the need for us as Christians to know and exercise our rights because our eternity hinges on it.

What The Bible Says

> And the Lord commanded the man, saying, Of every tree of the garden thou mayest freely eat But of the tree of the knowledge of good and evil, thou shalt not eat of it: for in the day that thou eatest thereof thou shalt surely die. (Genesis 2:16–17)

> And I have filled him with spirit of God, in wisdom, and in understanding, and in knowledge, and in all manner of workmanship. (Exodus 31:3)

> For the LORD is a God of knowledge, and by him actions are weighed. (1 Samuel 2:3)

> Give me now, wisdom and knowledge, that I may go out and come in before this people. (2 Chronicles 1:10)

> Therefore my people are gone into captivity, because they have no knowledge. (Isaiah 5:13)

> And wisdom and knowledge shall be the stability of thy times, and strength of salvation: the fear of the LORD is His treasure. (Isaiah 33:6)

> And the spirit of the Lord shall rest upon him, the spirit of wisdom and understanding, the spirit of counsel and might, the spirit of knowledge, and of the fear of the LORD. (Isaiah 11:2)

> The fear of the Lord is the beginning of knowledge: but fools despise wisdom and instruction. (Proverbs 1:7)

Receive my instruction, and not silver; and knowledge rather than choice gold. (Proverbs 8:10)

For wisdom and might are his. (Daniel 2:20)

My people are destroyed for lack of knowledge: because thou hast rejected knowledge, I will also reject thee. (Hosea 4:6)

To give knowledge of salvation unto his people by the remission of their sins. (Luke 1:77)

To desire that ye might be filled with knowledge of his will in all wisdom and spiritual understanding. (Colossians 1:9)

Who, (God our Savior) will have all men to be saved, and to come unto the knowledge of the truth. (1 Timothy 2:4)

For if we sin willfully after that we have received the knowledge of the truth, there remaineth no more sacrifice for sins. (Hebrews 10:26)

And thou, Solomon my son, know the God of thy father, and serve him with a perfect heart and a willing mind: for the Lord searcheth all hearts, and understandeth all imaginations of the thoughts: if thou seek him, he will be found of thee; but if thou forsake him, he will cast thee off for ever. (1 Chronicles 28:9)

The Lord is with you, while ye be with him; and if ye seek him, he will be found of you; but if ye forsake him, he will forsake you. (2 Chronicles 15:2)

My son, let not them, (Knowledge and wisdom) depart from thine eyes: Keep sound wisdom and discretion. (Proverbs 3:21)

Why You Need to Exercise Your Rights in God's Plan

- You can appropriate your promises.
- You can set your course for the future.
- You can become effective in your ministry.
- You can avoid unnecessary waste of time and energy.
- You can live a life of fulfillment and engage in the right activities.
- You can find your predetermined path to a predetermined end.
- You can achieve specific, measurable goals.
- You can focus and avoid distractions and pitfalls.

God's Rights for You

We cannot know our rights in the Bible outside the person and work of Jesus Christ at Calvary. He is our Justifier. He is our righteousness before God. We must find our position in Him so we can then appropriate our promises. Jesus gives us that perfect conformity to all the requirements of the law.

Sovereign God elected His chosen people and gave them to His Son in the Covenant of Grace, and as sovereign, he executes that Covenant when he makes the righteousness of Christ theirs by imputation. Justification on the other hand is God's judicial act proceeding upon that sovereign imputation and declaring the law to be perfectly satisfied in respect to us. This involves first pardoning of his sins; second, restoration to divine favor for those who obey the commands of the law. It is strictly legal, but we know that God is sovereign and will admits and credit to us a vicarious righteousness because that is what the law demands.

The Bible and the US Constitution

In the Bible, there are no checks and balances but unity of the deity, God the Father united with God the Son and God the Holy Spirit. In the Bible, our rights, position, and promises are inextricably tied to the person of Jesus Christ and His work on the cross. Under the Constitution, our rights, position, and promises are tied to the founding fathers and their revolution against the British monarchy that resulted in our political independence.

Under the Bible, our rights, position, and promises were determined before the foundation of the world, while with the Constitution, they were produced by the Constitution signed in 1787 and subsequent amendments.

Under the Bible, our rights, position, and promises came from God's unconditional love for us and His eternal commitment to our salvation. Under the Constitution, they were made out of political and social convenience.

Under the Bible, our rights, position, and promises are everlasting. Under the Constitution, they are good while we are alive.

Under the Bible, our rights, position, and promises are unchangeable and sealed with the Holy Spirit of promise. Under the Constitution, they are conditional and based on the law.

Under the Bible, our rights, position, and promises are enforced by the Holy Spirit that lives in us. Under the Constitution, they are enforced by government officials who may not be concerned about our welfare.

Under the Bible, our rights, position, and promises are obtained by our exercising faith in Jesus Christ. Under the Constitution, they are appropriated by our exercising our legal rights.

Under the Bible, our rights, position, and promises not amendable because they are eternal. Under the Constitution, they are amendable under article 5 of the Constitution.

Under the Bible, the testator of our position and promises still lives and lives forever more. The founding fathers are dead, and that means they personally have no power to enforce the Constitution.

Under the Bible, our rights, position, and promises are experienced by one way only—through Jesus Christ. Under the Constitution, they can be experienced by citizenship, which comes by blood, birth, or naturalization.

Under the Bible, our rights, position, and promises are not based on age or mental condition. Under the Constitution, they are based on age and sometimes mental condition and what is called legal standing.

We Have Rights because We Are Justified

We are justified without the deeds of the law by the blood of Christ by faith and grace through the agency of an advocate by means of a satisfaction and imputed righteousness. The term *righteousness* means obedience of suffering that satisfies the demands of the law and constitutes the grounds on which justification proceeds. Consequently, it signifies perfect conformity to the law, which was the original grounds of justification under the Covenant of Works, the vicarious obedience and suffering of Christ, our substitute, which he wrought in our behalf and which when imputed to us because our righteousness, or the ground of our justification. We appropriated justification through our faith in Christ Jesus and His work on the cross. The law consists essentially of a rule of duty and of a penalty for breaking that rule.

Justification Is by Faith

> Therefore by the deeds of the law there shall no flesh be justified in his sight: for the law is the knowledge of sin. (Romans 3:20)

> Even the righteousness of God which is by faith of Jesus Christ unto all and upon all them that believe: for there is no difference. For all have sinned, and come short of the glory of God. (Romans 3:22–23)

> Therefore we conclude that a man is justified by faith without the deeds of the law. (Romans 3:28)

> But to him that worketh not, but believeth on him that justifieth the ungodly, his faith is counted for righteousness. (Romans 4:5)

> Therefore being justified by faith, we have peace with God through our Lord Christ. (Romans 5:1)

> For therein (the gospel) is the righteousness of God revealed from faith to faith: as it is written, The Just shall live by faith. (Romans 1:17; Galatians 3:11).

> For Christ is the end of the law for righteousness to everyone that believeth. (Romans 10:4)

> Knowing that a man is not justified by the works of the law, but by the faith of Jesus Christ, even we have believed in Jesus Christ, that we might be justified by the faith of Christ, and not by the works of the law: for by the works of the law shall no flesh be justified. (Galatians 2:16)

And he is the propitiation for our sins: and not for ours only, but also for the sins of the whole world. (1 John 2:2)

And be found in him, not having mine own righteousness, which is of the law, but that which is through the faith of Christ, the righteousness which is of God by faith. (Philippians 3:9)

But of him are ye in Christ Jesus, who of God is made unto us wisdom, and righteousness, and sanctification, and redemption. (1 Corinthians 1:30)

For He hath made him to be sin for us, who knew no sin; that we might be made the righteousness of God in him. (2 Corinthians 5:21)

No Works Can Justify

When scriptures deny that justification can be by works, the term *works* is always used generally as obedience to the whole revealed will of God however made known. God demands perfect obedience to His will as revealed to any individual. But since everyone is a sinner, justification by the law is equally impossible for all. Believers are justified without the deeds of the law, and God justifies the ungodly in Christ. Justification is in the name of Christ, by His blood and grace, and by faith. Christ was our representative, and His perfect righteousness as imputed to us is the sole and strictly legal ground of our justification.

Thus, He is made for us the end of the law for righteousness, and we are made the righteousness of God in Him. Christ came to fulfill the law. The law failed in the hands of Adam. Christ, the second Adam, came under the Covenant of Grace and assumed all the responsibilities of humanity and discharged obligations of His people under the Covenant of Works. His suffering discharged the penalty, but only His active obedience fulfils the condition. All promises are attached to obedience, not suffering.

Justification Is the Fulfillment of the Law

Do we then make void the law through faith? God forbid: yea we establish the law. (Romans 3:31, 5:19)

For He hath made him to be sin for us, who knew no sin; that we might be made the righteousness of God in him. (2 Corinthians 5:21)

Behold the Lamb of God, which taketh away the sin of the world. (John 1:29)

Who his own self bare our sins in his own body on the tree, that we, being dead to sins, should live unto righteousness: by whose stripes ye were healed. (1 Peter 2:24)

But now the righteousness of God without the law is manifested, being witnessed by the law and the prophets. (Romans 3:21)

"Even as David also describeth the blessedness of the man, unto whom God imputeth righteousness without works. (Romans 4:6)

Therefore as by the offense of one judgement came upon all men to condemnation; even so the righteousness of one the free gift came upon all men unto justification of life. (Romans 5:18)

For by grace are ye saved through faith; and that not of yourselves: it is the gift of God. (Ephesians 2:8)

Knowing that a man is not justified by the works of the law, but by the faith of Jesus Christ, even we have believed in Jesus Christ, that we might be justified by the faith of Christ, and not by the works of the law: for by the works of the law shall no flesh be justified. (Galatians 2:16)

> For such an high priest became us, who is holy, harmless, undefiled, separate from sinners, and made higher than the heavens. (Hebrews 7:26)

Jesus Christ—Our Perfect Substitute

To accomplish the work of atonement for humankind, God needed a perfect substitute, His only begotten Son, Jesus Christ. This indeed was a full expression of His plan before the creation of humanity.

What The Bible Says

> And that he died for all, that they which live should not henceforth live unto themselves, but unto him which died for them, and rose again. (2 Corinthians 5:15)

> Even as the Son of man came not to be ministered unto, but to minister, and to give his life a ransom for many. (Matthew 20:28)

> Who gave himself a ransom for all, to be testified in due time. (1 Timothy 2:6)

> But with the precious blood of Christ, as of a lamb without blemish and without spot. (1 Peter 1:19)

> For ye are bought with a price: therefore glorify God in your body, and in your spirit, which are God's. (1 Corinthians 6:20)

> Know ye not, that so many of us as were baptized into Jesus Christ were baptized into his death? Therefore we are buried with him by baptism into death: that like as Christ was raised up from the dead by the glory of the Father, even so we also should walk in newness of life. (Romans 6:3–4)

Christ Holds Our Position

We cannot find our position and promises without Jesus Christ because God has set up all things on earth and in heaven to be controlled and administered by His Son.

What The Bible Says

> Being justified freely by his grace through the redemption that is in Christ Jesus. (Romans 3:24)
>
> Much more then, being now justified by his blood, we shall be saved from wrath through him. (Romans 5:9)
>
> For as by one man's disobedience many were made sinners, so by the obedience of one shall many be made righteous. (Romans 5:19)
>
> There is therefore no condemnation to them that are in Christ Jesus, who walk not after the flesh, but after the Spirit. (Romans 8:1)
>
> For Christ is the end of the law for righteousness to everyone that believeth. (Romans 10:4)
>
> But of him are ye in Christ Jesus, who of God is made unto us wisdom, and righteousness, and sanctification, and redemption. (1 Corinthians 1:30)
>
> And be found in him, not having mine own righteousness, which is of the law, but that which through the faith of Christ, the righteousness which is of God by faith. (Philippians 3:9)
>
> Therefore being justified by faith, we have peace with God through our Lord Jesus Christ. (Romans 5:1)
>
> To wit, that God was in Christ, reconciling the world unto himself, not imputing their trespasses unto them;

and hath committed unto us the word of reconciliation. (2 Corinthians 5:19)

And you, that were sometimes alienated and enemies in your mind by wicked works, yet now hath he reconciled. (Colossians 1:21)

Nevertheless death reigned from Adam to Moses, even over them that had not sinned after the similitude of Adam's transgression, who is the figure of him that was to come." But not as the offence, so also is the free gift, For if through the offence of one many be dead, much more the grace of God, and the gift by grace, which is by one man, Jesus Christ hath abounded unto many. (Romans 5:14–15)

For he as in Adam all die, even so in Christ shall all be made alive. (1 Corinthians 15:22)

As thou hast given him power over all flesh, that he should give eternal life to as many as thou hast given him. (John 17:2)

I am crucified with Christ: nevertheless I live; yet not I, but Christ liveth in me: and the life which I now live in the flesh I live by the faith of the Son of God, who loved me, and gave himself for me. (Galatians 2:20)

For by one Spirit are we all baptized into one body, whether we be Jews or Gentiles, whether we be bond or free; and have been all made to drink into one spirit. (1 Corinthians 12:13)

But now in Christ Jesus ye who sometimes were far off are made nigh by the blood of Christ. Having abolished in his flesh the enmity, even the law of commandments contained in the ordinances; for to make in himself of twain one new man, so making peace. (Ephesians 2:13, 15)

That Christ may dwell in your hearts by faith; that ye, being rooted and grounded in love. (Ephesians 3:17)

Blotting out the handwriting of ordinances that was against us, which was contrary to us, and took it out of the way, nailing it to the cross. (Colossians 2:14)

For he is our peace, who hath made both one, and hath broken down the middle wall of partition between us. (Ephesians 2:14)

There is one body, and one Spirit, even as ye are called in one hope of your calling. (Ephesians 4:4)

And as we have been borne the image of the earthy, we shall also bear the image of the heavenly. (1 Corinthians 15:49)

For he is our peace, who hath made both one, and hath broken down the middle wall of partition between us. (Ephesians 2:14)

How much more shall the blood of Christ, who through the eternal Spirit offered himself without spot to God, purge your conscience from dead works to serve the living God? (Hebrews 9:14)

Principles

- You must choose God's Covenant for your life, which is good for eternity.
- The Constitution is designed for the present age only.
- You need God's Covenant with humanity to live for eternity.
- Your promises in The Bible cannot and will not be amended
- You must be in Christ to enjoy your promises and your eternal purpose.
- Your hope and confidence must be in God's Covenant.

CHAPTER 6

The Rights of Christians and Jesus Christ

Jesus Christ holds our rights by imputation. Imputation is an act of God as sovereign judge whereby He makes the guilt and legal responsibilities of our sins really Christ's and punishes Him for them. He also makes the righteousness of Christ ours at the same time.

The transfer is of guilt from us to Him and of merit from Him to us. He justly suffered the punishment due to our sins, and we justly receive the rewards due to His righteousness. Being justified on the grounds of perfect righteousness, our whole relation to God and the law is changed; we receive the gift of the Holy Spirit, adoption, sanctification, perseverance, the working of all things together in this life, deliverance in death, the resurrection of the body, and final glorification. We also have peace with God, His justice being completely satisfied through the righteousness of Christ, and we can exercise our rights through Him.

Knowing Our Rights in Christ

Our rights are in Christ. This union is federal and representative in character whereby Christ as the second Adam (1 Corinthians 15:22) assumed in the Covenant of Grace those broken obligations of the Covenant of Works that the first Adam failed to discharge. Christ fulfilled the requirements of the law resulting in the imputation of our sins to Him and of His righteousness to us as well as all the forensic benefits of justification and adoption.

The eternal purpose of the triune God was expressed in the decree of election; we were chosen in Him before the foundation of the world (Ephesians 1:4) and provided for its own fulfillment in the Covenant of Grace between the Father as God absolute and the Son as Mediator (John 17:2–6; Galatians 2:20).

Jesus Christ assumed fellowship with us in community of nature and became our brother (Hebrews 2:16–17). The Holy Spirit quickens our spirit (1 Corinthians 15:45), and we are all constituted in the body of Christ and are members in particular (1 Corinthians 12:27). Our spiritual life is sustained and determined in its nature and movement by the life of Christ through the indwelling of His Spirit (John 14:19; Galatians 2:20).

This union determines our legal status on the same basis as His. All our legal or Biblical responsibilities rest upon Christ and His work on the Cross. This is also an indissoluble union. In God's appointed time, with each individual of His chosen, this union is established mutually by the inner workings of the Holy Spirit, who opens their eyes, renews their spirit and paves the way to their exercise of saving faith. Thus we come to Him, receive Him, eat of His flesh, and drink of His blood. Forensically, we are rendered complete in Him. His righteousness and His Father are ours too. We receive adoption in Him and are accepted. We are sealed by his Holy Spirit of promise; in Him, we obtain our inheritance and sit with him on His throne and behold his glory (Romans 8:1; Colossians 2:10; Ephesians 1:6, 11, 13; Philippians 3:8–9).

We have fellowship with Him in the transforming, assimilating power of His life, making us like Him; every grace of Jesus reproduces itself in us. This is true of our souls (Romans 8:9; Philippians 2:5; 1 John 3:2), and our bodies become the temples of the Holy Spirit (1 Corinthians 6:17, 19). Jesus Christ's resurrection allows us to be resurrected as well, and we also receive His body (Romans 6:5; 1 Corinthians 15:47, 49; Philippians 3:21). Thus as believers, we can bear fruit in Christ both in our bodies and spirits, which are His (John 15:5; 2 Corinthians 12:9; 1 John 1:6).

This leads to our fellowship with Christ in our experience, in our labors, sufferings, temptations, and death (Galatians 6:17; Philippians 3:10; Hebrews 12:3; 1 Peter 4:13) thus rendering sacred and glorious.

Definition of "Promises"

- concerning what God declares He will bring to pass
- the elements of The Covenant, contract, and pledge with blessings to the beneficiary
- fulfillment of what is properly expected
- commitment made, mediated, and inherited by someone
- binding on the part of the one who makes them

The substance of the Christian faith the Bible broadly speaking divides promises that the sanctification of God's people and their effectual preservation in a state and course of holiness to their final salvation. These promises are summarized in Hebrews 8:10–12.

Promises to Jesus

- the declaration that the Lord will write His laws in the hearts of those for whom Christ died
- the assurance that the Lord will be the God of His people giving Himself to them in all His perfection and relationships so the supply of their every need is guaranteed
- the powers of the Holy Spirit, who will teach, convict, show us the truth, and enable us to be effective witnesses of Jesus Christ
- the mercy He will show us for our unrighteousness

God provided enablement to the new Covenant. It is now God who works in us both to will and to do His good pleasure. Under the Covenant of Works, we were left to our own natural and created strength.

God gave the bare command; He furnished His grace and Spirit so we were empowered unto that sincere and evangelical obedience He accepts of us. When God bids us to come to Him, He draws us to Him.

The new Covenant has adequate provision for failure.

Promises to God's Children

God made promises not only to His only begotten Son, Jesus Christ, but also to us, His children. The Bible is full of promises that He made and will keep forever. God is faithful and will not lie. I will give a few examples as examples. What is critical is that these promises apply only to His children, those who have found their position in His Son, Jesus Christ. We cannot expect to enjoy our rights under the Constitution until we identify our legal position as specified by the Constitution. The Constitution makes a number of promises to those who are United States citizens including these.

- equal protection under the law
- due process
- citizenship

- fundamental rights listed in the Bill of Rights
- participation in the political processes of the US

God Promised to Adopt Us

God made some great promises we need to know as His adopted children. Below are some of those promises. The list is by no means comprehensive. I believe that we should dig into the Bible and come to the knowledge of these promises. Some of those promises come in the form of blessings, and others come in the form of deliverance. God has also promised to provide for His children, to hear their prayers, and to make them joint heirs with Jesus Christ.

We are forgiven under His promises. We can approach Him boldly before the throne of grace and ask for forgiveness of our sins. God has promised us rewards on earth and in heaven. When we consider God's promises for His children, we become anxious to know our position and find it so we can receive our promises under the new Covenant.

How to Obtain God's Promises

The Constitution makes a number of promises to all citizens. Those who are ignorant of their rights may find out that they are likely to enjoy fewer of their rights. Knowledge of one's rights is critical to the acquisition of those rights. Many people live in ignorance of their constitutional rights. It is indeed a pity because they end up blaming others for their ignorance.

We cannot exercise our rights if we do not know them. The seed, the Word of God, contains the exceedingly great and precious promises God has made to us, so God's Word ought to obtain and retain in us a place of honor, reverence, faith, love, obedience, trust, and authority.

We must stand on the promises of God; we must stand on His Word in faith that He will bring His Word to pass in our lives. We have to plant the Word in our hearts in order to have it fulfilled. It also means appropriating that blessing each promise reveals. That is our part as believers. We ought to esteem the Word, which has been given to us to unveil the Living Word to us, the Lord Jesus Christ. The Word of God ought to have the same place in our hearts that Jesus does. We have to esteem the Word so it can produce a harvest in our lives.

God Promised a New Seed

Just as seeds germinate in the ground, one verse of scripture allowed to germinate in our hearts can grow into a harvest of a thousand people being born again. Did you know that one kernel of wheat properly germinated and watered can in time cover a continent? One kernel of wheat properly planted can feed nations. And the results of cultivating the imperishable seed of God's Word are much greater and more desirable than the results of cultivating any material seed.

God Promised His Word

Every scripture is a seed that can bring forth a bountiful harvest. The Word of God is "the incorruptible seed" (1 Peter 1:23) and can bring forth incorruptible and imperishable results. Every seed brings forth after its kind (Genesis 1:11–12). Each promise in the Word reveals the nature of the harvest the seed will produce. God wants to fulfill His promises in us. We need to plant His promises in our hearts and watch Him bring forth a harvest in our lives.

God's Word Carries Our Promises

David watered the Word by taking it and hiding it in his heart (Psalm 119:11). This is an expression of his attitude toward God. He fully acknowledged his obligation to diligently keep God's precepts, His Word. David also rejoiced in God's testimonies (Psalm 119:14) and took delight in His statutes. Watering the Word is as critical as planting it. When we water, He gives the increase. If God's Word can be more precious to David, who was not even born again, how much more precious should the Word be to those of us who are born again?

What God Promises

> The Lord is far from the wicked: but he heareth the prayer of the righteous. (Proverbs 15:29)
>
> When a man's ways please the Lord, he maketh even his enemies to be at peace with him. (Proverbs 16:7)

He hath given meat unto them that fear him: he will even be mindful of his Covenant. (Psalm 111:5)

For whosoever shall do the will of God, the same is my brother, and my sister, and my mother. (Mark 3:35)

For as many as are led by the Spirit of God, they are the sons of God. (Romans 8:14)

That being justified by his grace, we should be made heirs according to his hope of eternal life. (Titus 3:7)

But rejoice, in as much as ye are partakers of Christ's sufferings; that, when his glory shall be revealed, ye may be glad also with exceeding joy. (1 Peter 4:13)

And for this cause, he is the mediator of the new testament, that by means of death, for the redemption of the transgressions that were under the first testament, they which are called might receive the promise of eternal inheritance. (Hebrews 9:15)

But if we walk in the light, as he is in the light, we have fellowship one with another, and the blood of Jesus Christ his Son cleanseth us from all sin. (1 John 1:7)

Therefore being by the right hand of God exalted, and having received of the Father the promise of the Holy Ghost, he hath shed forth this, which ye now see and hear. (Acts 2:33)

In whom ye also trusted, after that ye heard the word of truth, the gospel of your salvation: in whom also after that ye believed, ye were sealed with that Holy Spirit of promise. (Ephesians 1:13)

In hope of eternal life, which God, that cannot lie, promised before the world began. (Titus 1:2)

But now hath he obtained a more excellent ministry, by how much also he is the mediator of a better Covenant, which was established upon better promises. (Hebrews 8:6)

But now they desire a better country, that is, an heavenly: wherefore God is not ashamed to be called their God: for He hath prepared for them a city. (Hebrews 11:16)

Hath not God chosen the poor of this world rich in faith, and heirs of the kingdom which he hath promised to them that love him? (James 2:5)

Blessed are they which are persecuted for righteousness' sake: for theirs is the kingdom of heaven. (Matthew 5:10)

The Lord knoweth how to deliver the godly out of temptations, and to reserve the unjust unto the day of judgment to be punished. (2 Peter 2:9)

Nevertheless we, according to his promise, look for a new heavens and a new earth, wherein dwelleth righteousness. (2 Peter 3:13)

And this is the promise that he hath promised us, even eternal life. (1 John 2:25)

Who will render to every man according to his deeds: To them who by patient continuance in well doing seek glory and honor and immortality, eternal life (Romans 2:6–7)

But glory, honor, and peace to every man that worketh good, to the Jew first, and also of the Gentile. For there is no respect of persons with God. (Romans 2:10–11)

Now to him that worketh is the reward not reckoned of grace, but of debt. But to him that worketh not, but believeth on him that justifieth the ungodly, his faith is counted for righteousness. (Romans 4:4–5)

Take that thine is, and go thy way: I will give unto this last, even as unto thee. So the last shall be first, and the first last; for many be called, but few chosen. (Matthew 20:14, 16)

But now they desire a better country, that is, an heavenly: wherefore God is not ashamed to be called their God: for He hath prepared for them a city. (Hebrews 11:16)

In my Father's house are many mansions: if it were not so, I would have told you. I go to prepare a place for you. And if I go and prepare a place for you, I will come again, and receive you unto myself; that where I am, that ye may be also. (John 14:2–3)

Knowing that of the Lord ye shall receive the reward of the inheritance: for ye serve the Lord Christ. But he that doeth wrong shall receive for the wrong which he hath done: and there is no respect of persons. (Colossians 3:24–25)

If any man serve me, let him follow me; and where I am, there shall also my servant be: if any man serve me, him will my Father honor. (John 12:26)

As for me, I will behold thy face in righteousness: I shall be satisfied, when I awake, with thy likeness. (Psalm 17:15)

Father, I will that they also, whom thou hast given me, be with me where I am; that they may behold my glory, which thou hast given me: for thou lovedst me before the foundation of the world. (John 17:24)

And if children, then heirs; heirs of God, and joint-heirs with Christ; if so be that we suffer with him, that we may be also glorified together. For I reckon that the sufferings of this present time are not worthy to be compared with the glory which shall be revealed in us. (Romans 8:17–18)

When Christ, who is our life, shall appear, then shall ye also appear with him in glory. (Colossians 3:4)

Until the Ancient of days came, and judgment was given to the saints of the most High; and the time came that the saints possessed the kingdom. (Daniel 7:22)

Do ye not know that the saints shall judge the world? and if the world shall be judged by you, are ye unworthy to judge the smallest matters? (1 Corinthians 6:2)

And I saw thrones, and they sat upon them, and judgment was given unto them: and I saw the souls of them that were beheaded for the witness of Jesus, and for the word of God, and which had not worshipped the beast, neither his image, neither had received his mark upon their foreheads, or in their hands; and they lived and reigned with Christ a thousand years. (Revelation 20:4)

And Jesus said unto them, Verily I say unto me, That ye which have followed me, in the regeneration when the Son of man shall sit in the throne of his glory, ye also shall sit upon twelve thrones, judging the twelve tribes of Israel. But many that are first shall be last; and the last shall be first. (Matthew 19:28–30)

If we suffer, we shall also reign with him: if we deny him, he also will deny us. (2 Timothy 2:12)

And there shall be no night there; and they need no candle, neither light of the sun; for the Lord God giveth them light: and they shall reign for ever and ever. (Revelation 22:5)

And every man that striveth for the mastery is temperate in all things. Now they do it to obtain a corruptible crown; but we are an incorruptible. (1 Corinthians 9:25)

Henceforth there is laid up for me a crown of righteousness, which the Lord, the righteous judge, shall give me at that day: and not to me only, but unto all them also that love his appearing. (2 Timothy 4:8)

And when the chief Shepherd shall appear, ye shall receive a crown of glory that fadeth not away. (1 Peter 5:4)

Blessed is the man that endureth temptations: for when he is tried, he shall receive the crown of life, which the Lord hath promised to them that love him. (James 1:12)

He that overcometh shall inherit all things; and I will be his God, and he shall be my son. (Revelation 21:7)

And now, brethren, I commend you to God, and to the word of his grace, which is able to build you up, and to give you an inheritance among all them which are sanctified. (Acts 20:32)

And for this cause he is the mediator of the new testament, that by means of death, for the redemption of the transgressions that were under the first testament, they which are called might receive the promise of eternal inheritance. (Hebrews 9:15)

To an inheritance incorruptible, and undefiled, and that fadeth not away, reserved in heaven for you. (1 Peter 1:4)

Then shall the King say unto them on his right hand, Come, ye blessed of my Father, inherit the kingdom prepared for you from the foundation of the world. (Matthew 25:34)

Wherefore we receiving a kingdom which cannot be moved, let us have grace, whereby we may serve God acceptably with reverence and godly fear. (Hebrews 12:28)

And they that be wise shall shine as the brightness of the firmament; and they that turn many to righteousness as the stars for ever and ever. (Daniel 12:3)

And the Gentiles shall come to thy light, and kings to the brightness of thy rising. (Isaiah 60:3)

And he said unto them, Verily I say unto you, There is no man that hath left house, or parents, or brethren, or wife, or children, for the Kingdom sake. Who shall not receive manifold more in this present time, and in the world to come life everlasting. (Luke 18:29–30)

For ye had compassion of me in my bonds, and took joyfully the spoiling of your goods, knowing in yourselves that ye have in heaven a better and an enduring substance. (Hebrews 10:34)

For we know that if our earthly house of this tabernacle were dissolved, we have a building of God, an house not made with hands, eternal in the heavens. (2 Corinthians 5:1)

For he looked for a city which hath foundations, whose builder and maker is God. (Hebrews 11:10)

His Lord said unto him, Well done, thou good and faithful servant: thou hast been faithful over a few things, I will make thee ruler over many things: enter thou into the joy of thy Lord. (Matthew 25:21)

For if Jesus had given them rest, then would he not afterward have spoken of another day. There remaineth therefore a rest to the people of God. (Hebrews 4:8–9)

Thou wilt shew me the path of life: in thy presence is fullness of joy: at thy right hand there are pleasures for evermore. (Psalm 16:11)

As for me, I will behold thy face in righteousness: I shall be satisfied, when I awake, with thy likeness. (Psalm 17:15)

Thou shalt guide me with thy counsel, and afterward receive me to glory. (Psalm 73:24)

The wicked worketh a deceitful work: but to him that soweth righteousness shall be a sure reward. (Proverbs 11:18)

For since the beginning of the world men have not heard, nor perceived by the ear, neither hath the eye seen, O God, beside thee, what he hath prepared for him that waiteth for him. (Isaiah 64:4)

Look to yourselves, that we lose not those things which we have wrought, but that we receive a full reward. (2 John 8)

I press toward the mark for the prize of the high calling of God in Christ Jesus. (Philippians 3:14)

For our light affliction, which is but for a moment worketh for us a far more exceeding and eternal weight of glory. While we look not at the things which are seen, but at the things which are not seen: for the things which are seen are temporal; but the things which are not seen are eternal. (2 Corinthians 4:17–18)

Every man's work shall be made manifest: for the day shall declare it, because it shall be revealed by fire; and the fire shall try every man's work of what sort it is. If any man's work abide which he hath built thereupon, he shall receive a reward. If man's work shall be burned, he shall suffer loss: but he himself shall be saved; yet so as by fire. (1 Corinthians 3:13–15).

Principles

- God's Covenant with humanity was made before the foundation of the world.
- God's Covenant is in the hands of the great Shepherd, Jesus Christ.
- Our position and promises are secure in Jesus Christ.
- Knowledge of our position precedes obtaining our promises.
- God's predetermined position for us cannot be changed.
- Once we occupy our position, God can use us in His plan.
- God's position and promises for us are good for eternity.

CHAPTER 7

The Constitution and the Bible: Checks and Balances and the Unity of the Deity in God's Kingdom

The separation of powers devised by the framers of the Constitution was meant to do one primary thing: to prevent the majority from ruling with an iron fist. Based on their experience, the framers shied away from giving any branch of the new government too much power. The separation of powers provides a system of shared power known as checks and balances.

Three branches are created in the Constitution. The legislative, composed of the House and Senate, is set up in Article 1. The executive, composed of the president, vice president, and the departments, is set up in article 2. The judicial, composed of the federal courts and the Supreme Court, is set up in article 3.

Each of these branches has certain powers, and each of these powers is limited or checked by another branch. For example, the president appoints judges and departmental secretaries, but these appointments must be approved by the Senate. Congress can pass a law, but the president can veto it. The Supreme Court can rule a law unconstitutional, but Congress with the states can amend the Constitution.

All these checks and balances, however, are inefficient, but that was by design rather than by accident. By forcing the various branches to be accountable to the others, no one branch can usurp enough power to become dominant.

The following are the powers of the executive: veto power over all bills, appointment of judges and other officials, making treaties, ensuring all laws are carried out, being the commander in chief of the military, and the power to pardon.

Checks and Balances: The Constitution and the Unity of the Deity

The Constitution is based on the principle of checks and balances whereby each branch of government exercises a check on the actions of the others. Separation of powers, divided authority, and checks and balances limit government power by pitting power against power. For example, the president checks Congress by holding veto power, Congress holds the purse strings and approves presidential appointments. There are inbuilt conflicts and rivalry in our Constitution.

On the other hand, the Deity had no conflict. There is perfect unity in the operation of God the Father, Son, and Holy Spirit. That power was delegated in God's eternal plan for us through His infinite wisdom. They cooperated in the creation of all things, in the redemption of humanity, and in the sustenance of creation. God the Father made the laws, God the Son executed the plan of humanity's atonement faithfully, and God the Holy Spirit comes to indwell us as a seal for our eternal salvation as our Comforter and teacher and to give us the testimony of Jesus Christ. What a perfect unity!

This perfect relationship with God is what we receive if we confess Jesus Christ and believe in our hearts that God raised Him from the dead. God has faithfully forgiven us and given us eternal life. The perfect harmony between God the Father, Son, and Holy Spirit cannot be matched or duplicated.

What The Bible Says

> In the beginning was the Word, and the Word was with God, and the Word was God. (John 1:1)

> And he that sent me is with me: the Father hath not left me alone; for I do always those things that please him. (John 8:29)

> And Jesus increased in wisdom and stature, and in favor with God and man. (Luke 2:52)

> Then answered Jesus and said unto them, Verily, verily, I say unto you, The Son can do nothing of himself, but what

he seeth the Father do: for what things soever he doeth, these also doeth the Son likewise. For the Father loveth the Son, and sheweth him all things that himself doeth: and he will shew him greater works than these that ye may marvel. (John 5:19–20)

For the Father judgeth no man but hath committed all judgement unto the Son. (John 5:22)

Believe me that I am in the Father, and the Father in me: or else believe me for the very works' sake. (John 14:11)

As the Father knoweth me, even so know I the Father: and I lay down my life for the sheep. (John 10:15)

And I have declared unto them thy name, and will declare it: that the love wherewith thou hast loved me may be in them, and I in them. (John 17:26)

But he, being full of the Holy Ghost looked up steadfastly into heaven, and saw the glory of God, and Jesus, standing on the right hand of God. (Acts 7:55)

For God, who commanded the light to shine out of darkness, hath shined in our hearts, to give the light of the knowledge of the glory of God in the face of Jesus Christ. (2 Corinthians 4:6)

For it pleased the Father that in him should all fullness dwell. (Colossians 1: 19)

For in him dwelleth all the fullness of the Godhead bodily. (Colossians 2:9)

Hath in these last days spoken unto us by his Son, whom he hath appointed heir of all things, by whom also he made the worlds. (Hebrews 1:2)

If we receive the witness of men, the witness of God is greater for this is the witness of God which he hath testified of his Son. (1 John 5:9)

Behold my servant, whom I have chosen: my beloved, in whom my soul is well pleased: I will put my spirit upon him, and he shall shew judgement to the Gentiles. (Matthew 12:18)

And Jesus, when he was baptized, went up straightway out of the water: and lo, the heavens were opened unto him, and he saw the Spirit of God descending like a dove, and lighting upon him. And lo, a voice from heaven, saying, This is my beloved Son, in whom I am well pleased. (Matthew 3:16–17)

And John bare record, saying, I saw the Spirit descending from heaven like a dove, and it abode upon him. And I knew him not: but he that sent me to baptize with water, the same said unto me, Upon whom thou shalt see the Spirit descending, and remaining on him, the same is he which baptizeth with the Holy Ghost. (John 1:32–33)

But when the Comforter is come, whom I will send unto you from the Father, even the Spirit of truth, which proceedeth from the Father, he shall testify of me. (John 15:26)

He shall glorify me: for he shall receive of mine, and shall shew it unto you. (John 16:14)

Nevertheless I tell you the truth; It is expedient for you that I go away: for if I go not away, the Comforter will not come unto you; but if I depart, I will send him unto you. (John 16:7)

Wherefore I give you to understand, that no man speaking by the Spirit of God calleth Jesus accursed: and that no man can say that Jesus is the Lord, but by the Holy Ghost. (1 Corinthians 12:3)

But ye shall receive power, after that the Holy Ghost is come upon you: and ye shall be witnesses unto me both in Jerusalem, and in all Judea, and in Samaria, and unto the uttermost part of the earth. (Acts 1:8)

Therefore being by the right hand of God exalted, and having received of the Father the promise of the Holy Ghost, he hath shed forth this, which ye now see and hear. (Acts 2:33)

Searching what, or what manner of time the Spirit of Christ which was in them signify, when it testified beforehand the sufferings of Christ, and the glory that shall follow. (1 Peter 1:11)

Principles

- The Constitution is based on separation of powers held by many people.
- The Bible is based on separation of powers in one person.
- The government is based on checks and balances.
- God's Constitution is based on unity of the deity.
- The Constitution is based our human moral standards.
- God's Constitution is based on eternal truth.
- The Constitution limits power of officeholders.
- God's Constitution has no limitation on God's powers.

CHAPTER 8

The Constitution and the Bible: The Preamble

We the People of the United States, in order to form a more perfect Union, establish justice, insure domestic Tranquillity, provide for the common defence, promote the general Welfare, and secure the Blessings of Liberty to ourselves and our Posterity, do ordain and establish this Constitution for the United States.

The preamble to the Constitution is a brief expression of its fundamental purposes and guiding principles. It states in general terms, and courts have referred to it, as reliable evidence of the founding fathers' intentions regarding the Constitution's meaning and what they hoped it would achieve. It is an introduction to a document that specifies the intention of the document itself. It is a summary with a more goal-oriented text.

The "six purposes" line is usually used in reference to the Constitution; they are these.

- to form a more perfect union
- to establish justice
- to ensure domestic tranquility
- to provide for the common defense
- to promote general welfare
- to secure the blessings of liberty to ourselves and our posterity

The document then goes on to spell out exactly how the federal government will be formed to ensure each of these goals is met.

God's Kingdom Government for Us

God created His government based on kingdom principles to guide us to holy lives on earth. Sovereign God governs all creation because He made everything. He does whatever pleases Him and determines whether we can do what we have planned. He has absolute independence to do as He pleases; He has absolute control over all His creatures. Nobody or nothing can thwart His will or act outside the bounds of it. God planned everything in His infinite wisdom. We cannot know all the reasons God set up His government for us in the manner He did, but He is all knowing, and that places Him above what we know and what we did in constructing our Constitution. We will learn more about God and His sovereignty when we are willing to put our Constitution under His kingdom.

The reason the Constitution was made is clearly specified. The reason God made a Covenant with us is because He committed Himself to His creation forever. He was not forced by circumstances. He did not do it out of expediency. He did not do it out of selfish reasons. He did it for our good out of His grace, wisdom, and eternal omniscience and omnipotence in His Constitution.

What The Bible Says

> There is no wisdom, no insight, and no plan that can succeed against the LORD. (Proverbs 21:30)

> Who is he that saith, and have it cometh to pass, when the Lord commandeth? (Lamentations 3:37)

> These things saith he that is holy, he that is true, he that hath the key of David, he that openeth, and no man shutteth; and shutteth, and no man openeth. (Revelation 3:7)

> There are many devices in a man's heart; nevertheless the counsel of the LORD, that shall stand. (Proverbs 19:21)

> Whatsoever the Lord pleased, that did He in heaven, and in earth, in the seas, and all deep places. (Psalm. 135:6)

My counsel shall stand, and I will do my pleasure. (Isaiah. 46:10)

For we are his workmanship, created in Christ Jesus unto good works, which God hath before ordained that we should walk in them. (Ephesians 2:10)

Know ye that the LORD he is God: it is he that made us, and not we ourselves; we are his people, and the sheep of his pasture. (Psalm 100:3)

Thy people also shall be all righteous: they shall inherit the land for ever, the branch of my planting, the work of my hands, that I may be glorified. (Isaiah 60:21)

But now, O Lord, thou art our Father; we are the clay, and thou our potter; and we all are the work of thy hand. (Isaiah 64:8)

Do ye thus requite the Lord, O foolish people and unwise? is not he thy father that hath bought thee? hath he not made thee, and established thee? (Deuteronomy 32:6)

I have made the earth, and created man upon it: I even my hands, have stretched out the heavens, and all their host have I commanded. I have raised him up in righteousness, and I will direct all his ways: he shall build my city, and he shall let go my captives, not for price nor reward, saith the Lord of hosts. (Isaiah 45:12–13)

Behold I formed thee in the belly I knew thee: and before thou comest forth out of the womb I sanctified thee, and I ordained thee a prophet unto the nations. (Jeremiah 1:5)

Thus saith the Lord that made thee, and formed thee from the womb, which will help thee; Fear not, O Jacob, my servant; and thou, Jesurun, whom I have chosen. (Isaiah 44:2)

Ye are God's husbandry, ye are God's building. (1 Corinthians 3:9)

Surely your turning of things upside down shall be esteemed as the potter's clay: for shall the work say of him that made it, He made me not? or shall the thing framed say of him that framed it, He had no understanding? (Isaiah 29:16)

Woe unto him that striveth with his Maker! Let the potsherd strive with the potsherds of the earth. Shall the clay say to him that fashioneth it, What makest thou? or thy work, He hath no hands? (Isaiah 45:9)

Behold, as the clay is in the potter's hand, so are ye in mine hand, O house of Israel. (Jeremiah 18:6)

Shall the thing formed say to him that formed it, Why hast thou made me thus? (Romans 9:20)

Hath not the potter power over the clay, of the same lump to make one vessel unto honor, and another unto dishonor? (Romans 9:21)

For the Lord is a God of Knowledge, and by him actions are weighed. (1 Samuel 2:3)

Great is our Lord, and of great power, his understanding in infinite. (Psalm 147:5)

Thus saith the Lord, thy redeemer, and he that formed thee from the womb, I am the Lord that maketh all things; that stretcheth forth the heavens alone; that spreadeth abroad the earth by myself; That frustrateth the tokens of the liars, and maketh diviners mad; that turneth wise men backward, and maketh their knowledge foolish; That confirmeth the word of his servant, and performeth the counsel of his messengers. (Isaiah 44:24–26)

Principles

- God's government is not subject to our approval or consent.
- God's government is based on His eternal love for us.
- God's government was made for eternity.
- God's government is based on His truth and promises.
- God's government works for our good all the time.
- God's government expresses His kingship over us.

CHAPTER 9

Article 1: The Constitution and God's Constitutional Powers of Congress

All legislative Powers herein granted shall be vested in a Congress of the United States which shall consist of a Senate and House of Representatives.

> The Congress shall have Power
> To lay and collect Taxes Duties, Imposts and Excises, to pay the Debts and pro-vide for the common Defence and general Welfare of the United States;
> To borrow Money on the Credit of the United States;
> To regulate Commerce with foreign Nations, rib establish an uniform Rule of Naturalization, To coin Money,
> To establish Post Offices, and post Roads;
> To promote the Progress of Science and useful Arts,
> To declare War, To raise and support Armies,
> To provide and maintain a Nary;
> To make all Laws which shall be necessary and proper for carrying into Execution the foregoing Powers, and all other Powers vested by this Constitution in the Government of the United States, or in any Department or Officer thereof Under the US Constitution.

Congress makes all laws. Congress is made up of the House of Representative with 435 members and the Senate with 100 members.

God the Father Is Our Congress in His Government

The Bible clearly states that God made all the laws in His kingdom. These laws must be the final basis on which we can determine what is biblically correct today. While we are expected to follow human laws, we need to be aware that God's laws existed before human laws did and that His laws are designed for all His creation including us. His laws are made for our own good, while our laws are designed to accomplish our goals—to protect our interests and rights that may at times conflict with and violate others' interests and rights. God's laws are made in love and grace; they have no respect for persons. They apply to all races and genders and are not arbitrary. We cannot justify breaking God's laws for the sake of submission to the state.

What The Bible Says

> For the LORD is our judge, the LORD is our lawgiver, the LORD is our King, He will save us. (Isaiah 33:22)

> And it is easier for heaven and earth to pass, than one title of the law to fail. (Luke 16:17)

> And God spake all these words, saying, I am the LORD thy God, which have brought thee out of the land of Egypt, out of the house of bondage. Thou shall have no other gods before me. Thou shalt not make unto thee any graven image, or any likeness of anything that is in heaven above, or that is in the earth beneath, or that is in the water under the earth: Thou shall not bow down thyself to them, nor serve them: for I the LORD thy God am a jealous God, visiting the iniquity of the fathers upon the children unto the third and fourth generation of them that hate me; And shewing mercy unto thousands of them that love me, and keep my commandments. Thou shalt not take the name of the LORD thy God in vain; for the LORD will not hold him guiltless that taketh his name in vain.

> Remember the Sabbath day, to keep it holy. Six days shalt thou labor, and do all thy work: But the seventh day is

the Sabbath of the LORD thy God: in it thou shalt not do any work, thou, nor thy son, nor thy daughter, thy manservant, nor thy maidservant, nor thy cattle, nor thy stranger that is within thy gates: For in six days the LORD made heaven and earth, the sea, and all in them is, and rested the seventh day: wherefore the LORD blessed the Sabbath day, and hallowed it.

Honor thy father and thy mother: that thy days may be long upon the land which the LORD thy God giveth thee. Thou shalt not kill. Thou shalt not commit adultery. Thou shalt not steal. Thou shalt not bear false witness against thy neighbor. Thou shalt not covet thy neighbor's house, thou shalt not covet thy neighbor's wife, nor his manservant, nor his maidservant, nor his ox, nor his ass, nor any thing that is thy neighbor's. (Exodus 20:1–17)

And the LORD said unto Moses, Come up to me into the mount, and be there: and I will give thee tables of stone, and a law and commandments which I have written; that thou mayest teach them. (Exodus 24:12)

And the tables were the work of God, and the writing was the writing of God, graven upon the tables. (Exodus 32:16)

Saith the LORD, I will put my laws into their mind, and write them in their hearts: and I will be to them a God, and they shall be to me a people. (Hebrews 8:10)

Principles

- God makes laws for all creation.
- God's laws are made for eternity.
- God's laws supersede those in our Constitution.
- God's laws express His love for humankind.
- God's laws are immutable.
- God's laws are timeless.

CHAPTER 10

The Constitution and the Bible: Political Representation

US Constitution

Article 1, Section 2

> The House of Representatives shall be composed of Members chosen every second Year by the People of the several States, and the Electors in each State shall have the Qualifications requisite for Electors of the most numerous Branch of the State Legislature.
>
> No person shall be a Representative who shall not have attained to the Age of twenty five Years, and been seven years a citizen of the United States, and who shall not, when elected, be an Inhabitant of that State in which he shall be chosen.

Article 1, Section 3

> The Senate of the United States shall be composed of two Senators from each State, chosen by the Legislature thereof, for six years; and each Senator shall have one vote.
>
> No person shall be a Senator who shall not have attained to the age of thirty years, and been nine years a citizen of

> the United States, and who shall not, when elected be an Inhabitant of that State for which he shall be chosen.

Amendment 17

> The Senate of the United States shall be composed of two Senators from each State, elected by the people thereof, for six years; and each Senator shall have one vote.

What the Constitution Says

Our government is composed of elected officials. Citizens who meet specified constitutional standards are permitted to choose local, state, and national leaders to make political decisions and other critical social regulations that affect us. To choose our leaders is a critical part of our democratic system, and those who qualify to participate in the process have a sacred duty to exercise their right.

God is not an elected official. He is the King of Kings and Lord of Lords. In His kingdom, He has supreme authority He derives from Himself. We are subjects who cannot elect God. We receive orders and carry them out without questioning His authority. God has called us to be His ecclesia so we can take His official policies to the ends of the world.

The Bible does not provide for the right to choose or elect our heavenly government, which is God. On the contrary, God elected us into His kingdom. He adopted us before the foundation of the world. He gave us His Great Commission, a privileged call for all who accept it. In His sovereign and divine grace, He created us in Christ Jesus to do works he prepared in advance (Ephesians 2:10). Those elected share in His kingdom and are eligible for all spiritual blessings through Jesus Christ.

God's elect are called not on their own merit but through God's grace and through Jesus Christ for salvation and sanctification of the Spirit. They are individuals specially chosen to be heirs of salvation and witnesses for God before humanity not due to works but to free grace. They are special vessels of the Spirit chosen by God to carry out His purposes. In all ages, God chose such people to be His witnesses as an expression of His sovereignty and grace. Paul himself was so chosen. On the other hand, it should not be forgotten that salvation is by grace.

God called us to be His ambassadors. No one comes into His kingdom by his or her choice. We are called to lead the war against the devil; we are called unto holiness. We are called to be servants and prisoners for Christ. The apostle Paul gave us a clear understanding of our mission for Christ. He was on a mission to put Christians out of commission. Jesus Christ called him and made him His apostle to the Gentiles. No one is called to sit idly and do nothing. We are all called for the Great Commission, the sole and inescapable calling.

The powers of darkness must be eradicated, and we must press on toward the prize of our high calling in Christ Jesus. Our God is not a God of experiments; He is a God of infinite perfection. His plan is good forever.

It is indeed a privilege to be elected, chosen, called, and ordained by God to do His will. We must praise Him for that. Many are called, but few are chosen. This is a critical statement when we consider the size of the planet and the number of people inhabiting it. Many would like to enter the kingdom, but it is for the elect to enter and live in His presence forever. Glory to His name!

We are God's elect. We were chosen before the foundation of this world to be in Christ Jesus. We are not saved by our choice or will. We respond only to God's call. We receive His saving grace through faith. Many saints were called in the Old Testament as well. God is no respecter of persons. The Old Testament gave the children of Israel God's qualified status of the elect. Under the New Testament, all people, Jew and Gentile alike, qualify for God's election through the blood of His Son, Jesus Christ, which was shed for the remission of our sins.

Our status was defined before the beginning of this world. The Bible has many examples of men and women who were called and separated for His work in this world. This indeed is a special calling that no man can give or take away.

What The Bible Says

> Before I formed thee in the belly I knew thee; and before thou comest forth out of the womb, I sanctified thee, and I ordained thee a prophet unto the nations. (Jeremiah 1:5)

> Thus, saith the LORD that made thee, and formed thee from the womb, which will help thee; Fear not, O Jacob, my servant; and thou, Jesurun, whom I have chosen. (Isaiah 44:2)

> And now, saith the Lord that formed me from the womb to be his servant, to bring Jacob again to him. (Isaiah 49:5)

> For thou art an holy people unto the Lord thy God: the Lord thy God hath chosen thee to be a special people unto himself, above all people that are upon the face of the earth. (Deuteronomy 7:6)

> And did I choose him out of all the tribes of Israel to be my priest, to offer upon mine altar, to burn incense, to wear an ephod before me? (1 Samuel 2:28)

> And Samuel said to all the people, See ye him whom the Lord hath chosen, that there is none like him among all the people? And all the people shouted, and said, God save the king. (1 Samuel 10:24)

> Thou art the Lord the God, who didst choose Abram, and broughtest him forth out of the Chaldees, and gavest him the name Abraham. (Nehemiah 9:7)

> Blessed is the nation whose God is the LORD; and the people whom he hath chosen for his own inheritance. (Psalm 33:12)

The New Testament

Jesus Christ is the only one who made the New Testament legal and binding for humanity to receive God's grace. We are called or elected by grace through faith. God designed His calling on us to maintain His sovereignty over us, and He will not have any other form of political or civil representation in His kingdom.

We were called before the foundation of the world and are appointed for eternal life in His kingdom. Our assignments are predetermined; we cannot alter them. We are not voted into office but are called by God Himself into a position we occupy into eternity. The Bible is full of evidence of how God calls us into His kingdom for our assignments.

What The Bible Says

Paul, a servant of Jesus Christ, called to an apostle, separated unto the gospel of God. (Romans 1:1)

Paul, called to be an apostle of Jesus Christ through the will of God. (1 Corinthians 1:1; Ephesians 1:1; Colossians 1:1)

Paul, an apostle, (not of men, neither by man, but by Jesus Christ, and God the Father, who raised him from the dead). (Galatians 1:1)

Paul, an apostle of Jesus Christ by the commandment of God our Savior, and Lord Jesus Christ, which is our hope. (1 Timothy 1:1)

Paul, an apostle of Jesus Christ by the will of God, according to the promise of life which is in Christ Jesus. (2 Timothy 1:1)

Paul, a servant of God, and an apostle of Jesus Christ, according to the faith of God's elect, and the acknowledging of the truth which is after godliness. In hope of eternal life, which God, that cannot lie, promised before the world began. (Titus 1:1–2)

Behold my servant, whom I have chosen: my beloved, in whom my soul is well pleased: I will put my spirit upon him, and he shall shew judgement to the Gentiles. (Matthew 12:18)

If ye were of the world, the world would love his own; but because ye are not of the world, but I have chosen you out of the world, therefore the world hateth you. (John 15:19)

Paul, a prisoner of Jesus Christ. (Philemon 1:1)

Ye have not chosen me, but I have chosen you. (John 15:16)

Having predestined us unto the adoption of children by Jesus Christ to himself. (Ephesians 1:5)

Because God hath from the beginning chosen you to salvation. (2 Thessalonians 2:13)

But as He which hath called you is holy. (1 Peter 1:15)

Elect according to the foreknowledge of God the Father. (1 Peter 1:2)

But ye are a chosen generation, a royal priesthood, an holy nation, a peculiar people; that ye should shew forth the praises of him who hath called you out of darkness into his marvelous light. (1 Peter. 2:9)

Blessed is the nation whose God is the Lord; and the people whom he hath chosen for own inheritance. (Psalm 33:12)

For many be called, but few are chosen. (Matthew 20:16)

And when it was day, he called unto him his disciples: and of them he chose twelve, whom also he named apostles. (Luke 6:13)

Have not I chosen you twelve, and one of you is a devil? (John 6:70)

For the children being not yet born, neither having done any good or evil, that the purpose of God according to election might stand, not of works, but of him that calleth. (Romans 9:11)

For whom he did foreknow, he also did predestinate to be conformed to the image of his Son, that he might be the firstborn among many brethren. Moreover whom he did predestinate, them he also called: and whom he called, them he also justified: and whom he justified, them he also glorified. (Romans 8:29–30)

According as he hath chosen us in him before the foundation of the world, then we should be holy and blame before him in love. (Ephesians 1:4)

Because God hath from the beginning chosen you to salvation through sanctification of the Spirit and belief of the truth. (2 Thessalonians 2:13)

As they ministered to the Lord, and fasted, the Holy Ghost said, separate me Barnabas and Saul for the work whereunto I have called them. (Acts 13:2)

And when the Gentiles heard this, (the gospel), they were glad, and glorified the word of the Lord; and as many as were ordained to eternal life believed. (Acts 13:48)

And he saith unto them, Follow me, and I will make you fishers of men. And they immediately left the ship and their father, and followed him. (Matthew 4:19

But unto them which are called, both Jews and Gentiles, Christ the power of God, and the wisdom of God. (1 Corinthians 1:24)

For ye see your calling, brethren, how that not many wise men after the flesh, not many mighty, not many noble, are called. (1 Corinthians 1:26)

Let every man abide in the same calling wherein he was called. (1 Corinthians 7:20)

But when it pleased God, who separated me from my mother's womb, and called me by his grace, To reveal his Son in me, that I might preach him among the heathen;

> immediately I conferred not with flesh and blood. (Galatians 1:15–16)
>
> There is one body, and one Spirit, even as ye are called in one hope of your calling; One Lord, one faith, one baptism, One God and Father of all, who is above all, and through all, and in you all. (Ephesians 4:4–6)
>
> That ye would walk worthy of God, who hath called you unto his who hath called you unto his kingdom and glory. (1 Thessalonians 2:12)
>
> For God hath not called us unto uncleanness, but unto holiness. (1 Thessalonians 4:7)
>
> Who hath saved us, and called us with an holy calling, not according to our works, but according to his own purpose and grace, which was given us in Christ Jesus before the world began. (2 Timothy 1:9)
>
> But the God of all grace, who hath called us unto his eternal glory by Christ Jesus, after that ye have suffered a while, make you perfect, establish, strengthen, settle you. (1 Peter 5:10)
>
> And he said unto me, Write, Blessed are they which are called unto the marriage supper of the Lamb, And he saith unto me, These are the true sayings of God. (Revelation 19:9)

Why Are We Called?

We are on assignment. God has not called us by accident. He is not a God of accidents. We are specifically called to accomplish what He prepared in advance for us to do. We are called to serve Him. We are called to be His disciples. We are called to fellowship with Him. We are all called for a special reason. We must know our calling to fill our position in Christ and receive our provision for the calling.

What The Bible Says

If any man serve me, let him follow me; and where I am, there shall also my servant be: if any man serve me, him will my Father honor. (John 12:26)

And if it seem evil unto you to serve the LORD, choose you this day whom ye will serve; whether the gods which your fathers served that were on the other side of the flood, or the gods of the Amorites, in whose land ye dwell: but as for me and my house, we will serve the LORD. (Joshua 24:15)

And Samuel spake unto all the house of Israel, saying, If ye do return unto the LORD with all your hearts, then put away the strange gods and Ashtaroth from among you, and prepare your hearts unto the LORD, and serve him only: and he will deliver you out of the hand of the Philistines. (1 Samuel 7:3)

And Samuel said unto the people, Fear not: ye have done all this wickedness: yet turn not aside from following the LORD, but serve the Lord with all your heart. (1 Samuel 12:20)

And thou, Solomon my son, know thou the God of thy father, and serve him with a perfect heart and with a willing mind: for the LORD searcheth all hearts, and understandeth all the imaginations of the thoughts: if thou seek him, he will be found of thee; but thou forsake him, he will cast thee off for ever. (1 Chronicles 28:9)

Yea, all kings shall fall down before him: all nations shall serve him. (Psalm 72:11)

Also the sons of the stranger, that join themselves to the Lord, to serve him, and to love the name of the LORD, to be his servants, every one that keepth the Sabbath from polluting it, and taketh hold of my Covenant. (Isaiah 56:6)

For the nation and kingdom that will not serve thee shall perish: yea, those nations shall be utterly wasted. (Isaiah 60:12)

If it be so, our God whom we serve is able to deliver us from the burning fiery furnace, and he will deliver us out of thine hand, O king. (Daniel 3:17)

For then will I turn to the people a pure language, that they may all call upon the name of the LORD, to serve him with one consent. (Zephaniah 3:9)

No man can serve two masters: for either he will hate the one, and love the other; or else he will hold to the one, and despise the other. Ye cannot serve God and mammon. (Matthew 6:24)

And she was a widow of about fourscore and four years, which departed not from the temple, but served God with fasting and prayers night and day. (Luke 2:37)

But ye shall not be so: he that is greatest among you, let him be as the younger; and he that is chief, as he that doth serve. (Luke 22:26)

Serving the Lord with all humility of mind, and with many tears, and temptations, which befell me by the lying in wait of the Jews? (Acts 20:19)

For there stood by me this night the angel of God, whose I am, and whom I serve. (Acts 27:23)

Knowing this, that our old man is crucified with him, that the body of sin might be destroyed, that henceforth we should not serve sin. (Romans 6:6)

But now we are delivered from the law, that being dead wherein we were held; that we should serve in newness of spirit, and not in the oldness of the letter. (Romans 7:6)

For brethren, ye have called unto liberty; only use not liberty for an occasion to the flesh, but by love, serve one another. (Galatians 5:13)

Principles

- God's government is not elected.
- God's elect are qualified by grace through faith.
- God's church comprises His chosen representatives.
- God calls us to serve, not to make laws.
- God's calling is eternal.
- God's calling has eternal rewards.
- God calls according to His pleasure, not by our performance.
- God's calling supersedes all elective positions.

CHAPTER 11

Article 2: US Constitution—Powers of the President and the Bible

Section 1

The Executive Power shall be vested in a President of the United States of America.

Section 2: Powers and Duties of the President

The President shall be the Commander in Chief of the Army and Navy of the United States. He shall have Power, by and with the Advice and Consent of the Senate to make Treaties, provided two thirds of the Senators present concur.

Section 3: Powers and Duties of the President

He shall from time to time give to the Congress Information of the State of the Union, and recommend to their Consideration such Measures as he shall judge necessary and expedient.

Other Functions of the President

- negotiating treaties
- receiving foreign ambassadors
- vetoing bills from Congress
- pardoning persons convicted of federal offenses

While the Constitution has stipulated the powers of the president, the Bible shows that Christ is the President of God's kingdom appointed by God the Father, who rules forever.

Christ's Commission

"Christ received a certain charge or commission from the Father that He solemnly undertook. He was promised the actual bestowal of God's children, who had been given to Him." (A. W. Pink's "Studies in the Scriptures. Volume 2 of 17)

The Father made Christ the federal head of His people and He freed them from the dreadful condemnation God foresaw from eternity that they would fall into after Adam. This alone explains why Christ is denominated the "last Adam" (1 Corinthians 15:45, 47).

In Ephesians 5:23, Christ is the head of the church, and He is the Savior of the body. He could not have been the Savior unless He had first been the head. He voluntarily entered into the work of suretyship by divine appointment, serving as the representative of His people, taking upon Himself all their responsibilities, and agreeing to discharge all their legal obligations. He put Himself in the stead of His insolvent people, paid their debts, worked out for them a perfect righteousness, and legally merited for them the reward or blessing of the fulfilled law.

In order to execute His Covenant engagement, it was necessary for Christ to assume human nature and be made in all things like His brethren so that He might enter their place, be made under the law, and serve in their stead. He must have a soul and body in which He was capable of suffering and being paid the just wages of His peoples' sins. On the grounds of Christ's willingness to perform the work stipulated in The Bible, certain promises were made to Him by the Father.

What The Bible Says

> He was assured of divine endowment for the discharge of all specifications of The Kingdom. (Isaiah 11:1–3, 61:1; John 8:29)
>
> He was guaranteed them protection under the execution of His work. (Isaiah 42:6; Zechariah 3:8–9; John 10:18)

He was promised the divine assistance unto a successful conclusion. (Isaiah 42:4, 49:8–10; John 17:4)

Those promises were given to Christ for the stay of His heart, to be pleaded by Him. (Psalm 89:26, 2:8): and this He did (Isaiah 50:8–10; Hebrews 2:13).

Christ was assured of success in His undertaking and a reward for the same. (Isaiah 53:10, 11; Psalm 89:27–29, 110:1–3; Philippians 2:9–11)

Christ received promises concerning his people, gifts for them (Psalm 68:18; Ephesians 4:10–11): God would make them willing to receive Him as their Lord. (Psalm 110:3; John 6:44)

Christ was also promised eternal life for His people (Psalm 133:3; Titus 1:2); that a seed should serve Him., proclaim His righteousness, and declare what He had done for them (Psalm 22:30, 31) and that kings and princes should worship Him. (Isaiah 49:7)

Jesus Christ: The Foundation of Fallen Humanity

Christ laid a sure foundation for the recovery of God's fallen people and for their true fellowship with Him; yet more was still needed for the actualizing of the divine purpose of grace. As it is through Christ all blessings are conveyed, so it is by Him that the kingdom is administered. Consequently, upon His exaltation to the right hand of God, He received a further and higher anointing, obtaining the promise of the Father in the gift of the Holy Spirit, to be by Him dispensed to His church at His will (Acts 2:33; Hebrews 1:9; Revelation 3:1). Thus is He effectually equipped to secure that salvation of all His people? He has been exalted to be "a Prince and a Savior, for to give repentance to Israel, and forgiveness of sins" (Acts 5:31). He is endowed with "all power in heaven and in earth" (Matthew 28:18). He must "must reign till he hath put all in enemies under his feet" (1 Corinthians 15:25). God has assured Him that "He shall see of the travail of his soul, and shall be satisfied" (Isaiah 53:11). (A. W. Pink's "Studies in the Scriptures, Volume 2 of 17)

Jesus Christ: The Administrator of The Covenant of Grace:

The administration of the kingdom in the actual application of its blessings and securing beyond the possibility of the slightest failure its ordained results is an essential part of the mediatorial work of Christ. Therefore, was He exalted to the right hand of the majesty on high to exercise sovereign power? His cross was but the prelude to His crown. The latter was not only the appointed and appropriate reward of the former, but having begun the work of salvation by His death, to Him was reserved the honor of completing it by His reigning power. "God raised him from the dead and set him at his own right hand and hath put all things under his feet, and gave him to be the head over all things to the church which is his body" (Ephesians 1:20). The salvation of the church and the unlimited power and authority with which the Redeemer was now entrusted are indispensable to its successful attainment.

Administration of The Covenant

The administration of the Covenant by the Mediator as bearing on the salvation of sinners is a subject of vast importance. Christ now reigns, and nothing is more consoling and stabilizing than a deep conviction of this fact. His rule is not an imaginary one but a reality; His reign is not figurative but personal. He is now on the throne and is exercising the power and authority committed to Him as the Messiah in the complex constitution of His person for the accomplishment of His people's salvation. It is the holy privilege of the Christian to have personal dealings with One who is invested with supreme sovereignty and yet at the same time has his best interests at heart.

Jesus Christ is responsible for the execution of God's plan made before the foundation of the world. His function can be understood as that of chief executive officer. God gave him full authority to fulfill his plan for humanity's redemption; the scriptures make this abundantly clear.

Christ: The Mediator of the Covenant

When scripture refers to Christ as the Mediator, that term is comprehensive of the entire work of mediation in all its departments that as the spiritual deliverer of His people He voluntarily undertook.

As Mediator, Christ is the supreme prophet. He revealed the character and will of God. In the Sermon on the Mount, Jesus explained and vindicated the revelation previously given. In addition, He furnished in His own mission the supreme manifestation of God's love and grace. He also revealed the true nature of the salvation fallen humanity needed; the Holy Spirit must effect in them the certainty of a future life of bliss or woe according to their present character and the solemnities of that judgment with which the present order of things shall close.

To His apostles, He assigned the duty under His own superintendence of amplifying what He had in substance taught. Christ too is the source of all illumination whereby the truths is in any case practically apprehends and savingly believed. "No man knoweth … who the father is, but the Son, and he to whom the Son will reveal him" (Luke 10:22). A clear and scriptural knowledge of the truth is obtained only by divine teaching.

Christ: The High Priest

Christ as mediator is the great high priest, an office involving the making of expatiation and intercession.

> A merciful and faithful high priest in things pertaining to God, to make reconciliation for the sins of the people. (Hebrews 2:17)
>
> But this man, because he continueth ever, hath an unchangeable priesthood. Wherefore he is able also to save them to the uttermost that come unto God by him, seeing he ever liveth to make intercession for them. (Hebrews 7:24–25)

Christ was made sin legally that His people might be made righteous of God in Him. Such is the very essence of the gospel, and those who deny it place themselves outside the pale of divine mercy.

Christ: The Savior

As mediator, Christ is the King of Zion. His government abounds with truth and peace. The New Testament represents His exaltation and the authority with which He is now invested as the designed recompense of the work He accomplished (Ephesians 1:19–23; Philippians 2:8–11). It was part of the divine arrangement that the administration of the economy of grace should be committed to Him by whose sufferings and death the foundation had been laid for true intercourse between God and sinful humanity.

The supreme object for conferring the regal dignity on the Messiah was His own vindication and glory, but the subordinate design was that He should give practical effect to the divine purpose in the actual saving of all God's elect. The very nature of that purpose serves to determine the character and extent of the work committed to Him.

Christ: The Deliverer

The purpose includes the spiritual deliverance of God's people scattered throughout the world and therefore is a work affected against every conceivable opposition. The rule of the Messiah is supreme and universal because nothing short of that is adequate. "Who is gone into heaven, and is on the right hand of God; angels and authorities and powers being made subject unto him" (1 Peter 3:22). It is in the discharge of these three offices that Christ effectually executed the work of mediation.

In the performance of His duties, Christ made it abundantly clear that He was here to secure our rights with God and to do what the Father sent Him to do. The prophet Isaiah gave us a great account of the coming of the Lord and His mission in our lives as the chief executive officer.

The Bible Says

> For unto us a child is born, unto us a son is given: and the government shall be upon his shoulder: and his name shall be Wonderful, Counselor, The mighty God, The everlasting Father, The Prince of Peace. Of the increase of his government and peace there shall be no end, upon the throne of David, and upon his kingdom to order it, and to establish it with judgement, and with justice from henceforth even forever. The zeal of the Lord of hosts will perform it. (Isaiah 9:6–7)

> He will swallow up death in victory, and the Lord GOD will wipe away tears from off all faces; and the rebuke of

his people shall he take away from off all the earth: for the Lord hath spoken it. (Isaiah 25:8)

Thy dead men shall live, together with my dead body shall they arise. (Isaiah 26:19)

But he was wounded for our transgressions, he was bruised for our iniquities: the chastisement of our peace was upon him; and with his stripes was healed. (Isaiah 53:5)

The Spirit of the Lord GOD is upon me; because the LORD hath anointed me to preach the good tidings unto the meek; he hath sent me to bind up the brokenhearted, to proclaim liberty to the captives, and the opening of the prison to them that are bound. To proclaim the acceptable year of the LORD, and the day of vengeance of our God: to comfort all that mourn. To appoint unto them that mourn in Zion, to give unto them beauty for ashes. (Isaiah 61:1–3)

And she will bring forth a son and thou shalt call his name JESUS: for he shall save his people from their sins. (Matthew 1:21)

For the Son of man is come to save that which was lost. (Matthew 18:11)

But he answered and said, I am not sent but unto the lost sheep of the house of Israel. (Matthew 15:24)

And he said unto them, let us go into the next towns that I may preach there also: for therefore came I forth. (Mark 1:38; Luke 4:43)

And he shall reign over the house of Jacob for ever; and of his kingdom, there shall be no end. (Luke 1:33; Micah 4:7)

For I came down from heaven, not to do mine own will, but the will of him that sent me. (John 6:38)

These words spake Jesus, and lifted up his eyes to heaven, and said, Father, the hour is come; glorify thy Son. that thy Son also may glorify thee. (John 17:1)

For as in Adam all die, even so in Christ shall all be made alive. (1 Corinthians 15:22)

And being made perfect, he became the author of eternal salvation unto all them that obey him. (Hebrews 5:9)

For there is one God, and one mediator between God and men, the man Christ Jesus. (1 Timothy 2:5)

Jesus saith unto him, I am the way, the truth, and the life: no man cometh unto the Father, but by me. (John 14:6)

I am the door: by me if any man enter in, he shall be saved, and shall go in and out, and find pasture. I am come that they might have life, and that they might have it more abundantly. I am the good shepherd: the good shepherd giveth his life for the sheep. (John 10:9–11)

I am the good shepherd, and know my sheep and am known of mine. (John 10:14)

I am the light of the world: he that followeth me shall not walk in darkness, but shall have the light of life. (John 8:12)

I do nothing of myself; but as my Father hath taught me, I speak these things. And he that sent me is with me: the Father hath not left me alone; for I do always those things that please him. (John 8:28–29)

And the word which ye hear is not mine, but the Father's which sent me. (John 14:24)

And I seek not mine own glory: there is one that seeketh and judgeth. (John 8:50)

No man taketh it from me but I lay it down of myself. I have power to lay it down, and I have power to take it again This commandment have I received of my Father. (John 10:18)

And this is the will of him that sent me, that every one which seeketh the Son, and believeth on him, may have everlasting life: and I will raise him up at the last day. (John 6.40)

I am the living bread which came down from heaven: if any man eat of this bread, he shall live for ever: and the bread that I will give is my flesh, which I will give for the life of the world. (John 6:51)

For God sent not his Son into the world to condemn the world; but that the world through him might be saved. (John 3:17)

If ye shall ask any thing in my name, I will do it. (John 14:14)

Now ye are clean through the word which I have spoken unto you. (John 15:3)

But now he hath obtained a more excellent ministry, by how much also he is the mediator of a better Covenant, which was established upon better promises. (Hebrews 8:6)

But I have greater witness than that of John: for the works which the father hath given me to finish, the same works that I do bear witness of me, that the Father hath sent me. (John 5:36)

As the living Father hath sent me, and I live by the Father: so he that eateth me, even he shall live by me. (John 6:57)

For the Son of man is come to save that which was lost. (Matthew 18:11)

But he answered and said, I am not sent but unto the lost sheep of the house of Israel. (Matthew 15:24)

And he said unto them; Let us go into the next towns that I may preach there also: for therefore came I forth. (Mark 1:38; Luke 4:43)

These words spake Jesus, and lifted up his eyes to heaven, and said, Father, the hour is come; glorify thy Son, that thy Son also may glorify thee. (John 17:1)

For as in Adam all die, even so in Christ shall all be made alive. (1 Corinthians 15:22)

And being made perfect, he became the author of eternal salvation unto all them that obey him. (Hebrews 5:9)

Then answered Jesus, and said unto them, Verily, verily, I say unto you, The Son can do nothing of himself, but what he seeth the father do: for what things soever he doeth, these also doeth the Son likewise. (John 5:19)

And yet if I judge, my judgement is true, for I am not alone, but I and the Father that sent me. (John 8:16)

I am one that bear witness of myself, and the Father that sent me beareth witness of me. (John 8:18)

Jesus answered them, and said, My doctrine is not mine, but his that sent me. (John 7:16)

Then said Jesus unto them, When ye have lifted up the Son of man, then shall ye know that I am he, and that I do nothing of myself; but as my Father hath taught me, I speak these things. (John 8:28)

Christ Lived by Example

While we expect our president to lead the nation by exemplary behavior, it is evident that many presidents have failed to meet our expectations. Jesus Christ lived by example; He taught what He lived and lived what He taught. He showed the way, the truth, and the life. There was doubt that He was God. He fulfilled the plan of God to the letter but in word and deed. This is exactly what He expects from us.

We cannot expect to please the world and be full partakers of God's promises. We must make choices every day whether we will live according to God's laws or according to human laws even if they violate our Covenant with God.

What The Bible Says

> And he saith unto them, Follow me, and I will make you fishers of men. (Matthew 4:19)

> And when he had called the people unto him with his disciples also, he said unto them, whosoever will come after me, let him deny himself, and take up the cross, and follow me. "For whosoever will save his life shall lose it; but whosoever shall lose his life for my sake and the gospel's, the same shall save it. For what does it profit a man, if he shall gain the whole world, and lose his own soul. Or what shall a man give in exchange for his soul. (Mark 8:34–37)

> And he said to them all, If any man will come after me, let him deny himself, and take up his cross daily and follow me. (Luke 9:23)

> My sheep hear my voice, and I know them, and they follow me. (John 10:27)

> For I have given you an example, that ye should do as I have done to you. (John 13:15)

Jesus saith unto him, I am the way, the truth, and the life: no man cometh to the Father, but by me. (John 14:6)

Be ye therefore followers of God as dear children. (Ephesians 5:1)

For we have not an high priest which cannot be touched with the feeling of our infirmities; but was in all points tempted like as we are, yet without sin. (Hebrews 4:15)

Though he were a Son, yet learned he obedience by the things which he suffered. (Hebrews 5:8)

For even hereunto were ye called: because Christ also suffered for us, leaving us an example, that ye should follow his steps. (1 Peter 2:21)

Herein is our love made perfect, that we may have boldness in the day of judgement: because as he is so are we in this world. (1 John 4:17)

Principles

- Jesus Christ came to the world to save us sinners.
- Jesus Christ executed God's plan for our salvation.
- Jesus Christ reconciled us to God through His work.
- Jesus Christ was faithful to the end of His mission.
- Jesus Christ showed us the way to the Father.
- Jesus Christ was tested in all ways.
- Jesus Christ gave us a way to receive eternal life.
- Jesus Christ gave us a perfect example of obedience.
- Jesus Christ did only what He had been commissioned to do.

CHAPTER 12

The Constitution and the Bible: Qualifications for Holding the Office of the President of the United States

Section 1

No person except a natural born Citizen of the United States, at the time of the Adoption of this Constitution, shall be eligible to the Office of the President; neither shall nay Person be eligible to that Office who shall not have attained to the Age of thirty five Years, and been fourteen Years Resident within the United States. The President of the United States (POTUS) is the head of state and head of government of the United States of America. The president directs the executive branch of the federal government and is the commander-in-chief of the United States Armed Forces.

In contemporary times, the president is looked upon as the world's most powerful political figure and as the leader of the only current global superpower. The role includes responsibility for the world's most expensive military that has the second largest nuclear arsenal. The president also leads the nation with the largest economy by nominal GDP. The president possesses significant domestic and international hard and soft power.

Article II of the Constitution establishes the executive branch of the federal government. It vests the executive power of the United States in the president. The power includes the execution and enforcement of federal law, alongside the responsibility of appointing federal executive, diplomatic, regulatory, and judicial officers and concluding treaties with foreign powers with the advice and consent of the Senate.

The president is further empowered to grant federal pardons and reprieves, and to convene and adjourn either or both houses of Congress under extraordinary circumstances. The president is largely responsible for dictating the legislative agenda of the party to which the president is a member. The president also directs the foreign and domestic policies of the United States. In addition, as part of the system of checks and balances, Article One of the United States Constitution gives the president the power to sign or veto federal legislation. Since the office of president was established in 1789, its power has grown substantially, as has the power of the federal government as a whole.

Through the Electoral College, the registered voters indirectly elect the president and vice president to a four-year term. This is the only federal election in the United States which is not decided by popular vote. Nine vice presidents became president by virtue of a president's intra-term death or resignation.

The Twenty-second Amendment precludes any United States citizen from being elected president for a third term. It also prohibits a person from being elected to the presidency more than once if that person previously had served as president, or acting president, for more than two years of another person's term as president. In all, 44 individuals have served 45 presidencies (counting Grover Cleveland's two non-consecutive terms separately) spanning 57 full four-year terms.

Donald Trump is the 45th and current president, inaugurated on January 20, 2017. (https://en.wikipedia.org/wiki/President_of_the_United_States)

The Bible

While the Constitution has set conditions for holding the office of president, in the Bible, our president is Jesus Christ, but we are joint heirs with Him.

The national origin of the president is clearly specified in the Constitution. The birth and ministry of Jesus Christ were made known before time. The Old Testament is full of records that foretold His coming. Furthermore, He had to be born of a particular lineage. The Constitution requires that only natural-born citizens can hold this important office. Jesus met that requirement and fulfilled the Davidic Covenant. While He had the natural, physical features of human beings, He still retained the sonship of God.

He came as a Savior of the children of Israel, which necessitated His Davidic ancestry. However, we must recognize the race in God's plan included the Gentiles who had accepted Him as their Savior and Lord, those who had received the circumcision of the heart.

Jesus Christ fulfilled God's promise to the seed of Abraham, who was called the father of the faithful. The new Covenant was made to all who accepted the Messiah in the name of Jesus Christ and His finished work on the cross.

What the Bible Says

> The Lord hath sworn in truth unto David; he will not turn from it, of the fruit of thy body will I set upon thy throne. (Psalm 132:11)

> Thy seed will I establish and build up thy throne to all generations. Selah. (Psalm 89:4)

> He shall build a house for my name, and I will establish the throne of his kingdom for ever. I will be his father, and he shall be my son. (2 Samuel 7:13–14)

There will I make the horn of David to bud: I have ordained a lamp for mine anointed. (Psalm 132:17)

Behold, the days come, saith the LORD, that I will raise unto David a righteous Branch, and a King shall reign and prosper, and shall execute judgment and justice in the earth. (Jeremiah 23:5)

In those days, and at that time, will I cause the Branch of righteousness to grow up unto David; and he shall execute judgment and righteousness in the land. (Jeremiah 33:15)

The book of the generation of Jesus Christ, the sons of David, the son of Abraham. (Matthew 1:1)

Saying, what think ye of Christ? whose son is he? They say unto him, The Son of David. (Matthew 22:42)

He shall be great, and shall be called the Son of the Highest: and the Lord God shall give unto him the throne of his father David. (Luke 1:32)

And they said, Is not this Jesus the son of Joseph, whose father and mother we know? how is it then that he saith, I came down from heaven. (John 6:42)

Concerning his Son Jesus Christ our Lord, which was made of the seed of David according to the flesh. (Romans 1:3)

And again, Esaias saith, There shall be a root of Jesse, and he that shall rise to reign over the Gentiles; in him shall the Gentiles trust. (Romans 15:12)

Men and brethren, let me freely speak unto you of the patriarch David, that he is both dead and buried, and his sepulcher is with us unto this day. Therefore being a prophet, and knowing that God had sworn with an oath to him, that of the fruit of his loins, according to the flesh, he would raise up Christ to sit on his throne. (Acts 2:29–30)

And when he had removed him, he raised up unto them David to be their king, to whom also he gave testimony, and said I have found David, the son of Jesse, a man after mine own heart, which shall fulfill all my will. Of this man's seed hath God according to his promise raised unto Israel a Savior, Jesus. (Acts 13:22–23)

I Jesus have sent mine angel to testify unto you these things in the churches. I am the root and the offspring of David, and the bright and mourning star. (Revelation 22:16)

And there shall come forth a rod out of the stem of Jesse, and a Branch shall grow out of his roots. (Isaiah 11:1)

And the angel said unto her, Fear not Mary: for thou hast found favor with God. And behold, thou shalt conceive in thy womb, and bring forth a son and shalt call his name, JESUS. He shall be great, and shall be called the Son of the Highest: and the Lord God shall give unto him the throne of his father David. (Luke 1:30–32)

Therefore thus saith the Lord God, Behold, I lay in Zion for a foundation a stone, a tried stone, a precious corner stone, a sure foundation: he that believeth shall not make haste. (Isaiah 28:16)

I shall see him, but not now: I shall behold him, but not nigh: there shall come a Star out of Jacob, and a Scepter shall rise out of Israel, and shall smite the corners of Moab, and destroy all the children of Sheth. (Numbers 24:17)

But thou, Bethlehem Ephratah, though thou be little among the thousands of Judah, yet out of thee shall he come forth unto me that is to be ruler in Israel; whose goings forth have been from of old, from everlasting. (Micah 5:2)

When Israel was a child, then I loved him, and called my son out of Egypt. (Hosea 11:1)

The Birth of Jesus Christ

Now when Jesus was born in Bethlehem of Judea in the days of Herod the king, behold, there came wise men from the east to Jerusalem, Saying, where is he that is born King of the Jews? for we have seen his star in the east, and are come to worship him. (Matthew 2:1–2)

And the Word was made flesh, and dwelt among us, (and we beheld his glory, the glory as the only begotten of the Father,) full of grace and truth. (John 1:14)

But when the fullness of the time was come, God sent forth his Son, made of a woman, made under the law. (Galatians 4:4)

Now the birth of Jesus Christ was on this wise: When as his mother Mary was espoused to Joseph, before they came together, she was found with child of the Holy Ghost. (Matthew 1:18)

But while he thought on these things, behold, the angel of the LORD appeared unto him in a dream, saying, Joseph, thou son of David, fear not to take unto thee Mary thy wife: for that which is conceived in her is of the Holy Ghost. And she shall bring forth a son, and thou shalt call his name, JESUS: for he shall save his people from their sins. (Matthew 1:20–21)

And when they were come into the house, they saw the young child with Mary his mother, and fell down, and worshipped him: and when they had opened their treasures, they presented unto him gifts; gold, and frankincense, and myrrh. (Matthew 2:11)

Principles

- Jesus Christ met the natural requirements for God's plan.
- Jesus Christ was born in the designated geographical area.
- Jesus Christ's birth and life were prophesied.
- Jesus Christ redeemed humankind.
- Jesus Christ was born of a virgin and the Holy Spirit.
- Jesus Christ was born from the Davidic tribe as prophesied.

CHAPTER 13

The Constitution and the Bible: Article 3—Judicial Powers, Courts, and Judges

Section 1

> The judicial power shall extend to all cases, in law and equity, arising under this Constitution, the Laws of the United States, and Treaties made, or which shall be made, under their authority.

The Judiciary of the United States:

Judges are nominated by the president and confirmed by the Senate. Some of the nominees for the presidency may hold the same views, philosophy, and ideology as those of the president. This is designed to perpetuate the ideas and views of the party in power even after the term of the president has expired. The main function of this branch of government is to interpret the Constitution for the people when necessary.

The Holy Spirit Is Our Judiciary

The Holy Spirit is equal with the Father and Son in power and glory. He is the divine helper, assistant, counselor, and instructor, and His office is to carry forward the great work of teaching and saving humanity that Christ began. He is to the disciples of Christ what Christ was to them while on earth (John 15:26; 1 Corinthians 12:4–11). He is the divine Spirit commissioned to guide, inspire, and energize believers to do the work of God on earth interceding, directing, bearing witness and giving gifts, special spiritual qualifications. It is only by the power of the Holy Spirit working through consecrated men and women that souls can interpret scripture references to the Holy Spirit and the experiences of Christian people in regard to Him.

The Holy Spirit Came the Day of Pentecost

Jesus said He would send the Holy Spirit. Peter declared on the day of Pentecost that He had been exalted to the right hand of God, who had sent Him in fulfillment of the promise (Acts 2:16–33). His work was to convict us of sin, to lead us to repentance, to guide us, to reveal Christ, to be the Comforter in trouble, to strengthen and to sanctify our souls, and to be the guide, the energizer, and the sanctifier of the church.

The Holy Spirit Reveals Christ

Christ administers the government by wise means. Chief among these means in the matter of salvation are His Word and Spirit, the former containing all that it is necessary for us to know for our spiritual deliverance. The Word reveals the character of the Lord God and the nature of our relationship with Him. It sustains us and tells us what He requires of us and the principles by which He will deliver us.

It depicts what we are as fallen creatures, what sin is, and what its wages are. It unfolds the divine method of salvation through the sacrifice and mediation of the Son, His all-sufficiency for the work assigned Him, the way in which we become interested in its blessings and the character of that obedience that as the subjects of His grace we must render to Him.

The Holy Spirit Is Our Assurance

By His power, the Spirit dispels the darkness of our own understanding and subdues the enmity of the heart. This He does by regenerating us, which imparts to us a capacity for receiving and loving the truth. Christ fulfils the promises of The Bible by means of the ministry of the Word under the agency of the Holy Spirit. We may rest fully assured that everyone in whom the work of the Holy Spirit has begun will continue and persevere in the course on which they have entered until their salvation is completed.

The Holy Spirit Represents Christ

The Holy Spirit comes to represent Jesus Christ in our lives. He has a number of responsibilities that include teaching us the truth, interpreting the Word for us, and showing the way. We cannot understand the Word without the power of the Holy Spirit. Many scriptures need interpretation, which comes solely from the Holy Spirit.

The Spirit will show us nothing of Himself. He must reflect only those things that come from Christ. His ideology, views, opinions, and philosophy are replicas of those held by Christ. The scriptures below will shed some light on this fact.

What The Bible Says

> Howbeit when he, the Spirit of truth, is come, he will guide you into all truth: for he shall not speak of himself; but whatsoever he shall hear, that shall he speak: and he will shew you things to come. He shall glorify me: for he shall receive of mine, and shall shew it unto you. All things that the Father hath are mine: therefore said I, that he shall take of mire, and shall shew it unto ye. (John 16:13–15)

> But the Comforter, which is the Holy Ghost, whom the Father will send in my name, he shall teach you all things, and bring all things to your remembrance, whatsoever I have said unto you. (John 14:26)

> But ye shall receive power, after that the Holy Ghost is come upon you: and ye shall be witnesses unto me both in Jerusalem, and in all Judea, and in Samaria, and unto the uttermost part of the earth. (Acts 1:8)

> Nevertheless I tell you the truth; It is expedient for you that I go away: for if I go not away, the Comforter will not come unto you; but if I depart, I will send him unto you. And when he is come, he will reprove the world of sin, and of righteousness and judgement. Of sin, because they believe

not on me; Of righteousness, because I go to my Father, and ye see me no more; Of judgement, because, the prince of this world is judged. (John 16:7–11)

And when they had prayed, the place was shaken where they were assembled together; and they were all filled with the Holy Ghost, and they spake the word of God with boldness. (Acts 4:31)

While Peter yet spake these words, the Holy Ghost fell on all them which heard the word. And they of the circumcision which believed were astonished, as many as came with Peter, because that on the Gentiles also was poured out the gift of the Holy Ghost. For they heard them speak with tongues, and magnify God. (Acts 10:44–46)

No man speaking by the Spirit of God calleth Jesus accursed: and that no man can say that Jesus is the Lord, but by the Holy Spirit. (1 Corinthians 12:3)

But the fruit of the Spirit is love, joy, peace, longsuffering, gentleness, goodness, faith, meekness, temperance: against such there is no law. (Galatians 5:22–23)

The Spirit of God came upon him, and he prophesied among them. (1 Samuel 10:10)

The Spirit of the Lord GOD is upon me; because the LORD hath anointed me to preach good tidings unto the meek; he hath sent me to bind up the brokenhearted, to proclaim liberty to the captives, and the opening of the prison to them that are bound; to proclaim the acceptable year of the LORD, and the day of vengeance of our God; to comfort all that mourn. (Isaiah 61:1–2)

But if I cast out devils by the Spirit of God … (Matthew 12:28)

Through mighty signs and wonders, by the power of the Spirit of God … (Roman 15:19)

Thou givest also thy good spirit to instruct them, withheldest not thy manna from their mouth, and gavest them water for their thirst. (Nehemiah 9:20)

But ye are washed, but ye are sanctified, you are justified in the name of the LORD Jesus, and by the spirit of our God. (1 Corinthians 6:11)

Now we have received, not the spirit of the world but the spirit which is of God; that we might know the things are freely given to us. Which things also we speak, not in the words which man's wisdom teacheth, but which the Holy Spirit teacheth; comparing spiritual things with spiritual. But he that is spiritual judgeth all things, yet he himself is judged by no man. (1 Corinthians 2:12–13, 15)

But when the Comforter is come, whom I will send unto you from the Father, even the Spirit of truth, which proceedeth from the Father, he shall testify of me. (John 15:32)

But God has revealed to them unto us by His Spirit: for the Spirit searcheth all things, yea, the things of God. (1 Corinthians 2:10)

The grace of the Lord Jesus Christ, and the love of God, and the communion of the Holy Ghost, be with you all. (2 Corinthians 13:14)

Not by works of righteousness which we have done, but according to his mercy he saved us, by the washing of regeneration, and renewing of the Holy Ghost. (Titus 3:5)

And the spirit of the Lord shall rest upon him, the spirit of wisdom, and understanding, the spirit of counsel and might, the spirit of knowledge and the fear of the Lord. And shall make him quick of understanding in the fear of the Lord: and he shall not judge after the sight of his eyes, neither reprove after the hearing of his eyes. But with righteousness shall he judge the poor, and reprove with equity for the meek of the earth: and he shall smite the earth with the rod of his mouth, and with the breath of his lips shall he slay the wicked. (Isaiah 11:2–4)

He that believeth on me, as the scripture hath said, out of his belly shall flow rivers of living water. But this spake he of the Spirit, which they that believe on him should receive: for the Holy Ghost was not vet given; because that Jesus was not yet glorified. (John 7:38–39)

Then said Jesus to them again, Peace be unto you: as my Father bath sent me, even so send I you. And when he had said this, he breathed on them, and saith unto them, Receive ye the Holy Ghost. (John 20:21–22)

And we are his witnesses of these things; and so is also the Holy Ghost, whom God hath given to them that obey him. (Acts 5:32)

But he, (Stephen), being filled of the Holy Ghost, looked up steadfastly into heaven, and saw that glory of God and Jesus standing on the right hand of God. (Acts 7:55)

Now then when they heard this, they were pricked in their hearts and said unto Peter, and to the rest of the apostles, Men and brethren, what shall we do? The Peter said unto them, Repent, and be baptized every one of you in the name of Jesus Christ for the remission of sins, and ye shall receive the gift of the Holy Ghost. (Acts 2:37–38)

Ananias went his way. and entered into the house; and putting his hands on him said, Brother Saul, the Lord, even Jesus, that appeared unto thee in the way as thou comest, hath sent me, that thou mightiest receive thy sight, and be filled with the Holy Ghost. (Acts 9:17)

How God anointed Jesus of Nazareth with the Holy Ghost and with power: who went about doing good, and healing all that were oppressed of the devil; for God was with them. (Acts 10:38)

And I have filled him with the spirit of God, in wisdom, and in understanding, and in knowledge, and in all manner of workmanship. To devise cunning works, to work in gold, and in silver, and in brass. And in cutting of stones, to set them and in carving of timber, to work in all manner of workmanship. (Exodus 31:3–5)

Then wrought Bezaleel and Aholiab, and every wise hearted man, in whom the Lord put wisdom and understanding to know how to work all manner of work for the service of the sanctuary, according to all the Lord had commanded. (Exodus 36:1)

Principles

- The Holy Spirit comes to represent Jesus Christ.
- He has the power to interpret scriptures for us.
- He is our teacher.
- He is our comforter.
- He is our counselor.
- He is here to convict the world of sin.
- He draws us close to Christ.

CHAPTER 14

The Constitution and the Bible: Article 4—Interstate Relations

All states are required to

> give full faith and credit to one another's public acts, records, and judicial proceedings; And Congress may by general laws prescribe the manner in which such Ads, Records and Proceedings shall be proved, and the effect thereof.

Article 4: Privileges and Immunities for Citizens

> The citizens of each state shall be entitled to all privileges and immunities of citizens in the several states
>
> Extradition Any person charged in any state with treason, or any other crime, who shall lee from justice, and be found in another state, shall on demand of the executive authority of the state from which he fled, be delivered up, to be removed to the state having the jurisdiction of the crime.
>
> The Privileges and Immunities Clause (U.S. Constitution, Article IV, Section 2, Clause 1, also known as the Comity Clause) prevents a state from treating citizens of other states in a discriminatory manner. Additionally, a right of interstate travel may plausibly be inferred from the

> clause. (https://en.wikipedia.org/wiki/Privileges_and_Immunities_Clause)

The Fourteenth Amendment was ratified in 1868, and on November 1, 1869, the Supreme Court finally addressed this issue. In the case of *Paul v. Virginia*, 75 U.S. 168 (1868), the Court said the following.

> It was undoubtedly the object of the clause in question to place the citizens of each State upon the same footing with citizens of other States, so far as the advantages resulting from citizenship in those States are concerned. It relieves them from the disabilities of alienage in other States; it inhibits discriminating legislation against them by other States; it gives them the right of free ingress into other States, and egress from them; it insures to them in other States the same freedom possessed by the citizens of those States in the acquisition and enjoyment of property and in the pursuit of happiness; and it secures to them in other States the equal protection of their laws.

The Bible Says We Have a Relationship with the Deity

Our relationship with God through His Word or The Bible has "full faith and credit."

The Word is timeless.

> In the beginning was the Word, and the Word was with God and the Word was God. (John 1:1)

The Word created all things.

> By the word of the LORD were the heavens made; and all the host of them by the breath of his mouth. (Psalm 33:6)

The Word fulfilled itself.

> For I am the LORD: I will speak, and the word that I shall speak shall come to pass; it shall be no more prolonged:

> for in your days, O rebellious house, will I say the word, and will perform it, saith the LORD God. (Ezekiel 12:25)

The Word came to us.

> And the Word was made flesh, and dwelt among us, (and we beheld his glory, the glory of the begotten of the Father,) full of grace and truth. (John 1:14)

The Word stands forever.

> All the remnant of Judas that are gone into the land of Egypt to sojourn there, shall know whose words shall stand, mine or theirs. (Jeremiah 44:28)

The Word sets us free.

> If ye continue in my word, then are ye my disciples indeed. And ye shall know the truth, and the truth shall make you free. (John 8:31–32)

The Word works signs and wonders.

> And they went forth, and preached everywhere, the Lord working with them, and confirming the word with signs following. Amen. (Mark 16:20)

The Word gives life.

> Verily, verily, I say unto you, He that heareth my word, and believeth on him that sent me, hath everlasting life, and shall not come into condemnation, but is passed from death unto life. (John 5:24)

The Word sealed us with the Holy Spirit.

> In whom ye also trusted, after that ye heard the word of truth, the gospel of your salvation: in whom also after

> that ye believed, ye were sealed with that Holy Spirit of promise. Which is the earnest of our inheritance until the redemption of the purchased possessed, until the praise of his glory? (Ephesians 1:13–14)

Privileges and Immunities in The Bible

All citizens of the United States are granted equal privileges and immunities in the fifty states. They are not subjected to discrimination in some states because of the protection granted by the Constitution. The power of the blood of Jesus on the cross gives those who are redeemed certain guarantees.

- peace with God
- pardon for our sins
- protection from physical and spiritual defects
- permanent presence of God in our lives
- purity from the cleansing power of the blood of Jesus
- partaking rights of heirs to the Covenant

The Holy Spirit is deposited in your spirit as a guarantee of your salvation. Great benefits come from your membership in God's kingdom.

Eternal Life Is Yours

When we become God's children, we are given eternal life through His Son, Jesus Christ, and that life is imparted to us by the Holy Spirit. We can depend on God to fulfill His Word through His Constitution when He says we will receive eternal life.

What The Bible Says

> For God so loved the world that he gave his only begotten Son, that whosoever believeth in him should not perish, but have everlasting life. (John 3:16)

> But as many as received him, to them gave he power to become the Sons of God. (John 1:12)

> That if thou shalt confess with thy mouth the Lord Jesus, and shalt believe in thine heart that God hath raised him from the dead, thou shalt be saved. (Romans 10:9)
>
> For the eyes of the Lord are over the righteous, and his ears are open unto their prayers: but the face of the lord is against them that do evil. (1 Peter 3:12)
>
> And if children, then heirs; heirs of God and joint-heirs with Christ: if so be that we suffer with him, that we may be also glorified together. (Romans 8:17)

Forgiveness Is Ours

God has also promised us complete forgiveness of our sins when we accept His plan for salvation. We have the right to be cleansed of all sins that have separated us from Him since the fall of Adam. This forgiveness is eternal and is good for all sins we commit.

What The Bible Says

> Therefore is any man be in Christ, he is a new creature: old things are passed away; behold, all things are become new. (2 Corinthians 5:17)
>
> If we confess our sins, he is faithful and just to forgive us our sins, and to cleanse us from all unrighteousness. (1 John 1:9)
>
> There is therefore now no condemnation to them which are in Christ Jesus, who walk not after the flesh, but after the Spirit. (Romans 8:1)
>
> For I am persuaded, that neither death, nor life, nor angels, nor principalities, nor powers, nor things present, nor things to come, nor height, nor depth, nor any other creature, shall be able to separate us from the love of God, which is in Christ Jesus our LORD. (Romans 8:38–39)

The LORD is longsuffering, and of great mercy, forgiving iniquity and transgression, and by no means clearing the guilty, visiting the iniquity of the fathers upon the children unto the third and forth generation. (Numbers 14:18)

I said, I will confess my transgressions unto the Lord, and thou forgavest the iniquity of my sin. Selah. (Psalm 32:5)

For thou, Lord, art good, and ready to forgive; and plenteous in mercy unto all them that call upon thee. (Psalm 86:5)

Come now, and let us reason together, saith the LORD: though your sins be as scarlet, they shall be as white as snow; though they be red like crimson, they shall be as wool. (Isaiah 1:18)

I, even I, am he that blotteth out thy transgressions for mine own sake, and will not remember my sins. (Isaiah 43:25)

And I will cleanse them from all their iniquity, whereby they have sinned against me; and I will pardon all their iniquity, whereby they have transgressed against me. (Jeremiah 33:8)

And his transgressions that he hath committed, they shall not be mentioned unto him: in his righteousness that he hath done he shall live. (Ezekiel 18:22)

None of his sins that he hath committed shall be mentioned unto him: he hath done that which is lawful and right; he shall surely live. (Ezekiel 33:16)

To the Lord our God belong mercies and forgiveness, though we have rebelled against him. (Daniel 9:9)

> Who is a God like unto thee, that pardoneth iniquity and passeth by the transgression of the remnant of his heritage? he retaineth not his anger for ever, because he delighteth in mercy. (Micah 7:18)

> And forgive us our debts, as we forgive our debtors. (Matthew 6:12)

> But ye may know that the Son of man bath power on earth to forgive sins. (Mark 2:10)

> Then said Jesus, Father, forgive them; for they know not what they do. (Luke 23:34)

> For I will be merciful to their unrighteousness, and their sins, and their iniquities will I remember no more. (Hebrews 8:12)

Divine Health Is Ours

Through the death of Jesus Christ, we can receive divine healing from His blood. Christ is sufficient to heal all diseases that infect us, and He demonstrated His power to heal during His earthly ministry.

We thank God for modern medicine, which is also a gift from Him. Doctors play a major role in maintaining our physical health, but let us not forget that their intelligence is a gift from God. God has given them a gift of healing people through their skills and ability to cure diseases. God has the last word on our health. All our gifts must be used for His glory.

What The Bible Says

> Who his own self bare our sins in his own body on the tree, that we, being dead to sins, should live unto righteousness: by whose stripes ye were healed. (1 Peter 2:24)

> Confess your faults one to another, and pray one for another, that ye may be healed. (James 5:16)

> But when Jesus knew it, he withdrew himself from thence: and great multitudes followed him, and he healed them all. (Matthew 12:15)
>
> Then was brought unto him one possessed with a devil, blind, and dumb: and he healed him, insomuch that the blind and dumb both spake and saw. (Matthew 12:22)
>
> And Jesus went forth, and saw a great multitude, and was moved with compassion toward them, and he healed their sick. (Matthew 14:14)
>
> And great multitudes came unto him, having with them those that were lame, blind, dumb, maimed, and many others, and cast them down at Jesus' feet; and he healed them. (Matthew 15:30)
>
> And Jesus rebuked the devil; and he departed out of him: and the child was cured from that very hour. (Matthew 17:18)

Prosperity Is Ours

As God's children, we have been guaranteed all spiritual blessings through our Lord and Savior, Jesus Christ. While material wealth has been the focus of humanity on earth, we are promised God's provision to accomplish all things He has prepared for us in this world and the world to come. God is a faithful provider of all things. We can depend on His inexhaustible supply.

What The Bible Says

> Beloved, I wish above all things that thou mayest prosper and be in health, even as thy soul prospereth. (3 John 2)
>
> Let the LORD be magnified, which hath pleasure in the prosperity of his servant. (Psalm 35:27)
>
> Hitherto have ye asked nothing in my name: ask, and ye shall receive, that your joy may be full. (John 16:24)

Jesus said unto him, If thou canst believe, all things are possible to him that believeth. (Mark 9:23)

And his master saw that the LORD was with him, and that the LORD made all that he did to prosper in his hand. (Genesis 39:3)

And he shall be like a tree planted by the rivers of water, that bringeth forth his fruit in his season; his leaf also shall not wither, and whatsoever he doeth shall prosper. (Psalm 1:3)

For he shall be as a tree planted by the waters, and that spreadeth out her roots by the river, and shall not see when heat cometh, but her leaf shall be green; and shall not be careful in the year of drought, neither shall cease from yielding fruit. (Jeremiah 17:8)

Keep therefore the words of this Covenant, and do them, that ye may prosper in all that ye do. (Deuteronomy 29:9)

And keep the charge of the Lord thy God, to walk in his ways, to keep his statutes, and his commandments, and his judgements, and his testimonies, as it is written in the law of Moses, that thou mayest prosper in all that thou doest and whithersoever thou turnest thyself. (1 Kings 2:3)

Believe in the LORD your God, so shall ye be established; believe his prophets, so shall ye prosper. (2 Chronicles 20:20)

And he sought God in the days of Zechariah, who had understanding in the visions of God; and as long as he sought the LORD, God made him to prosper. (2 Chronicles 26:5)

Beloved, I wish above all things that thou mayest prosper and be in health, even as thy soul prospereth. (3 John 1:2)

Total Victory Is Ours

In Christ, we have a special right to claim total and everlasting victory over all problems, situations, pitfalls, and challenges that test our moral, physical, and spiritual strength. Without Jesus Christ, we are bound to look for victory in the wrong places.

Constitutional scholars, psychologists, and psychiatrists have made professions out of our social, political, and economic problems, but their solutions seem to get us deeper into more problems. Jesus Christ gives us victory over all situations in life. His work on the cross gave us a way out of the war with the devil, a spiritual warfare that no one could win with only natural abilities.

What The Bible Says

> We are more than conquerors through him that loved us. (Romans 8:37)
>
> I can do all things through Christ which strengthened me. (Philippians 4:13)
>
> But thanks be to God, which giveth us the victory through our LORD Jesus Christ. (1 Corinthians 15:57)
>
> For whatsoever is born of God overcometh the world: and this is the victory that overcometh the world, even our faith. (1 John 5:4)
>
> Now he which establisheth us with you in Christ, and hath anointed us, is God. Who hath also sealed us, and given the earnest of the Spirit in our hearts. (2 Corinthians 1:21–22)
>
> If God be for us, who can be against us? (Romans 8:31)
>
> He will swallow up death in victory; and the Lord GOD, will wipe away tears from off all faces; and the rebuke of his people shall he take away from all the earth: for the Lord hath spoken it. (Isaiah 25:8)

> A bruised reed shall he not break, and smoking flax shall he not quench, till he send forth judgement unto victory. (Matthew 12:20)

> And I saw as it were a sea of glass mingled with fire: and them that had gotten victory over the beast, and his image, and over his mark, and over the number of his name, stand on the sea of glass, having the harps of God. (Revelation 15:2)

We Have the Right to Partake

We have the right to partake of God's divine nature. We are joint heirs with Jesus Christ in all things God has prepared for us, His children. We have the privilege of being partakers of Christ's suffering on the cross knowing we will meet Him when His glory is revealed.

What The Bible Says

> Ye are partakers of sufferings, so shall ye be also of the consolation. (2 Corinthians 1:7)

> That the Gentiles should be fellowheirs, and of the same body, and partakers of his promise in Christ by the gospel. (Ephesians 3:6)

> We are partakers of Christ, if we hold the beginning of our confidence steadfast unto the end. (Hebrews 3:14)

> For they verily for a few days chastened us after their own pleasure; but he for our profit, that we might be partakers of his holiness. (Hebrews 12:10)

> But rejoice, inasmuch as ye are partakers of Christ's sufferings; that, when his glory shall be revealed, ye may be glad also with exceeding joy. (1 Peter 4:13)

> Whereby are given unto us exceeding great and precious promises: that by these ye might be partakers of the divine

> nature, having escaped the corruption that is in the world through lust. (2 Peter 1:4)
>
> For or sakes, no doubt, this is written: that he that ploweth should plow in hope; and that he thresheth in hope should be partaker of his hope. (1 Corinthians 9:10)
>
> For we being many are one bread, and one body: for we are all partakers of that one bread. (1 Corinthian 10:17)
>
> Wherefore, holy brethren, partakers of the heavenly calling, consider the Apostle, and High Priest of our profession, Christ Jesus Who was faithful to him that appointed him, as Moses was faithful in all his house. (Hebrews 3:1–2)
>
> For it is impossible for those who were once enlightened, and have tasted of the heavenly gift, and were made partakers of the Holy Ghost. And have tasted of the good word of God, and the powers of the world to come. If they shall fall away, to renew them again unto repentance; seeing they crucify to themselves the Son of God afresh, and put him to open shame. (Hebrews 6:4–6)

The Mystery of Salvation Has Been Removed

The gospel, which gives us access to salvation, has been hidden from us for a long time. We are to become what God planned for us from eternity. For a long time, we lived in darkness without knowledge or hope.

What The Bible Says

> For I would not, brethren, that ye should be ignorant of this mystery, lest ye should be wise in your own conceits; that blindness in part is happened to Israel, until the fullness of the Gentiles be come in. (Romans 11:25)
>
> Now to him that is of power to establish you according to my gospel, and the preaching of Jesus Christ, according to

the revelation of the mystery, which was kept secret since the world began. (Romans 16:25)

But we speak the wisdom of God in a mystery, even the hidden wisdom, which God ordained before the world unto our glory. (1 Corinthians 2:7)

Having made known unto us the mystery of his will, according to his good pleasure. which he hath purposed in himself. (Ephesians 1:9)

Whereby, when ye read, ye may understand my knowledge in the mystery of Christ. (Ephesians 3:4)

If ye have heard of the dispensation of the grace of God which is given to you-ward. Whereby that by revelation he be made known unto me the mystery. (Ephesians 3:2–3)

And to make all men see what is the fellowship of the mystery, which from the beginning of the world hath been hid in God, who created all things by Christ. (Ephesians 3:9)

And for me, that utterance may be given unto me, that I may open my mouth boldly, to make known the mystery of the gospel. (Ephesians 6:19)

Even the mystery which hath been hid from ages, and from generations, but now is made manifest to his saints. (Colossians 1:26)

And without controversy great is the mystery of godliness: God was manifest in the flesh, justified in the Spirit, seen of angels, preached unto the Gentiles, believed on in the world, received up into glory. (1 Timothy 3:16)

The Holy Spirit Will Extradite God's Children

The extradition laws of the United States in article 4 require the full cooperation of all the states in the union to bring criminals to justice. Scripture makes it clear that in God's eyes, we are all sinners who must stand trial on Judgment Day. We all rebelled against God and are busy running away from Him. Adam gave us our sin nature through his rebellion against God's commands in the Garden of Eden. God's extradition laws are designed to restore us to our original state of spiritual perfection, complete fellowship with Him, and the fulfillment of His plan for our lives.

We Christians are His creation in Christ Jesus; we are predestined to do what He prepared in advance for us to do. His extradition of the elect goes on all the time as an expression of His love for us, not for retribution or to bring us to justice. His love is so deep that He made provision for our inevitable fall.

God extradites sinners because of His sovereign love and grace. At the same time, we are given the right to choose to respond positively or negatively to that extradition. When we respond positively, we are given our rightful position and promises in Christ Jesus. If we do not respond to God's call, we face eternal damnation for our sins. God respects our will.

The Constitution does not provide for voluntary extradition. All who must stand trial will be extradited against their will and stand trial. God promises to judge us one day; that is inescapable.

The prophets warned us of God's impending wrath and His plan to redeem us from it. Christ is the only adequate provision God made for our successful extradition and redemption. He gave us the Holy Spirit as a guarantee of our eternal salvation and to reinforce the Covenant. We have the power to live and walk in God's way every day. God is omnipotent, omniscient, and omnipresent.

His extradition plan is not subject to human laws; we cannot control or avoid it. He dictates the laws and executes them according to His will. Scriptures abound with people who were extradited to serve God when they had fallen from His plan for their lives. We must recognize the absolute independence and sovereignty of God. Moses killed an Egyptian boy and ran away into the desert, but he met God's call on his life there.

Elijah reacted to Jezebel's threats by fearing for his own life, giving in to despair, and fleeing even after a great victory. God restored him and eventually took him up in a whirlwind.

David committed sin, failed to repent, and lost hope, but God restored him in due season. Jonah, displeased at the workings of God's sovereignty, became angry with God, which resulted in his wanting to die, but God extradited him and sent him to Nineveh. Peter denied Jesus by lying and cursing, which led him to weep bitterly. He was also restored by God's grace.

We see God working in people sovereignly then and today. King Nebuchadnezzar lived a life of spiritual inconsistency between submission to the Lord and rebellion. The Holy Spirit kept bringing him back to the truth, and at the end of his reign, his eyes were unto heaven, his understanding returned to him, and he blessed, praised, and honored God.

Spiritual extradition is the work of the Holy Spirit in us. God is constantly working in the lives of His children to bring them to a state of regeneration so they can become His ambassadors. This happens independent of our mental and physical capacity and orientation, but we must respond to this by yielding the members of our bodies to His plan and purpose.

What The Bible Says

> In whom also we have obtained an inheritance, being predestined according to the purpose of him who worketh all things after the counsel of his own will. (Ephesians 1:11)

> Now unto him that is able to exceeding abundantly above all that we ask or think, according to the power that worketh in us. (Ephesians 3:20)

> Being confident of this very thing, that he which hath begun a good work in you will -perform it until the day of Jesus Christ. (Philippians 1:6)

> For it is God which worketh in you both to will and to do of his good pleasure. (Philippians 2:13)

> Having predestined us unto the adoption of children by Jesus Christ to himself, according to the good pleasure of his will. (Ephesians 1:5)

Thy kingdom come, Thy will be done in earth, as it is in heaven. (Matthew 6:10)

My sheep hear my voice, and I know them, and they follow me. (John 10:27)

And other sheep I have, which are not of this fold: them also I must bring, and they shall hear my voice; and there shall be one fold, and one shepherd. (John 10:16)

My Father, which gave them me, is greater than all; and no man is able to pluck them out of my Father's hand. (John 10:29)

God Has Extradition Laws for His Children

For God so loved the world, that he gave his only begotten Son, that whosoever believeth in him should not perish, but have everlasting life. (John 3:16)

He that believeth on him is not condemned: but he that believeth not is condemned already, because he hath not believed in the name of the only begotten Son of God. (John 3:18)

He that believeth on the Son hath everlasting life: and he that believeth not the Son shall not see life; but the wrath of god abideth on him. (John 3:36)

The Spirit itself beareth witness with our spirit, that we are children of God. And if children, then heirs; heirs of God, and joint-heirs with Christ; if so be that we suffer with him, that we may also be glorified together. (Romans 8:16–17)

Whosoever therefore shall confess me before men, him will I confess also before my Father which is in heaven. (Matthew 10:32)

For the Son of man is come to seek and save that which was lost. (Luke 19:10)

But God commandeth his love towards us, in that, while we were yet sinners, Christ died for us. (Romans 5:8)

Who gave himself for our sins, that he might deliver us from this present evil world, according to the will of God and our Father. (Galatians 1:4)

A Wall of Sin Separates Humanity from God

As it is written, There is none righteous, no, not one. (Romans 3:10)

For all have sinned, and come short of the glory of God. (Romans 3:23)

For there is not a just man upon earth, that doeth good, and sinneth not. (Ecclesiastes 7:20)

But we are all as an unclean thing, and all our righteousness are as filthy rags; and we all do fade as a leaf; and our iniquities like the wind, have taken us away. (Isaiah 64:6)

If we say we have no sin, we deceive ourselves, and the truth is not in us. (1 John 1:8)

Therefore by the deeds of the law there shall no flesh be justified in his sight: for by the law is the knowledge of sin. (Romans 3:20)

Principles

- God's kingdom has rights, not privileges or immunities.
- God's rights include forgiveness of sin and divine healing.
- We are entitled to God's eternal security.

- We become partakers of God's divine nature.
- The mystery of salvation is removed from our minds.
- The Holy Spirit works in us to do God's will in our lives.
- God's plan for our lives begins to take effect in us.

CHAPTER 15

The Constitution and the Bible: Article 5—Powers to Amend the Constitution

The Congress, whenever two thirds of both Houses shall deem it necessary, shall pro-pose Amendments to this Constitution, or, on the Application of the Legislatures of two thirds of the several States, shall call a Convention for proposing Amendments, which, in either Case, shall be valid to all Intents and Purposes, as Part of this Constitution, when ratified by the Legislatures of three fourths of the several States, or by Conventions in three fourths thereof, as the one or the other Mode of Ratification may be proposed by the Congress.

Power to Amend the Constitution

> The United States Constitution is unusually difficult to amend. As spelled out in Article V, the Constitution can be amended in one of two basic ways. First, amendment can take place by a vote of two-thirds of both the House of Representatives and the Senate followed by a ratification of three-fourths of the various state legislatures or conventions in three-fourths of the states (ratification by thirty-eight states would be required to ratify an amendment today). This first method of amendment is the only one used to date, and in all but the case of the 21st Amendment, state ratification took place in legislatures rather than state conventions. Second, the Constitution might be amended by a Convention called for this purpose by two-thirds of the state legislatures, if the Convention's

> proposed amendments are later ratified by three-fourths of the state legislatures (or conventions in three-fourths of the states).
>
> Any amendment can be blocked by a mere thirteen states withholding approval (in either of their two houses). That means amendments don't come easy. In fact, only 27 amendments have been ratified since the Constitution became effective, and ten of those ratifications occurred almost immediately—as the Bill of Rights. The very difficulty of amending the Constitution greatly increases the importance of Supreme Court decisions interpreting the Constitution, because reversal of the Court's decision by amendment is unlikely except in cases when the public's disagreement is intense and close to unanimous. Even unpopular Court decisions (such as the Court's protection of flag burning) are likely to stand unless the Court itself changes its collective mind. (http://law2.umkc.edu/faculty/projects/ftrials/conlaw/articlev.htm)

God's Covenant, The Bible Cannot Be Amended

The Bible was written by God through humans. There is no other book that contains God's instruction for humanity. Our instructions are clear in regard to the Bible. From what is stated in the verses below, we cannot tamper with the Bible, who wrote the scriptures. While the Constitution can be amended with some difficulty, the Bible cannot and will not be amended without one facing eternal repercussions. It is eternal and the Constitution is not.

While we have been able to retain the essential framework of the Constitution, we have amended the document twenty-seven times, and it is conceivable that it will be amended many more times in future. The social, political, and economic pressures that have brought about changes to the Constitution are not found in God's kingdom. God is eternal, and His plan is everlasting. He does not make mistakes and does not need to change His plan to accommodate changes in the feelings and thinking of His creation. What He made with the Old Testament saints and prophets is a Covenant, which cannot change. The Bible is good for eternity. Words that the authors of The Bible wrote under God's instruction are not subject to change because God wrote those words Himself.

Scripture needs no updating, editing, or refining. Whatever time or culture you live in, it is eternally relevant. It needs no help in that regard. It is pure, sinless, inerrant truth; it is enduring. It is God's revelation for every generation. It was written by the omniscient Spirit of God, who is infinitely more sophisticated than anyone who dares stand in judgement on Scripture's relevancy for our society and infinitely wiser than all the best philosophers, analysts, and psychologists who pass like a childhood parade into irrelevancy. (John MacArthur, Truth Matters (Nashville, Tenn.: Thomas Nelson Publishers, 2004) 7-8.)

What The Bible Says

> And the Lord said unto Moses, Come up to me into the mount, and be there: and I will give thee tables of stone, and a law, and commandments which I have written; that thou mayest teach them. (Exodus 24:12)

> And He gave unto Moses, when he had made an end of communing with him upon the mount Sinai, two tables of testimony, tables of stone, written with the finger of God. (Exodus 31:18)

> And the tables were the work of God, and the writing was the writing of God, graven upon the tables. (Exodus 32:16)

> And the LORD said unto Moses, Write thou these words: for after the tenor of these words I have made a Covenant with thee and with Israel. (Exodus 34:27)

> And he wrote on the tables, according to the first writing, the ten commandments which the LORD spake unto you in the mount out of the midst of the fire in the day of the assembly: and the LORD gave them unto me. (Deuteronomy 10:4)

> Then Jeremiah called Baruch the son of Neriah: and Baruch wrote from the mouth of Jeremiah all the words of the LORD, which he had spoken unto him, upon a roll of a book. (Jeremiah 36:4)

> Ye shall not add unto the word which I command you, neither shall ye diminish ought from it, that ye may keep the commandments of the LORD your God which I command you. (Deuteronomy 4:2)

We Cannot Amend The Bible

The scriptures contain explicit instructions from God that we cannot add anything to. If we do, there is a punishment that no child of God is willing to take.

What The Bible Says

> Ye shall not add unto the word which I command you, neither shall ye diminish ought from it, that ye may keep the commandments of the Lord your God which commanded you. (Deuteronomy 4:2)

> What thing soever I command you, observe to do it: thou shalt not add thereto, not diminish from it. (Deuteronomy 12:32)

> This shall be written for the generation to come: and the people which shall be created shall praise the Lord. (Psalm 102:18)

> The law of the Lord is perfect, converting the soul: the testimony of the LORD is sure, making wise the simple. The statutes of the Lord are right, rejoicing the heart; the commandment of the Lord is pure, enlightening the eyes. The fear of the Lord is clean, enduring forever: the judgements of the Lord are true and righteous altogether. (Psalm 19:7–9)

Add thou not unto his words, lest he reprove thee, and thou be found a liar. (Proverbs 30:6)

Now go, write it before them in a table, and note it in a book, that it may be for the time to come for ever and ever. (Isaiah 30:8)

For I testify unto every man that heareth the words of the prophecy of this book, If any man shall add unto these things, God shall add unto him the plagues that are written in this book. And if any man shall take away the words of the book of this prophecy, God shall take away his part out of the book of life, and out of the holy city, and from the things which are written in this book. (Revelation 22:18–19)

Forever, O Lord, Thy word is settled in heaven. I esteem right all Thy precepts concerning everything, I hate every false way. Righteous art Thou, O Lord, And upright are Thy judgements.

Thou hast commanded Thy testimonies in righteousness, And exceeding faithfulness.

Thy righteousness is an everlasting righteousness, And Thy law is truth.

The sum of Thy word is truth, And every one of Thy righteous ordinances is ever lasting. (Psalms 119:89, 128, 137–38, 142, 160)

God Is Perfect: His Work Is Perfect

Out of our study of the Bible, we can confidently say that He is perfect. There are no mistakes in His work. His plan and all its parts are good for eternity. We must expect His Word to be perfect as well. Whatever He writes is inerrant, infallible, and irrevocable because of His perfect nature.

What The Bible Says

For I am the LORD, I change not; therefore ye sons of Jacob are not consumed. (Malachi 3:6)

The words of the LORD are pure words: as silver tried in a furnace of earth, purified seven times. (Psalm 12:6)

The grass withereth, the flower fadeth: but the word of our God shall stand for ever. (Isaiah 40:8)

For the word of the LORD is right; and all his works are done in truth. (Psalm 33:4)

As for God, his way is perfect: the word of the LORD is tried: he is a buckler to all those that trust in him. (Psalm 18:30)

Be ye therefore perfect, even as your Father which is in heaven is perfect. (Matthew 5:48)

He is the Rock, his work is perfect: for all his ways are judgement: a God of truth and without iniquity, just and right is he. (Deuteronomy 32:4)

And also the Strength of Israel will not lie nor repent: for he is not a man, that he should repent. (1 Samuel 15:29)

As for God, his ways are perfect; the word of the LORD is tried: he is a buckler to them that trust in him. (2 Samuel 22:31; Psalm 18:30)

And Jesus said unto him, Why callest thou me good? none is good, save one, that is God. (Luke 18:19)

I know that, whatsoever God doeth, it shall be forever: nothing can be put to it, nor anything taken from it: and God doeth it, that men should fear before him. (Ecclesiastes 3:14)

Jesus Christ Fulfilled the Old Testament

The Old Testament is full of prophetic scriptures about the coming of our Lord Jesus Christ. The new Covenant was promised in the Old Testament and fulfilled in the New Testament.

The prophets helped us prepare for the coming of the Lord. This is important for those who may be ignorant of the reason we have an Old and a New Testament in the Christian faith. The New Testament is not and will not be considered an amendment to the Old Testament but its fulfillment.

What The Bible Says

> Think not that I am come to destroy the law or the prophets: I am not come to destroy, but to fulfill. (Matthew 5:17)
>
> All things must be fulfilled which were written. (Luke 24:44)
>
> Thinkest thou that I cannot now pray to my Father, and he shall presently give me more than twelve legions of angels. But how then the scriptures shall be fulfilled, that thus it must be? (Matthew 26:53–54)
>
> And Jesus answering said unto him, suffer it to be so now: for thus it becometh us to fulfill all righteousness. Then he suffered him. (Matthew 3:15)
>
> That it might be fulfilled which was spoken by Esaias, the prophet. (Matthew 4:14)
>
> Think not that I am come to destroy the law, or the prophets: I am come not to destroy, but to fulfill. (Matthew 5:17)
>
> For verily I say unto you, Till heaven and earth pass, one jot or one title shall in no wise pass from the law, till all be fulfilled. (Matthew 5:18)

Verily I say unto you, This generation shall not pass, till all these things be fulfilled. (Matthew 24:34)

But how then shall the scripture be fulfilled, that thus it must be? (Matthew 26:54)

And they crucified him, and parted his garments, casting lots: that it might be fulfilled, which was spoken by the prophet. (Matthew 27:35)

And the Scripture was fulfilled, which saith, And he was numbered with the transgressors. (Mark 15:28)

And he began to say unto them. This day is the Scripture fulfilled in your ears. (Luke 4:21)

For I say unto you, I will not any more eat thereof, until it be fulfilled in the Kingdom of God. (Luke 22:16)

Principles

- The Word of God is perfect.
- The Word of God shall not be subject to amendments.
- The Word of God is the same yesterday, today, and forever.
- The Word of God is the work of His Spirit.
- The Word of God is an unbreakable Covenant with humanity.
- The Word of God was completely fulfilled in the New Testament.

CHAPTER 16

The Constitution and the Bible: Article 6—The Supremacy Act

This Constitution, and the Laws of the United States which shall be made in Pursuance thereof; and all treaties made, or which shall be made, under the Authority the United States, shall be the supreme Law of the Land; and the judges in every states shall be bound thereby any Thing in the Constitution or Laws of any State to the Contrary notwithstanding.

The Supremacy of the Bible

The Constitution contains laws that are supreme to all laws made by the fifty states in the union individually. No state can legally make laws that violate the Constitution. For God's citizens, the supremacy of His Constitution, The Bible in our lives over any other constitution cannot be compromised.

God set up His laws to be our final authority when He created us. Only God knows our position and promises because He determined everything before the foundation of the world. We are not accidents. Psalm 139 describes how God planned us and ordained our days before we drew our first breath. He saw us before we were born; He knew what we would accomplish, and He made full provision for the successful attainment of His goals in our lives. The Bible contains all we need to know about this matter.

The absolute and universal supremacy of God is plainly and positively affirmed in many scriptures. The Bible is the supreme law that governs our everyday conduct. If we live by the Word, we will naturally respect and obey all the laws of the United States.

God expects us to make His Word our final authority on all matters affecting our relationship with the secular world. The Word is abundantly clear on this question. We need to know that God's government was the first government for humanity, and all subsequent earthly governments cannot make laws that are superior to God's laws. His omnipotence, omniscience, and omnipresence in our lives today and forever dictate that it is our first duty to obey Him and His commands.

God's Supremacy

> Thine, O LORD, is the greatness, and the power, and the glory, and the victory, and the majesty: for all that is in heaven and in the earth is thine: thine is the kingdom, O Lord, and thou art exalted as head above all … And thou reignest over all. (1 Chronicles 29:11–12)
>
> And said, O Lord God of our fathers, art not Thou God in heaven? and rulest not thou over all the kingdoms of the heathen? and in thine hand is there not power and might, so that none is able to withstand thee? (2 Chronicles 20:6)
>
> I know that Thou canst do everything, and that no thought can be withholden from thee. (Job 42:2)
>
> Whatsoever the LORD pleased, that did he in heaven, and in earth, in the seas, and all deep places. (Psalm 135:6)
>
> The king's heart is in the hand of the LORD, as the rivers of water: He turneth it whithersoever he will. (Proverbs 21:1)

The Word Must Be Supreme for God's Children

Scriptures that give us clear instructions on how we should treat the Bible abound. It is indeed our supreme authority in all matters pertaining to life. From the Old to the New Testament, God has not changed His instructions on the primacy of the scriptures in dictating our position on all issues affecting our diplomatic mission from heaven.

What The Bible Says

This book of the law shall not depart out of thy mouth; but thou shalt meditate therein day and night, that thou mayest observe to do according to all that is written therein: for then thou shalt make thy way prosperous, and then thou shalt have good success. (Joshua 1:8)

Blessed is the man that walketh not in the counsel of the ungodly, nor standeth in the way of sinners, nor sitteth in the seat of the scornful. But his delight is in the law of the LORD; and in his law doth he meditate day and night. And he shall be like a tree planted by the rivers of water, that bringeth forth his fruit in his season; his leaf also shall not wither; and whatsoever he doeth shall prosper. (Psalm 1:1–3)

I will meditate on thy precepts, and have respect unto thy ways. I will delight myself in the statutes: I will not forget thy word. (Psalm 119:15–16)

And keep the charge of the LORD thy God, to walk in his ways, to keep his statutes, and his commandments, and his judgements, and his testimonies, as it is written in the law of Moses, that thou mayest prosper in all that thou doest, and withersoever thou turnest thyself. (1 Kings 2:3)

God is greater than our heart, and knoweth all things. (1 John 3:20)

For my thoughts are not your thoughts, neither are your ways my ways saith the LORD. For as the heavens are higher than the earth, so are my ways higher than your ways, and my thoughts than your thoughts. (Isaiah 55:8–9)

But as for thee, stand thou here by me, and I will speak unto thee all the commandments, and statutes, and the judgements, which thou shalt teach them, that they may do them in the land which I give them to possess it. Ye shall observe to do therefore as the LORD your God hath commanded you: ye shall not turn aside to the right hand or to the left. Ye shall walk in all the ways which the LORD your God hath commanded you, that ye may live, and that it may be well with you, and that ye may prolong your days in the land which ye shall possess. (Deuteronomy 5:31–33)

And these words, which I command thee this day, shall be in thine heart: And thou shalt teach them diligently unto thy children, and shalt talk of them when thou sittest in thine house, and when thou walkest by the way, and when thou liest down, and when thou risest up. And thou shalt bind them for a sign upon thine hand, and they shall be as frontlets between thine eyes. And thou shalt write them upon the posts of thy house, and on thy gates. (Deuteronomy 6:6–9)

Go ye therefore, and teach all nations, baptizing them in the name of the Father, and of the Son, and of the Holy Ghost: Teaching them to observe all things whatsoever I have commanded you: and, lo, I am with you always, even unto the end of the world. Amen. (Matthew 28:19–20)

All Scripture is given by inspiration of God, and is profitable for doctrine, for reproof, for correction, for instruction in righteousness: That the man of God may perfect, thoroughly furnished unto all good works. (2 Timothy 3:16–17)

For the word of God is quick, and powerful, and sharper than any two-edged sword, piercing even to the dividing asunder of soul and spirit, and of the joints and marrow and is a discerner of the thoughts and intents of the heart. (Hebrews 4:12)

But he said, Yea rather, blessed are they that hear the word of God and keep it. (Luke 11:28)

Thy word is a lamp unto my feet, and a light unto my path. (Psalm 119:105)

Take heed unto thyself, and unto the doctrine; continue in them; for in doing this thou shalt save thyself, and them that hear thee. (1 Timothy 4:16)

Do all to the glory of God. (1 Corinthians 10:31)

We need to rely upon God's word to distinguish between the folly of man's wisdom and the promises of God. (Psalm 19:7–14; 2 Timothy 3:16–17)

We are rooted, built up, and established in the LORD Jesus Christ, not to be con formed to this world. We must practice God's Word to grow into maturity. (Matthew 7:24–27; James 1:21–22)

And Moses with the elders of Israel commanded the people, saying, Keep all the commandments which I command you this day. (Deuteronomy 27:1)

Whoso eateth my flesh, and drinketh my blood … dwelleth in me, and I in him. (John 6:54, 56)

But he answered and said, It is written, Man shall not live by bread alone, but by every word that proceedeth out of the mouth of God. (Matthew 4:4)

And Jesus said unto them, I am the bread of life: he that cometh to me shall never hunger; and he that believeth on me shall never thirst. (John 6:35)

But whosoever drinketh of the water that I shall give him shall never thirst; but the water that I shall give him shall be in him a well of water springing up into everlasting life. (John 4:14)

Jesus stood and cried, saying, If any man thirst, let him come to me, and drink. He that believeth on me, as the Scripture hath said, out of his belly shall flow rivers of living water. (John 7:37–38)

And it shall come to pass, if thou shalt hearken diligently unto the voice of the LORD thy God, to observe and to do all his commandments which I command thee this day, that the LORD thy God will set thee on high above all nations of the earth. (Deuteronomy 28:1)

The secret things belong unto the LORD our God: but those things which are revealed belong unto us, and to our children for ever, that we may do all the words of the law. (Deuteronomy 29:29)

In that I command thee this day to love the LORD thy God, to walk in his ways, and to keep his commandments and his statutes and his judgements, that thou mayest live and multiply: and the LORD thy God shall bless thee in the Land whither thou goest to possess it. (Deuteronomy 30:16)

Keep therefore the words of this Covenant, and do them, that ye may prosper in all that ye do. (Deuteronomy 29:9)

Principles

- The Word of God must be the supreme authority over our lives.
- The Word of God must our standard of truth.
- The Word of God must dictate our search for truth.
- The Word of God must shape our lives.
- The Word of God is our constitution with God for eternity.
- The Word of God gives us life today and forever.
- The Word of God must be to our souls as food and drink are to our bodies.

CHAPTER 17

The Constitution and the Bible: Article 7—Ratification of the Constitution

The Ratification of the Conventions of nine States, shall be sufficient for the Establishment of this Constitution between the States so ratifying the Same.

> While the Constitution needed a number of states to ratify it so it would become a legal document binding all parties, the Bible tells us that Jesus ratified the Covenant for all children of God.
>
> The Federalists believed the Constitution provided just the right mix of power and limitations on power. The first government of the US was a one-house legislature with no executive. It couldn't raise money, it relied on the states for military power, and was generally seen as ineffective and weak. The US Constitution was written to remedy those weaknesses and provide the US with a better, more representative form of government. It tried to balance power between the small and large states by having a two house legislature. It tried to balance power between the central and state governments. And, it split power between three branches of government. All of this elaborate 'check and balance' system was intended to strengthen the central government while making sure that there were always forces in place to keep it from becoming too powerful. Federalists campaigned to support

> ratification because they believed the Constitution was the best way to balance these needs. Those opposed to the Constitution called themselves Democratic Republicans. The battle over the Constitution was fought, state by state. And when critics of the Constitution were successful in persuading many Americans that it took too much power from ordinary people, the Federalists promised to write a Bill of Rights that would also secure certain rights to the people themselves. These became the first ten amendments to the US Constitution. (https://socratic.org/questions/what-were-federalist-reasons-for-supporting-ratification-of-the-constitution)

Ratification of Covenant by Jesus with man in God's Kingdom

In Hebrews 12:24, we learn that Jesus was the ratifier or mediator of the new the Covenant between God and humanity, which required a mediator, Jesus Christ. It pleased God to demonstrate to us His matchless wisdom in such a constitution of things as the mediatorship of Christ discloses.

The Constitution was ratified by nine states before it became effective in all the states. God required the blood of Jesus to ratify our relationship with Him. This is what the law demanded for the remission of our sins. Sin is an evil before God so offensive and malignant as to necessitate a separation between God and humanity. God hates sin and justly punishes it. Hence, when He seeks the return of sinners to Himself, it is by mediation, which vindicates His perfection and magnifies His law.

As sinners, we need a mediator. We are enemies with God. We love darkness rather than light. We do not retain the knowledge of God in our minds; we do all we can to dismiss Him from our thoughts. It is neither carelessness nor involuntary ignorance that occasions this feeling but positive hostility; the carnal mind is enmity against God. When confronted with truth and made to feel we are under divine condemnation, we regard God as our worst enemy committed to our punishment, and we are conscious of feelings of aversion.

Christ Himself is thereby greatly glorified. This is the supreme end in the divine administration for He is the Alpha and the Omega in all the counsels of God. The perfect love of Christ for the Father evidenced by His voluntary self-abasement and obedience unto death shines forth in meridian splendor. He is the perfect lamb of sacrifice that God used to ratify His Covenant with humanity. The book of Hebrews helps us gain insight into the conditions Christ had to meet to ratify our Covenant with God.

What The Bible Says

> And for this cause he is the mediator of the new testament, that by means of death, for the redemption of the transgressions that were made under the first testament, they which are called might receive the promise of eternal inheritance. For where a testament is, there must also of necessity be the death of the testator. For a testament is of force after men are dead: otherwise it is of no strength all while the testator liveth. Whereupon neither the first testament was dedicated without blood. (Hebrews 9:15–18)

> And almost all things are by the law purged with blood; and without shedding of blood is no remission. (Hebrews 9:22)

Old Testament Ratification

The old the Testament Covenant between God and the children of Israel required the shedding of the blood of bulls and goats to maintain its status. This was done every year by the high priest, whose main function was to lead the worship of God by the people and present the blood of animals on the altar in the holy of holies to God for the atonement of the sins of the people.

What The Bible Says

> And Aaron shall make atonement upon the horns of it once in a year with the blood of the sin offering of atonements: once in the year shall he make atonement upon it throughout your generations: it is most holy unto the LORD. (Exodus 30:10)

> For the life of the flesh in is the blood: and I have given it to you upon the altar to make atonement for your souls: for it is the blood that maketh an atonement for the soul. (Leviticus 17:11)

> He was oppressed, and he was afflicted, yet he opened not his mouth: he is brought as a lamb to the slaughter, and as a sheep before her shearers is dumb, so he openeth not his mouth. (Isaiah 53:7)

> As for thee also, by the blood of thy Covenant I have sent forth thy prisoners out of the pit wherein is not water. (Zechariah 9:11)

New Testament Ratification

In the Old Testament, God instructed the priests to kill animals and present the blood to Him for the atonement of the sins of the children of Israel. This ritual was necessary to maintain the old Covenant. The new Covenant was completed by the blood of Jesus at Calvary once and for all covering the sins of humanity for eternity. His death and resurrection ratified the Covenant for all who accepted His plan of salvation.

What The Bible Says

> But God commandeth his love toward us, in that, while we yet sinners, Christ died for us. (Romans 5:8)

> For the wages of sin is death; but the gift of God is eternal life through Jesus Christ our Lord. (Romans 6:23)

> Neither is there salvation in any other: for there is none other name under heaven given among men, whereby we must be saved. (Acts 4:12)

> For the Son of man is come to seek and save that which was lost. (Luke 19:10)

For I delivered unto you first of all that which I also received, how that Christ died for our sins according to the scriptures. (1 Corinthians 15:3)

For this is the blood of the new testament, which is shed for many for the remission of sins. (Matthew 26:28)

Then Jesus said unto them, Verily, verily, I say unto you, Except ye eat the flesh of the Son of man, and drink his blood, ye have not life in you. Whoso eateth my flesh, and drinketh my blood, hath eternal life, and I will raise him up at the last day. For my flesh is meat indeed, and my blood is drink indeed. He that eateth my flesh, and drinketh my blood, dwelleth in me, and I in him. (John 6:53–56)

Take heed therefore unto yourselves, and to all the flock, over which the Holy Ghost hath made you overseers, to feed the church of God, which he hath purchased with his own blood. (Acts 20:28)

Much more then, being now justified by his blood, we shall be saved from wrath through him. (Romans 5:9)

The cup of blessing which we bless, is it not the communion of the blood of Christ? The bread which we break, is it not the communion of the body of Christ? (1 Corinthians 10:16)

After the same manner also, he took the cup, when he had supped, saying, this cup is the new testament in my blood: this do ye, as oft as ye drink it, in remembrance of me. (1 Corinthians 11:25)

In whom we have redemption through his blood, the forgiveness of sins, according to the riches of his grace. (Ephesians 1:7)

And to Jesus, the mediator of the new Covenant, and to the blood of sprinkling, that speaketh better things than that of Abel. (Hebrews 12:24)

And they overcame him by the blood of the Lamb, and by the word of their testimony; and they loved not their lives unto death. (Revelation 12:11)

And he said to him, Sir, thou knowest. And he said to me, These are they which came out of the great tribulation, and have washed their robes, and made them united in the blood of the Lamb. (Revelation 7:14)

This is he that came by water and blood, even Jesus Christ; not by water only, but by water and blood. And there are three that bear witness in earth, the spirit, and the water, and the blood: and these three agree in one. (1 John 5:6, 8)

How much more shall the blood of Christ, who through the eternal Spirit offered himself without spot to God, purge your conscience from dead works to serve the living God? (Hebrews 9:14)

Now the God of peace, that brought again from the dead our Lord Jesus, that great shepherd of the sheep, through the blood of the everlasting Covenant. (Hebrews 13:20)

For this is my blood of the new testament, which is shed for many for the remission of sins. (Matthew 26:28)

Likewise also the cup after supper, saying, This cup is the new testament in my blood, which is shed for you. (Luke 22:20)

Whom God hath sent forth to be a propitiation through faith in his blood, to declare his righteousness for the remission of sins that are past, through forbearance of God. (Romans 3:25)

Wherefore Jesus also, that he might sanctify the people with his own blood, suffered without the gate. (Hebrews 13:12)

But if we walk in the light, as he is in the light, we have fellowship one with another, and the blood of Jesus Christ his Son cleanseth us from all sin. (1 John 1:7)

Who needeth not daily, as those high priests, to offer up sacrifice, first for his own sins, and then for the people's: for this he did once when he offered up himself. (Hebrews 7:27)

And he is the propitiation for our sins; and not for ours only, but also for the sins of the whole world. (1 John 2:2)

Herein is love, not that we loved God, but that he loved us, and sent his Son to be the propitiation for our sins. (1 John 4:10)

Forasmuch as ye know that ye were not redeemed with corruptible things, as silver and gold, from your vain conversation received by tradition from your fathers. But with the precious blood of Christ, as a lamb without blemish and without spot. (1 Peter 1:18–19)

Jesus Is Our Assurance of Ratification

All God's children, whose salvation was ratified by Jesus Christ, can rest assured that they are His forever. He has promised to tend his sheep His Father gave him for eternity. He has given them everlasting life and has promised to protect them from the devil forever. Once ratified, the Covenant remains ratified forever with no amendments to it.

What The Bible Says

My sheep hear my voice, and I know them, and they follow me. And I give unto them eternal life; and they shall never

> perish, neither shall any man pluck them out of my hand. My Father, which gave them me, is greater than all; and no man is able to pluck them out of my Father's hand. (John 10:27–29)

> Jesus said unto her, I am the resurrection, and the life: he that believeth in me, though he were dead, yet shall he live. And whosoever liveth and believeth in me shall never die. Believest thou this? (John 11:25–26)

> Verily, verily, I say unto you, he that heareth my word, and believeth on him that sent me, hath everlasting life, and shall not come into condemnation; but is passed from death unto life. (John 5:24)

> For I am persuaded, that neither death, nor life, nor angles, nor principalities, nor powers, nor things present, nor things to come, nor height, nor depth, nor any other creature, shall be able to separate us from the Love of God, which is in Christ Jesus our Lord. (Romans 8:38–39)

> Being confident of this very thing, that he which hath begun the good work in you will perform it until the day of Jesus Christ. (Philippians 1:6)

> To an inheritance incorruptible, and undefiled, and that fadeth not away, reserved in heaven for you. (1 Peter 1:4)

The Covenant of Christ Is Ratified by Faith

The Covenant between humanity and God is ratified by faith. The Constitution required nine states to make it binding for all the states. This was not an easy process because some of the states were reluctant to join the union. However, it was eventually done.

Christ shed the blood needed to ratify our Covenant with God. By faith, we accept His work as complete to grant us full pardon for all sins. We believe and accept by faith that we are now God's children and will remain so forever. Without faith, it is impossible to ratify this Covenant.

The scriptures make this explicit and critical for all who want to be party to this Covenant.

What The Bible Says

> For by grace are ye saved through faith; and that not of yourselves: it is the gift of God. (Ephesians 2:8)
>
> Therefore being justified by faith, we have peace with God through our Lord Jesus Christ. By whom we have access by faith into this grace wherein we stand, and rejoice in hope of the glory of God. (Romans 5:1–2)
>
> Therefore we conclude that man is justified by faith without the deeds of the law. (Romans 3:28)
>
> For ye are all the children of God by faith in Christ Jesus. (Galatians 3:26)
>
> Now faith is the substance of things hoped for, the evidence of things not seen. (Hebrews 11:1)
>
> But without faith it is impossible to please him. (Hebrews 11:6)
>
> Looking unto Jesus the author and finisher of our faith … (Hebrews 12:2)
>
> Knowing that a man is not justified by the works of the law, but by the faith of Jesus Christ, even we have believed in Jesus Christ, that we might be justified by the faith of Christ, and not by the works of the law: for by the works of the law shall no flesh be justified. (Galatians 3:16)
>
> And God, which knoweth the hearts, bare them (Gentiles) witness, giving them the Holy Ghost, even as he did unto us; And put no difference between us (Jews) and them (Gentiles), purifying their hearts by faith. (Acts 15:8–9)

Principles

- Only the blood of Jesus can ratify our Covenant with God.
- Only the blood of Jesus can wash away our sins.
- Only the blood of Jesus can give us eternal life.
- Only the blood of Jesus can reconcile us with God.
- Only Jesus Christ can give us faith and hope in God.
- Only Jesus secures our position and promises in God.

CHAPTER 18

The Constitution and The Bible: The Bill of Rights

The Bill of Rights is a formal declaration of the legal and civil rights of all US citizens. It was included in the amendments to the Constitution. In the Bible, we do not have a Bill of Rights, but as children of God, we have privileges and blessings guaranteed and eternal. The Constitution attempts to address issues that were considered important at the time it was framed, but in the Bible, the blessings and privileges were prepared from eternity into eternity. It is important for us to understand God's perspective on what we consider to be crucial issues of our time.

The amendments to the Constitution were critical for its ratification. They expressed heartfelt concerns of the people. They reflect the priorities of citizens over time. As Christians, we have civil and spiritual provisions that God prepared for us. He has promised to meet our physical and social needs as well as our spiritual requirements for now and eternity. We need to look at the same issues and ask ourselves what God's Word teaches today.

Rights given by human beings are limited and short sighted, but those coming from God last forever. We must consider God's perspective on these matters since we must seek "His thoughts and His ways" (Isaiah 55:8), which are eternally higher than ours.

We do not need to challenge the Constitution per se but merely gain insight into God's modus operandi in the same matters. God speaks to us in all situations and has expressly commanded us to obey civic responsibilities, but our accountability to God supersedes every law in the land.

A biblical analysis of the same issues that are covered in the amendments may help us understand what God expects from us. Since we have declared ourselves dead to sin and alive to God, our mental and physical beings must conform to the image of Christ by the constant renewal of our minds. We are now new creatures in Christ. Behold—the old is gone and the new is come. It is not us living but Christ living in us. What then would He say about these amendments to us?

Freedom

Under the Constitution, there are freedoms that belong to the American people and must be protected and guarded as fundamental rights. Each person is born to live and exercise freedom of expression, speech, association, owning guns, and so on. We live under authority only because of our common social contract. The freedoms in the Constitution have produced debate that seems to consume society with a passion to protect individuals at the expense of the whole society. Is this the freedom we are looking for? Can it give us all we need to live abundant lives?

Apart from God, we are slaves to sin (Romans 6:16). Those who focus on saving their lives will lose them, but those who are willing to lose their lives for His sake will be saved (Luke 9:23–24). Be subject to those in authority over you (Romans 13:1; Hebrews 13:17).

We need the liberty only Christ can give us. It allows us live in conformity with God's plan of our lives, to destroy the power of sin over our lives, and achieve victory over the gods of this world. Many social ills can be cured if we adopt God's plan for our freedom.

The Bible Has No Bill of Rights

Christians are God's children who enjoy privileges, not rights. Rights can be taken away. We have privileges of being children of God set out by Paul in Romans 8:14–17.

> For those who are led by the Spirit of God are the children of God. The Spirit you received does not make you slaves, so that you live in fear again; rather, the Spirit you received brought about your adoption to son ship. And by him we cry, "Abba, Father." The Spirit himself testifies with our spirit that we are God's children. Now if we are children, then we are heirs-heirs of God and co-heirs with Christ, if indeed we share in his sufferings in order that we may also share in his glory.

A. Security

We are not to fear, but enjoy son ship (v 15a). An employee or a servant basically obeys out of fear of punishment, loss of job, etc. But a child-parent relationship is not characterized by a fear of losing the relationship.

B. Authority

We have the status not of "a slave" but of "sonship" (v 15a). In a house, slaves have no authority. They can only do what they are told. But under their parents, children do have authority in the house—they are not mere servants. The children of God are given authority over sin and the devil. They are to move about in the world knowing that it belongs to their Father. There should be a confidence and poise about them. Children have the honor of the family name. There is a wonderful new status conferred on us.

C. Intimacy

"By him we cry, 'Abba'" (v. 15b). We need to know the original language here. Abba was an Aramaic term which is best translated "Daddy"—a term of the greatest intimacy. A child does not always (or even often) address his father as "Father"; likely, he has a different term for him that shows his loving, trusting familiarity with his father, such as "Dad" or "Papa" or "Daddy." And this is how Christians can approach the all-powerful Creator of the universe, who sustains every atom in existence moment by moment!

D. Assurance

"The Spirit himself testifies with our spirit that we are God's children" (v 16). When we cry out to God as "Abba," the Spirit of God somehow comes alongside us ("with our spirit") and gives us assurance that we truly are in God's family. There is a lot of debate about the nature of this "testimony," but it appears to be an inner witness in the heart, a sense that yes, he really loves me.

Notice, Paul says our spirit is already testifying: "The Spirit … testifies with our spirit." This means we already have evidence that we are Christians. We know we trust Christ. We have his promises. We see our lives changing and growing. All these pieces of evidence lead our "spirit"—our hearts—to have a measure of confidence that we really are his. But Paul says that the Spirit can come alongside us and, in addition to all we see, "testify." This seems to refer to a direct testimony of the Spirit in our hearts. This probably is a sense of God's immediate presence and love that sometimes comes to us (something Paul has already spoken of back in 5:5). We don't get this all the time, or even often; and it may not be a very strong feeling. But there will be times when, as we cry out to Abba, we find ourselves deeply assured that he really is our Abba. That is the Spirit's work, testifying for us and to us that we truly are sons of the living God.

E. Inheritance

"Now if we are children, then we are heirs" (v 17). This means we have an incredible future. In more ancient times, the first son was the heir. There may have been many children, and all were loved, but the heir got the largest share of the wealth and carried on the family name. This was the way a great family kept its influence intact and did not have it divided and dissipated. (Paul's reference should not be read as either supporting or rejecting this practice. It is simply illustrative.) Now, in a breathtaking turn, he calls all Christians "heirs of God." This is a miracle, of course, because the heir got the lion's share of the parent's wealth. Paul is saying that what is in store for us is so grand and glorious that it will be, and will feel, as though we each had alone gotten most of the glory of God.

F. Family likeness

"We share in his sufferings" (Romans 8:17). Christians will suffer, not simply in the pains of this world that all people face, but specifically because they are brothers and sisters of Christ. Christ faced rejection because of who he was, and because he had come to expose sinfulness, warn of judgment and offer salvation through himself. Likewise, his family will suffer in the same ways as they live for him and speak of him. We get to be like him! God works in us and through our circumstances so that we would "be conformed to the likeness of his Son, that he might be the firstborn among many brothers" (v 29). Though we are adopted, God actually implants Christ's nature in us. As sons of God, we actually come to resemble the Son of God. As we bear the family likeness of suffering, we become more and more like the Son, and our Father, in our characters and attitudes. This is how the Christian looks at persecution and counts it as a privilege (e.g.: Acts 5:41; 1 Peter 4:13, 16). We get to be like him! (https://www.thegoodbook.com/blog/interestingthoughts/2016/12/08/seven-breathtaking-privileges/)

Principles

- Every issue in the Constitution is in God's Word.
- Every amendment has been answered by God in His Word.
- The freedoms we seek must be spiritual freedoms.
- God has given us freedom from the sin and death forever.
- Freedom on earth may not be God's freedom for humanity.
- We must seek God's freedom that guarantees eternal life.
- The source of true freedom is God and God only.

CHAPTER 19

The Constitution and The Bible: Amendment 1—Freedom of Religion, Speech, Press, Assembly, and Petition of the Government

Congress shall make no law respecting an establishment of religion, or prohibiting the free exercise thereof; or abridging the freedom of speech, or of the press, or the right of the people peaceably to assemble, and to petition the Government for a redress of grievances.

Separation of Church and State

> Ancient history is replete with examples of political leaders who derived legitimacy through religious titles. Sargon of Akkad claimed to have been given the right to rule by the god Anand the goddess Inanna. Many ancient Kings of Judah claimed to rule with a mandate from Heaven. Julius Caesar was elected as Pontifex Maximus, the chief priest of the Roman state religion before he became the consul of Rome. Caligula referred to himself as a god when meeting with politicians and he was referred to as Jupiter on occasion in public documents.[6][7]

In the US Constitution,

> the concept was implicit in the flight of Roger Williams from religious oppression in the Massachusetts Bay Colony to found the Colony of Rhode Island and Providence Plantations on the principle of state neutrality in matters of faith.

> Williams was motivated by historical abuse of governmental power, and believed that government must remove itself from anything that touched upon human beings' relationship with God, advocating a "hedge or wall of Separation between the Garden of the Church and the Wilderness of the world" in order to keep the church pure.
>
> Through his work Rhode Island's charter was confirmed by King Charles II of England, which explicitly stated that no one was to be "molested, punished, disquieted, or called in question, for any differences in opinion, in matters of religion."
>
> Williams is credited with helping to shape the church and state debate in England, and influencing such men as John Milton and particularly John Locke, whose work was studied closely by Thomas Jefferson, James Madison, and other designers of the US Constitution. Williams theologically derived his views mainly from Scripture and his motive is seen as religious, but Jefferson's advocation of religious liberty is seen as political and social. (https://en.wikipedia.org/wiki/Separation_of_church_and_state)

It was essential to separate the church and the state because of the political experiences of those who had come from England, where the church was controlled by the state. However, the Establishment Clause has resulted in the Supreme Court declaring that it is unconstitutional for prayer to be held in all public institutions. There are lawsuits year after year on where and when one can pray in public places. We have a war between the church and the state over many religious issues.

God made all things. He is interested in the state since He appointed our leaders by providence and permits them to lead our civic affairs. God cannot ignore our relationship with the state, which rules with His authority. Any government that ignores God is bound to fail its people. This appears to be our present experience. There is nothing that happens in our society that God cannot stop or change if He so desires. Our political and social lives are visible to Him. We must be aware that God is judging nations and blessing some for their actions concerning Him.

Role of the Church

The church is a divine institution designed

- to secure instrumentally the salvation of humanity,
- to bring humanity to the knowledge of truth,
- to secure their obedience to the truth, and
- to exercise their graces by the public confession of Christ, the fellowship of the brethren, and the administration of the ordinances and discipline.

Role of the State

The state is a divine institution, and the officers thereof are God's ministers. In Romans 13:1–4, Christ, the Mediator, is "Ruler among the Nations, King of Kings and Lord of Lords" (Revelation 19:16; Matthew 28; Philippians 2:9–11; Ephesians 1:17–23). All scriptures are infallible rules of faith and practice to all people under all conditions.

The Functions of the State to the Christian Faith

It follows therefore that every nation should explicitly acknowledge the Christ of God

- to be the supreme governor and His revealed will the supreme fundamental law of the land,
- to be the general principle to which all their laws should conform,
- to make the glory of God their end and His revealed will their guide,
- to promote perfect liberty of conscience and worship,
- to promote piety as well as civil order by the personal example of its civil officers,
- to give impartial protection to church property and facility to church work by the enactment and enforcement of laws conceived in the spirit of the gospel, and
- to provide for Christian instruction in the public affairs.

God's children must know that God's kingdom has no separation of church and state. God Himself is the State, and the church is the body ordained to accomplish His plan on earth.

The Constitution divides and separates the role of the church from that of the state. In God's kingdom, the two are fused. The church works to glorify the Father in its testimony to the world.

Our spirits are in God's kingdom today and forever. Our bodies are in the Constitution. God wants to control our bodies through His Spirit that dwells in us. Our minds must be renewed.

What The Bible Says about Freedom of Religion

> Blessed is the nation whose God is the LORD; and the people whom he hath chosen for his own inheritance. (Psalm 33:12)

> And it shall come to pass in the last days, that the mountain of the Lord's house shall be established in the top of the mountains, and shall be exalted above the hills; and all nations shall flow unto it. (Isaiah 2:2)

> Righteousness exalteth a nation. But sin is a reproach to any people. (Proverbs 14:34)

> All nations whom thou hast made shall come and worship before thee, O Lord; and shall glorify thy name. (Psalm 86:9)

> And many nations shall be joined to the LORD in that day, and shall be my people. (Zechariah 2:11)

> Yea, many people and strong nations shall come to seek the LORD of hosts in Jerusalem, and to pray before the LORD. (Zechariah 8:22)

> I saw in the night visions, and, behold, one like the Son of man came with the clouds of heaven, and came to the Ancient of days, and they brought him near before him.

And there was given him dominion, and glory, and a kingdom, that all people, nations, and languages, should serve him: his dominion is an everlasting dominion, which shall not pass away, and his kingdom that which shall not be destroyed. (Daniel 7:13–14)

And he that overcometh and keepeth my works unto the end, to him will I give power over the nations. (Revelation 2:26)

But in every nation he that feareth him, and worketh righteousness, is accepted with him. (Acts 10:35)

And God said unto him, (Jacob), I am God Almighty: be fruitful and multiply; a nation and a company of nations shall be of thee, and kings shall come out of thy loins. (Genesis 35:11)

By me kings reign, and princes decree justice. (Proverbs 8:15)

But they shall serve the LORD their God, and David their king, whom I will raise up unto them. (Jeremiah 30:9)

But the Lord said unto him, (Ananias), God thy way: for he (Saul), is a chosen vessel unto me, to bear my name before the Gentiles, and kings, and the children of Israel. (Acts 9:15)

I will speak if thy testimonies also before kings, and will not be ashamed. (Psalm 119:46)

And ye shall be brought before governors and kings for my sake, for a testimony against them and the gentiles. (Matthew 10:18)

Principles

- God will bless godly nations.
- God will judge all nations one day.
- God's children will face persecution from world governments.
- God's testimony must be preached to all kings.
- God has ordained us to represent Him before kings.
- God allows kings to dispense justice on earth.

CHAPTER 20

The Constitution and The Bible: Freedom of Speech

Congress shall make no law respecting an establishment of religion, or prohibiting the free exercise thereof; or abridging the freedom of speech, or of the press, or the right of the people peaceably to assemble, and to petition the Government for a redress of grievances.

Freedom of Speech

Based on the First Amendment, people have a right to freely express themselves. But that right has come under fire from those who believe in political correctness and moral relativism. The debate is over speech codes—what is permissible in schools, workplaces, and other settings. No doubt the proponents of free speech are incensed by those who are attempting to curb their freedom.

The Constitution has no clear definition of the freedom of speech. Many people feel that moral standards should dictate our freedom of speech. But whose moral standards are we going to adopt? The questions about this freedom have brought about our focus on the diversity of ethnic and cultural groups that make up the United States. Colleges have generated academic discussions on political correctness and many other topics designed to address this question.

God's Constitution is clear on what kind of speech He allows His children to use in His kingdom. What then is our freedom of speech as Christians? Is our standard of speech the same as that of the secular world? God forbid. God gave us lips and freedom of speech governed by His statutes. We are under orders to know what the statutes say about this freedom. Christianity is called the Great Confession. Romans 10:8 say, "But saith it? The word is nigh thee, even in thy mouth, and in thy heart, that is the word we preach."

It is vital that every day we confess with our lips the following.

- What we believe is true.
- There is evidence of what we know in our hearts.
- We testify to the truth we have accepted.
- We praise Him who called us out of darkness into His marvelous light.
- We are called to repentance through Jesus Christ.

As children of the kingdom, our confession is centered around five areas that form the cardinal points of our position and promises in eternity.

- What God in Christ did for us in the plan of redemption.
- What God through the Word and the Holy Spirit did for us in the new birth and baptism in the Holy Spirit.
- What we are to God the Father.
- What Jesus is doing for us now as He sits at the right hand of the Father and intercedes for us. (Hebrews 7:25)
- What God is able to do through us or what His Word will do as we speak it.

What The Bible Says

> Let no corrupt communication proceed out of your mouth, but that which is good to the use of edifying, that it may minister grace unto the hearers. (Ephesians 4:29)

> That if thou shalt confess with your mouth the Lord Jesus, and shalt believe in thine heart that God hath raised him from the dead, thou shalt be saved. (Romans 10:9)

> The Spirit of the Lord GOD is upon me, because the LORD hath anointed me to preach good tidings unto the meek. (Isaiah 61:1)

Sing aloud unto God our strength: make a joyful noise unto God of Jacob. (Psalm 81:1)

I will sing of the mercies of the LORD for ever: with my mouth will I make known thy faithfulness to all generations. (Psalm 89:1)

O give thanks unto the LORD; call upon his name: make known his deeds among people. (Psalm 105:1)

Praise ye the LORD. O give thanks unto the LORD; for he is good: for his mercy endureth for ever. (Psalms 106:1, 107:1)

O God, my heart is fixed; I will sing and give praise, even with my glory. (Psalm 108:1)

I love the Lord, because he hath heard my voice, and my supplications. (Psalm 116:1)

I will keep my mouth with a bridle, while the wicked is before me. (Psalm 39:1)

Everyone that sweareth by him shall glory: but the mouth of them that speak lies shall be stopped. (Psalm 63:11)

Whoso keepeth this mouth and his tongue keepeth his soul from troubles. (Proverbs 21:23)

The mouth of the just bringeth forth wisdom. (Proverbs 10:31)

A soft answer turneth away wrath, but grievous words stirs up anger. (Proverbs 15:1)

Let the words of my mouth, and the meditation of my heart, be acceptable in thy sight, O LORD, my strength, and my redeemer. (Psalm 19:14)

This book of the law shall not depart out of thy mouth. (Joshua 1:8)

Set a watch, O LORD, before my mouth; keep the door of my lips. (Psalm 141:3)

Let your speech be always with grace, seasoned with salt, that ye may know how ye ought to answer every man. (Colossians 4:6)

Wherefore putting away lying, speak every man truth with his neighbor: for we are members one of another. (Ephesians 4:25)

For I will give you a mouth and wisdom, which all your adversaries shall not be able to gainsay nor resist. (Luke 21:15)

The Lord GOD hath given me the tongue of the learned, that I should know how to speak a word in season to him that is weary. (Isaiah 50:4)

But now ye also put off all these; anger, wrath, malice, blasphemy, filthy communication out of your mouth. (Colossians 3:8)

Let the word of Christ dwell in you richly in all wisdom; teaching and admonishing one another in psalms and hymns and spiritual songs, singing with grace in your hearts to the Lord. (Colossians 3:16)

Be not rash with thy mouth, and let not thine heart be hasty to utter anything before God: for God is in heaven, and thou upon earth: therefore let thy words be few. (Ecclesiastes 5:2)

Suffer not thy mouth to cause thy flesh to sin; neither say thou before the angel, that it was an error: wherefore should God be angry at thy voice, and destroy the work of thine hands? (Ecclesiastes 5:6)

But I say unto you, That every idle word that men shall speak, they shall give account thereof in the day of judgement. For by thy words thou shalt be justified, and by thy words thou shalt be condemned. (Matthew 12:36–37)

Death and life are in the power of the tongue: and they that love it shall eat the fruit thereof. (Proverbs 18:21)

A fool's lips enter into contention, and his mouth calleth for strokes. (Proverbs 18:6)

A fool's mouth is his destruction, and his lips are the snare of his soul. (Proverbs 18:7)

The words of a man's mouth are as deep waters, and the wellspring of wisdom as a flowing brook. (Proverbs 18:4)

Whoso keepeth his mouth and his tongue keepeth his soul from troubles. (Proverbs 21:23)

In the multitude of words there wanteth not sin: but he that refraineth his lips is wise. (Proverbs 10:19)

In the mouth of the foolish is a rod of pride: but the lips of the wise shall preserve them. (Proverbs 14:3)

The desire of a man is his kindness: and a poor man is better than a lair. (Proverbs 19:22)

Pleasant words are as an honeycomb, sweet to the soul, and health to the bones. (Proverbs 16:24)

The tongue of the wise useth knowledge aright: but the mouth of the fools poureth out foolishness. (Proverbs 15:2)

A wholesome tongue is a tree of life: but perverseness therein is a breach in the spirit. (Proverbs 15:4)

A divine sentence is in the lips of the king: his mouth transgresseth not in judgment. (Proverbs 16:10)

Whoso curseth his father or his mother, his lamp shall be put out in obscure darkness. (Proverbs 20:20)

Every man shall kiss his lips that giveth a right answer. (Proverbs 24:26)

Be not a witness against thy neighbor without cause; and deceive not with thy lips. (Proverbs 24:28)

Let it not be once named among you, as becometh saints; Neither filthiness, nor foolish talking, nor jesting, which are not convenient: but rather giving of thanks. (Ephesians 5:3–4)

Let all bitterness, and wrath, and anger, and clamour, and evil speaking, be away from you, with all malice. (Ephesians 4:31)

The law of truth was in his mouth, and iniquity was not found in his lips: he walked with me in peace and equity, and did turn many away from iniquity. For the priest's lips should keep knowledge, and they should seek the law at his mouth: for he is the messenger of the LORD of hosts. (Malachi 2:6–7)

Principles

- Our speech must be holy in God's sight.
- Our speech must edify others.
- Our speech must be truthful and gracious.
- Our speech must avoid bitterness, wrath, and anger.
- Our speech must be based on what is acceptable to God.
- Our speech must show godly wisdom.

CHAPTER 21

The Constitution and The Bible: Amendment 1—Freedom of the Press, the Right to Peaceably Assemble, and the Right to Petition the Government

Congress shall make no law respecting an establishment of religion, or prohibiting the free exercise thereof; or abridging the freedom of speech, or of the press, or the right of the people peaceably to assemble, and to petition the Government for a redress of grievances.

Freedom of the Press

Millions of people in our nation look to the internet, newspapers, and television and radio programs for information and answers to their business, professional, and personal problems. We want a free press to inform and educate us.

The following article from the Center for Foreign Journalists epitomizes the complexity of the American press today.

> The communications industry is the largest private sector employer in the United States, and the news media make up the largest segment of that industry. Generating information, not just delivering it, is a growth business in the United States.
>
> The American news business used to be a largely domestic enterprise, but no longer. Satellite delivery of 24-hour Cable

News Network broadcasts and same-day publication of the Wall Street Journal in Asia and Europe are symptomatic of the U.S. media's new global reach.

Change has occurred in other aspects of the industry besides mere growth, however. American journalism itself has undergone a fundamental transformation in recent years, partly as a result of new technology and partly as a result of the changes in the society it has chosen to mirror. This is not surprising, since change itself is a hallmark of American culture. Whether it chooses to call itself an observer or not, the American news industry is a full-fledged participant in that culture, as well as in its country's democratic political system and its free-market economy.

Protected by government interference by a brief, 200-year-old clause in the American constitution, the press has emerged as the self-appointed monitor of official life, recorder of public events, and even unofficial arbiter of public behavior. The U.S. news industry is also a very big business. Daily newspapers alone generate some $32 billion in advertising revenue a year. Magazines—and there are more than 11,000 of them—circulate more copies than there are Americans to read them. Every household has at least three radios, and more than 95 percent own televisions.

Today, the press is better known as the media—the plural for "medium" (or means of conveyance) and a reflection of its many components in the electronic age. For it is no longer the written word but sight and sound that dominate the communications industry.

Some recent studies claim that 65 percent of Americans depend on television for their daily diet of news. Nevertheless, that statistic can be misleading because it assumes that television fully satisfies the public's appetite for news. Within that same 65 percent there are many who read newspapers and magazines, listen to the radio, and receive a vast array of newsletters and brochures (much of it unsolicited advertising in their mailboxes). Now they must deal with the newest member of the communications family: the fax. Add the VCR, computerized mail, and something called interactive video, and it is no wonder Americans complain about "no time in the day" to do all the things they want or need to do.

One of the consequences of all these choices is increased competition in the information and advertising marketplace for a person's attention, and this scramble has helped blur the once-clear line between information, entertainment, and commerce. Journalism is no longer quite so easy to define as it was just a decade ago. The American news business is currently facing what the psychiatric profession calls an "identity crisis." This is particularly true in the newspaper industry, which is watching its role (and its revenue) shrink in the electronic age. Connected with this is the concern, as well as some evidence that America's reading habit is diminishing, largely as a result of television and home video.

The story of the American press is a complex one, reflecting the pluralism of the country itself. A favored description is diversity. Nevertheless, there are some common threads that bind the media in the United States. Here are some of the most important of its common traits:

The American news industry is a business.
The industry views itself as a public trust.
The news industry is largely unregulated.
There is no uniform definition of news.
The mainstream press is generally non-ideological.
America's press tradition is community based.

A Business: The American press and broadcast industries are mostly profit-seeking enterprises and must be financially healthy in order to survive. Only a small percentage are subsidized (less than 20 percent of the broadcast industry, less than 1 percent of the print media). Most depend upon commercial advertising for the bulk of their income—about 75 percent. In 1991, the media overall earned $130 billion in advertising revenue.

A newspaper owner/publisher is often more a business person than a journalist, while the editor is usually the keeper of the paper's news mission. The publisher, who has the ultimate say in what the product looks like, may not want to carry news that will hurt his business, while the editor in the American system is usually ruled by the dictum: "If it's news, publish it." In the best of the business, the publisher gives the editor ultimate authority over the news.

A Public Trust: Treating itself as both a business and a public trust can cause conflict, if not confusion, within the news industry, not to mention in the eyes of the public.

Nevertheless, the "public's right to know" remains at the core of America's free-press philosophy and guides the way it conducts itself, particularly in relations with government. Some call this relationship "adversarial." Others prefer to think of it more benignly as simply a monitoring role, without the influence of opposition.

In short, the American press enjoys its role as the "watchdog of government." The power that comes from this largely self-appointed role has earned the press the honorific title "the fourth estate," after the three official branches of government (legislative, judicial, and executive). It is also this role that prompted Thomas Jefferson, one of the founders of American democracy, to say some 200 years ago that if he had to choose between government without newspapers or newspapers without government, he "should not hesitate a moment to prefer the latter."

It was this vision of how a democracy should work that prompted the framers of the U.S. Constitution to make free expression the first amendment of this charter's "Bill of Rights." In reality, the amendment simply said that Congress cannot enact a law infringing free speech or a free press. That brief clause has been the beacon and the shield for the American press for over two centuries, but it is not carved in stone for eternity. It is tested almost daily in the courts, on the streets, and in the corridors of power. So far, this First Amendment protection has withstood these tests.

News: There is no universally accepted definition or set of definitions for "news" in the American media. This is because there is no single role designated for the press. Among the roles the American press has chosen for itself are to inform, to educate, to reform, to entertain, to incite, or all of the above.

For better or for worse, the American media will remain a strong force in public life. Modern society has become too dependent upon quick and reliable information for it to be otherwise. But the shape of that future remains uncertain. In just a handful of years, the American news business has already undergone tremendous changes as a result of a transformation in technology, market forces, and public tastes. Too many new players have entered the information field for journalism to ever be the same as it was. But the profession never really stood still for long anyway. The daily newspaper industry, trying to catch up with the electronic media and other newcomers, seems to have suffered most in this recent transformation. But as long as the American press remains largely immune from government interference, there will always be new opportunities for the industry and new choices for the public. Whatever happens, it will be the public that decides the future of the American news industry. That, free-press advocates say, is the beauty of the system. (https://usa.usembassy.de/etexts/media/unfetter/press01.htm)

The Bible as the Press for Christians

While we are concerned about the secular press, we must remember that God has given us The Bible as His press for our truth. The truth in The Bible is unchangeable and inerrant; it must take first place in our daily walk with the Lord. Every day, we must read our press and seek God's direction in our lives.

When Jesus was tempted in the wilderness, He was hungry, and the devil used his hunger as a trap. "But he answered and said, it is written, Man shall not live by bread alone, but by every word that proceeds out of the mouth of God" (Matthew 4:4). This is the food we need to please God and make that are right all the time.

Pastor Haley wrote this in his devotional "A Prescription for Peace."

> As much as is humanly possible, our Thoughts need to be 100% pure and need to be generated from the truth of god's Word. We are literally ASSAULTED and BOMBARDED with a mixture of sinful, sexual and sensual sources of thought very day. Again, TV, internet, Social media, Music, Advertising, magazines, and Books, Improper and immodest dress, all of these combine to paint pictures of thought in our mind that lead to lustful and licentious thinking. Pornography and perversion is everywhere and the battle to keep a god's and pure mind is very real and very constant. Take inventory of what goes into your mind every day and how it goes in. It may be that you need to "turn off" or "tune out" some sources of impure input. As we are constantly exposed to impure and immoral thoughts so we must combat them by being constantly exposed and focused on THE SINGLE SOURCE OF PURE THOUGHTS—THE WORD OF GOD!" [28]

Many times, the secular press gives us bad news about the economy, our government, and world affairs. I believe the good news for us Christians is that the bad news is wrong because we are "more than conquerors," "can do all things through Christ who strengthens us," and "greater is he who is in us that the one that is in the world."

The Bible must have first place on our reading list and in our decisions about what is right or wrong. It is our lighthouse, the source of authority for everything we do. When in doubt, it is our duty to find out what God would have us does or say. The world may have its own standards for making critical decisions, but for you and me, God's statutes must have the final say.

The Bible Is Our Holy, Official Press

The Bible is there to give us clear direction as to how we should live our lives so we will remain undefiled by the world while we pursue our dreams. We must live without sinning, which comes from what we do and what we expose ourselves to daily.

What The Bible Says

> But seek ye first the Kingdom of God and his righteousness; and all these things shall be added unto you. (Matthew 6:33)
>
> Thy word have I hid in mine heart, that I might not sin against thee. (Psalm 119:11)
>
> Blessed are the undefiled in the way, who walk in the law of the Lord. (Psalm 119:1)
>
> The law of his God is in his heart; none of his steps shall slide. (Psalm 37:31)
>
> For the commandment is a lamp; and the law is light; and reproofs of instruction are the way of life. (Proverbs 6:23)
>
> Thy words were found, and I did eat them; and thy word was unto the joy and rejoicing of mine heart: for I am called by thy name, O LORD God of hosts. (Jeremiah 15:16)
>
> So I opened my mouth, and he caused me to eat the roll. And he said unto me, Son of man, cause thy belly to eat, and fill thy bowels with this roll that I give thee. Then I

did eat; and it was in my mouth as honey for sweetness. (Ezekiel 3:2–3)

Open thy mouth, and eat that I give thee. (Ezekiel 2:8)

And I took the little book out of the angel's hand, and ate it up, and it was in my mouth sweet as honey: and as soon as I had eaten it, my belly was bitter. (Revelation 10:10)

Now therefore, if ye will obey my voice indeed, and keep my Covenant, then you shall be a peculiar treasure unto me above all the people, for all the earth is mine. (Exodus 19:5)

But this thing commanded I them, saying, Obey my voice, and I will be your God, and you will be my people: and will walk ye in all the ways that I have commanded you, that it may be well unto you. (Jeremiah 7:23)

Beware of him, and obey his voice, provoke him not; for he will not pardon your transgressions, for my name is in him. (Exodus 23:21)

Casting down imaginations, and every high thing that exalteth itself against the knowledge of God, and bringing into captivity every thought to the obedience of Christ. (2 Corinthians 10:5)

By whom we have received grace and apostleship, for obedience to the faith among all nations, for his name. (Romans 1:5)

But God thanked, that ye were servants of sin, but ye have obeyed from the heart that form of doctrine which was delivered you. (Romans 6:17)

But they have not all obeyed the gospel. For Esaias saith, Lord, who hath believed our report? So then faith cometh by hearing, and hearing by the word of God. (Romans 10:16–17)

Let every soul be subject unto the higher powers. For there is no power but of God: the powers that be are ordained of God. (Romans 13:1)

And Samuel said, "Hath the LORD as great delight in burnt offerings and sacrifices, as in obeying the voice of the LORD? Behold, to obey is better than sacrifice, and to hearken than the fat of rams." (1 Samuel 15:22)

As obedient children, not fashioning yourselves according to the former lusts in your ignorance.(1 Peter 1:14)

Elect according to the foreknowledge of God the Father, through sanctification of the Spirit, unto to obedience and sprinkling of the blood of Jesus Christ: Grace unto you, and peace, be multiplied. (1 Peter 1:2)

Therefore now amend your ways and your doings, and obey the voice of the LORD your God; and the LORD will repent him of the evil that he hath pronounced against you. (Jeremiah 26:13)

But Jeremiah said, "They shall not deliver thee. Obey, I beseech thee, the voice of the LORD, which I speak unto thee: so it shall be well unto thee, and they soul shall live." (Jeremiah 38:20)

And it shall come to pass, if ye shall hearken diligently unto my commandments which I command you this day, to love the LORD your God, and to serve him with all your heart and with all your soul. (Deuteronomy 11:13)

As soon as they hear of me, they shall obey me; the strangers shall submit themselves unto me. (Psalm 18:44)

If ye be willing and obedient, ye shall eat the good of the land. (Isaiah 1:19)

And said unto them, ye have kept all that Moses the servant of the LORD commanded you, and have obeyed my voice in all that I commanded you. Ye have not left your brethren these many days unto this day, but have kept the charge of the commandment of the LORD your God. (Joshua 22:2–3)

And thou shalt not go aside from any of the words which I command thee this day, to the right hand, or to the left, to go after other gods to serve them. (Deuteronomy 28:14)

Wherefore, my beloved, as ye have always obeyed, not as in my presence only, but now much more in my absence, work out your salvation with fear and trembling. (Philippians 2:12)

The Right to Peaceably Assemble

The Supreme Court has held that the First Amendment protects the right to conduct a peaceful public assembly. The right to assemble is not, however, absolute. Government officials cannot simply prohibit a public assembly, but the government can impose restrictions on the time, place, and manner of peaceful assembly, provided that constitutional safeguards are met. Time, place, and manner restrictions are permissible so long as they are "justified without reference to the content of the regulated speech, … are narrowly tailored to serve a significant governmental interest, and … leave open ample alternative channels for communication of the information" (United States Library of Congress, 2017).[37]

Overall, the Right to Assemble is of significant importance to U.S. society as it gives all citizens the freedom to have a voice and freely associate with one another in public

> under a common cause or shared value. (https://www.learningtogive.org/resources/right-assemble)

A study of the New Testament clearly reveals that when believers were converted to Christ and baptized, they immediately joined themselves to the local church in their community. When people responded to Peter's sermon at Pentecost, The Bible says, "And the same day, there were added unto them about three thousand souls." Next, we read that the church continued preaching the message of the gospel and sharing in every aspect of the life of the church: "The Lord added to the church daily such as should be saved" (Acts 2:47). The book of Acts demonstrates the inevitable growth of the church wherever the gospel was preached.

It is important for believers to assemble for praise and corporate worship, for edification, and for inspiration. If you are not part of a church, locate one and join it to grow in the service of Lord.

The world wants to assemble for political reasons. We Christians want to be guaranteed this freedom but only for the glory of God. We want the right to assemble for praise, worship, the glory of our Father, and for the edification of fellow Christians.

What The Bible Says

> Not forsaking the assembling of ourselves together, as the manner of some is; exhorting one another: and so much the more, as ye see the day approaching. (Hebrews 10:25)

> Teaching and admonishing one another in psalms and hymns and spiritual songs, singing with grace in your hearts to the Lord. (Colossians 3:16)

> Speaking to yourselves in psalms and hymns, and spiritual songs, singing and making melody in your heart to the Lord. (Ephesians 5:19)

> For as the body is one, and hath many members, and all the members of that one body, being many are one body: so also is Christ. (1 Corinthians 12:12)

> That there should be no schism in the body; but that the members should have the same care one for another. (1 Corinthians 12:25)

> And when they had prayed, the place was shaken where they were assembled together; and they were all filled with the Holy Ghost, and they spake the word of God with boldness. (Acts 4:31)

> And when the day of Pentecost was fully come, they were all with one accord in one place. And they were all filled with the Holy Ghost, and began to speak with other tongues as the Spirit gave them utterance. (Acts 2:1, 4)

> All the congregation blessed the LORD GOD of their fathers, and bowed down their heads, and worshipped the LORD, and the King. (1 Chronicles 29:20)

> Praise shall be of thee in the great congregation. (Psalms 22:25, 26:12, 111:1)

> For where two or three are gathered together in my name, there am I in the midst of them. (Matthew 18:20)

> And upon the first day of the week … the disciples came together to break bread. (Acts 20:7)

The Right to Petition Our Government and God Almighty

The Constitution specifically guarantees our right to petition our government for redress of grievances. By and large, this right has been exercised in association with others. We Christians must participate in affairs that are crucial to our welfare in society. At the same time, our desire to associate with others must be related to our deep commitment to Jesus Christ and His precepts to us concerning this issue. We have a right to petition God individually and collectively every day. God is ever present in our lives. He wants to communicate with us consistently, and I believe we have a right to present our needs to Him and expect Him to meet them.

God has a government that can be petitioned and is ready to listen to His children's requests.

> When we pray in the name of Jesus, we come to God on the basis of Jesus' accomplishment.
>
> And having an high priest [Jesus] over the house of God; let us draw near with a true heart in full assurance of faith. (Hebrews 10:21–22)
>
> As our high priest, Jesus offers our prayers to God. His prayers are always heard.
>
> Verily, Verily, I say unto you, whatsoever ye shall ask the Father in my name, he will give it you. (John 16:23)
>
> There are those who say, "Prayer changes things because it changes us." I agree but only in part. Prayer changes things because prayer appeals to the top power in the universe. Prayer is not a magical formula or a mystical chant. It is the yes to God's invitation to invoke His name.
>
> Mark it down: it won't have the last word. Jesus will.
>
> God raised [Christ] from death and set Him on a throne in deep heaven, in charge of running the universe, everything from galaxies to governments, no name and no power exempt from His rule. And not just for the time being, but forever. He is in charge of it all, has the final word on everything.—Ephesians 1:20–22 MSG.
>
> The phrase "In Jesus' name" is not an empty motto or talisman. It is a declaration of truth: My cancer is not in charge; Jesus is. The economy is not in charge; Jesus is. The grumpy neighbor doesn't run the world; Jesus, You do! You, Jesus, are the Head Coach, CEO, President, King, Supreme Ruler, Absolute Monarch, High and Holy Baron, Czar, Overlord, and Rajah of all history."

> Pray! Since God works, prayer works. (Max Lucado, December, 2015, "*God Is with You Every Day*" 365-day Devotional, Grace for the Moment)

Our Petitions Are Granted through Christ

When entering God's presence in the morning, we Christians must realize who He is and where he stands in relation to God. Each person who claims access to and an audience with the Most High must have a living sense of the place he or she has in Christ before God.

We Need to Approach God through Christ

> Knowing who you are in Christ is a prerequisite for knowing your rights in Christ. Then you can come to ask God to meet you and provide all that you need in life. You are the one who knows, by the Word and Spirit of God, that you are in Christ and that your life is hid with Christ in God. In Christ you died to sin and the world. You have been taken out of the world, separated from it, and delivered from its power. You have been raised together with Christ; and in Him, live unto God. Your life is hid with Christ in God. You can come to God to claim and obtain all the divine life that is hidden away in Him for today's need and supply.
>
> Yes, this is who you are. You say it to God in humble, holy reverence, "I expecting abundant grace to live the hidden life of heaven here on earth. I am one who says, Christ is my life. The longing of my soul is for Christ, revealed by the Father Himself within the heart. Nothing less can satisfy me. My life is hid with Christ. He can be my life in no other way than as He is in my heart. I can be content with nothing less than Christ in my heart. Christ is the Savior from sin, the gift and instrument of God's love. Christ is my indwelling friend and Lord.

If God should ask, "Who are you?" I would reply, "I live in Christ and Christ in me. Lord, you alone can make me know and be all that truly means." Andrew Murray 2005" The Andrew Murray Daily Reader", Bethany House Publishers.

Living the Life of Christ

I come as one who desires, who seeks, to be prepared to live the life of Christ today on earth and to translate His hidden, heavenly glory into the language of daily life. As Chris lived on earth only to do the will of God, it is my great desire to stand perfect and complete all His will. My ignorance of that will is very great. My power to do His will is even greater and yet I come to God as one who must not compromise, as one who in all honesty accepts the high calling of living out fully the will of God in all things.

This desire brings me to the prayer closet. As I think of all my failures in fulfilling: God's will, as I look ahead to all the temptations and dangers that await me, I can say God -I come to claim the life hid in Christ, that I may live for Christ. I cannot be content without the quiet assurance that God will go with me and bless me.

Who am I that I should ask these great and wonderful things of God? Can I expect to live the life hid with Christ in God and manifest it in my mortal body? I can, because Himself will work it in me by the Holy Spirit dwelling in me. The same God, who raised Christ from the dead and then set Him at His right hand, has raised me with Him and give me the Spirit of the glory of His Son in my heart, A life in Christ, given up to know and all God's will, is the life God Himself will work and maintain increasingly in me by the Holy Spirit. (Andrew Murray, *The Practice of God's Presence*)

Presenting Myself To God

I come every morning and present myself before Him to receive hidden life so I can live it out in the flesh. I can wait confidently and quietly, as one in the Spirit dwells, for the Father to give the fresh anointing that teaches all things. I can for Him to take charge of the new day He has given me. I am sure you realize how important the morning hour is o secure God's presence for the day. During that time you take firm stand on the foundation of full redemption. Believe what God says to you. Accept what God has bestowed on you in Christ. Be what God has made you to be. Take time before God to confess your position in Christ. In a battle much depends upon an impregnable position. Take your place where God has placed you.

The very attempt to do this may at times interfere with your ordinary Bible study or prayer. That will be no loss. It will be fully recompensed later. Your life depends upon knowing who your God is and who you are as His redeemed one in Christ. Your daily Christian walk depends on this knowledge. When you have learned the secret, it will, own you do not think of it, be the strength of your heart, both in going in before God and out with Him to the world. (Andrew Murray, *The Practice of God's Presence*)

What The Bible Says

Be careful for nothing; but in everything by prayer and supplication with thanksgiving let your requests be made known unto God. (Philippians 4:6)

For we have not a high priest, which cannot be touched with the feelings of our infirmities; but was in all points tempted like as we are, yet without sin. (Hebrews 4:15)

Let us therefore come boldly unto the throne of grace, that we may obtain mercy, and find grace to help in time of need. (Hebrews 4:16)

Daniel … maketh his petition three times a day. (Daniel 6:13)

And if we know that he hear us, whatsoever we ask, we know that we have the petitions that we desired of him. (1 John 5:15)

Ask and it shall be given you; seek, and ye shall find; knock, and it shall be opened unto you. (Matthew 7:7)

Then shalt thou call, and the LORD shall answer; thou shalt cry, and he shall say, Here I am. (Isaiah 58:9)

If my people, which are called by my name, shall humble themselves, and pray, and seek my face, and turn from their wicked ways; then I will hear from heaven, and will forgive their sin, and will heal their land. (2 Chronicles 7:14)

Then shall ye call upon me, and ye shall go and pray unto me, and I will hearken unto you. (Jeremiah 29:12)

And whatsoever we ask, we receive of him, because we keep his commandments, and do those things that are pleasing in his sight. (1 John 3:22)

And whatsoever ye shall ask in my name, that I will do. (John 14:13)

I will offer to thee the sacrifice of thanksgiving, and will call upon the name of the LORD. (Psalm 116:17)

Take heed, watch and pray: for ye know when the time is. (Mark 13:33)

Then began men to call upon the name of the Lord. (Genesis 4:26)

Therefore the people came to Moses, and said, We have sinned, for we have spoken against the LORD, and against thee, pray unto the LORD, that he take away the serpents' from us. And Moses prayed for the people. (Numbers 21:7)

Even them will I bring to my holy mountain, and make them joyful in my house of prayer: their burnt offerings and their sacrifices shall be accepted upon mine altar; for mine house shall be called an house of prayer for all people. (Isaiah 56:7)

Then shall ye call upon me, and ye shall go and pray unto me, and I will hearken unto you. And ye shall seek me, and find me, when ye shall search for me with all your heart. (Jeremiah 29:12–13)

Evening, and morning, and at noon, will I pray, and cry aloud: and he shall hear my voice. (Psalm 55:17)

Pray for them that despitefully use you, and persecute you. (Matthew 5:44)

Watch ye therefore, and pray always, that ye may be accounted worthy to escape all these things that shall come to pass, and to stand before the Son of man. (Luke 21:36)

And she was a widow of about fourscore, and four years, which departed not from the temple, but served God with fastings and prayers night and day. (Luke 2:37)

And whatsoever ye shall ask in my name, that will I do, that the Father may be glorified in the Son. If ye shall ask any thing in my name, I will do it. (John 14:13–14)

If ye abide in me, and my words abide in you, ye shall ask what ye will, and it shall be done unto you. (John 15:7)

If my people, which are called by my name, shall humble themselves, and pray, and seek my face, and turn from their wicked ways, then will I hear from heaven, and will forgive their sin, and will heal their land. (2 Chronicles 7:14)

But when they in their trouble did turn unto the LORD GOD of Israel, and sought him, he was found of them. (2 Chronicles 15:4)

But the end of all things is at hand: be ye therefore sober, and watch unto prayer. (1 Peter 4:7)

And whatever we ask, we receive of him, because we keep his commandments, and do those things that are pleasing in his sight. (1 John 3:22)

And if we know that he hears us, whatsoever we ask, we know that we have the petitions that we desired of him. (1 John 5:15)

I will therefore that all men pray every where, lifting up holy hands, without wrath and doubting. (1 Timothy 2:8)

Principles

- The Word of God must be our daily press.
- The Word of God must be our daily guide in critical decisions.
- The Word of God must be our source of truth for life.
- The Word of God must be our mirror for life.
- The Word of God must shape and mold our thinking.
- We must spend time petitioning God every day.
- We must make opportunities to talk to God and listen to Him.
- We must grow in our spiritual and prayer life.
- God gives us time to fellowship with Him through prayer.
- Fellowship with other members of our faith is important.
- Spiritual growth comes out of fellowship with others.
- The Bible encourages us to fellowship with others.
- Christ gives us a good example in the Last Supper.
- God's children must share their faith through fellowship.

CHAPTER 22

The Constitution and the Bible: Amendment 2—Militia and the Right to Bear Arms

A well regulated Militia, being necessary to the security of a free State, the right of the people to bear arms, shall not be infringed.

The United States Armed Forces are the military forces of the United States. It consists of the Army, Marine Corps, Navy, Air Force and Coast Guard. The President of the United States is the commander-in-chief of the US Armed Forces and forms military policy with the US Department of Defense (DoD) and US Department of Homeland Security (DHS), both federal executive departments, acting as the principal organs by which military policy is carried out. All five armed services are among the seven uniformed services of the United States.

From the time of its inception, the US Armed Forces played a decisive role in the history of the United States. A sense of national unity and identity was forged as a result of victory in the First Barbary War and the Second Barbary War. Even so, the founders of the United States were suspicious of a permanent military force. It played a critical role in the American Civil War, continuing to serve as the armed forces of the United States, although a number of its officers resigned to join the military of the Confederate States. The National Security Act of 1947, adopted following World War II and during the Cold War‘s onset, created the modern US military framework. The Act merged the previously Cabinet-level Department of War and the Department of the Navy into the National Military Establishment (renamed the Department of Defense in 1949), headed by the Secretary of Defense; and created the Department of the Air Force and the National Security Council.

The US Armed Forces are one of the largest militaries in terms of the number of personnel. It draws its personnel from a large pool of paid volunteers. Although conscription has been used in the past in various times of both war and peace, it has not been used since 1972, but the Selective Service System retains the power to conscript males, and requires that all male citizens and residents residing in the US between the ages of 18–25 register with the service.

As of 2016, the US spends about US$580 billion annually to fund its military forces and Overseas Contingency Operations. Put together, the US constitutes roughly 40 percent of the world's military expenditures. The US Armed Forces has significant capabilities in both defense and power projection due to its large budget, resulting in advanced and powerful equipment and its widespread deployment of force around the world, including about 800 military bases outside the United States. The US Air Force is the world's largest air force, the US Navy is the world's largest navy by tonnage, and the US Navy and the US Marine Corps combined are the world's second largest air arm. (https://en.wikipedia.org/wiki/United_States_Armed_Forces#cite_note-8)

The second amendment has become a badge and bumper sticker, a shield for gun activists and scripture for much of the American right. But like other cherished texts, it is not as clear as many make it out to be. The amendment reads: “A well regulated militia, being necessary to the security of a free state, the right of the people to keep and bear arms, shall not be infringed." For most of the republic's lifespan, from 1791 to 2008, those commas and clauses were debated by attorneys and senators, slave owners and freedmen, judges, Black Panthers, governors and lobbyists. For some, the militia was key; for others the right that shall not be infringed; for yet others, the question of states versus the federal government. For the most part, the Supreme Court stayed out it.

"Americans have been thinking about the second amendment as an individual right for generations," said Adam Winkler, a law professor at UCLA and author of Gunfight: The Battle over the Right to Bear Arms in America. "You can find state supreme courts in the mid-1800s where judges say the second amendment protects an individual right." But for the 70 years or so before a Supreme Court decision in 2008, he said, "the supreme court and federal courts held that it only applied in the context of militias, the right of states to protect themselves from federal interference." In 2008, the Supreme Court decided the District of Columbia v Heller, 5–4, overturning a handgun ban in the city. The conservative justice Antonin Scalia wrote the opinion in narrow but unprecedented terms: for the first time in the country's history, the supreme court explicitly affirmed an individual's right to keep a weapon at home for self-defense. Justice John Paul Stevens dissented, saying the decision showed disrespect "for the well-settled views of all of our predecessors on the court, and for the rule of law itself." Two years later, he dissented from another decision favoring gun rights, writing:

The reasons that motivated the framers to protect the ability of militiamen to keep muskets, or that motivated the Reconstruction Congress to extend full citizenship to freedmen in the wake of the Civil War, have only a limited bearing on the question that confronts the homeowner

> in a crime-infested metropolis today. (http://oursalon.ning.com/profiles/blog/show?id=6524927%3ABlogPost%3A727448&commentId=6524927%3AComment%3A727568)

In the Bible, Christians are urged to bear arms of a different nature. The warfare is spiritual, so the weapons of warfare are also spiritual.

The Army and the Right to Bear Arms

This is a fundamental right for all US citizens, but for Christians, there are spiritual weapons they must use to fight their enemies. Guns are a common sight in American movies. Homes are no longer safe because people can be robbed at any time by people who may own guns illegally. America is growing into a society that is riddled with gun outlets.

The need for an army in all societies is beyond question. America has invested tremendously in its army through sophisticated technology, weaponry, training, and dollars. Some think that since the Cold War is over, we need to put our military production capabilities to new uses for a new industrial society. Some are unhappy with America's strength because of threats from Russia. The world is confused about security matters. The UN has made decisions affecting many nations and has deployed troops to quell disturbances. Are these lasting solutions? A few lessons from the Bible should help us understand the power of God to intervene in human affairs.

The Bible has many stories of wars. Christians must be aware that God can and will intervene in our wars. He has a different view and approach. When we are God's, our wars are His.

> We're in a battle in this world. We may not see it, we might forget it's there. But the enemy would love nothing more than to start our year off with discouragement and defeat, bringing fear and stress. Don't let him win. If you're a believer who is living like salt and light in a dark world, you won't go for long without encountering spiritual warfare - obstacles and attacks he'll hurl your direction. God reminds us in His word to stay aware of Satan's schemes, to live alert in this world, and to stay close to Him. He arms us with the sword, the Word of God, to stand against the enemy's lies. He equips us with

> strength, wisdom, and discernment through His own Spirit to stay strong in the spiritual warfare battle. He invites us to spend time in His Presence, through prayer and worship, pressing in to know Him more. As we grow to know God's Truth and what is real, we also know more what is false, and we are stronger to stand against it in the powerful name of Jesus. He never leaves us to fend for ourselves in a dark world, but reminds us He is constantly with us, fighting for us, even when we cannot see. Praying God's words back to Him, is a powerful weapon against the forces of evil. It is Truth going out. It reminds us that God knows our way and understands what we face today. It builds our faith and our trust in God. It guards our hearts and focuses our minds back on Him. It wins the battle. (http://debbiemcdaniel.com/2016/06/28/31-spiritual-warfare-scriptures-help-facing-lifes-battles/)

The Bible and Spiritual Warfare

God has made us soldiers of the cross. IN THE Kingdom of God, God's children do not need protection by human soldiers and we not need any soldiers to le in our homes. We are soldiers under the command of Jesus Christ.. We are engaged as soldiers of the Cross and are fighting a spiritual war against the Devil. We must stand up for Jesus. The Word makes it clear that we are soldiers in two camps stand in eternal opposition to each other—the camp of our Lord Jesus Christ, the Prince of Peace, and the camp of the Satan, Devil, the prince of darkness. We cannot stand in the middle. We are either following the devil and his demonic plans to destroy the work of God or we are God's children commissioned to stand up for the cross.

The life of a Christian is actually warfare in which believers are beset by a conniving, artful, and persistent foe—the devil, our greatest enemy. We need help. We cannot cope with the devil in our own strength because we are just no match for him. We are not wise enough, strong enough, or good enough. The conflicts are unavoidable and continuous. The devil is on all sides doing everything he can to keep us from walking with God. He is real, and we are in a fight with him whether we like it or not. The devil raises questions about the ways of God, and he flatters us by appealing to our self-importance.

Put On the Whole Armor

Fortunately, God has provided us adequate armor that will enable us Christians to be victorious in the conflict. Paul was very familiar with Roman soldiers' armor, and he advised Christians to put on the whole armor of God so they could "stand against the wiles of the devil." Paul had no question in his mind about the devil being real. Believers are advised to remember that the devil is active, hostile, cunning, and a lot smarter than any human being. God can and will protect believers for which they can thank Him. He will do it in His way.

With reference to the devil, we should never forget that Michael, the archangel, did not dare rail against him. Whatever you do, do not joke about the devil. Paul has in mind that the devil was real and was not bound at that time. He is prowling, and he is after us to do us harm. He is cunning. He comes at us always on our weak side. Everyone has some weakness.

Jesus of Nazareth warned Peter that Satan planned to sift him like wheat; He said to Peter, "I have prayed for thee, that thy faith fail not" (Luke 22:32). Jesus would not allow Peter to withstand that testing alone. Our Lord is in heaven now praying for us, which is a great comfort to all believers.

God has made provision for believers for this battle against the enemy, and He has made these provisions as we read in Ephesians by preparing a certain armor that Christians can put on to help them defend themselves against the devil. The armor includes truth, "having your loins girt about with truth"; righteousness, "the breastplate of righteousness"; the gospel of peace, "Your feet shod with the preparation of the gospel of peace"; and faith, "taking the shield of faith, wherewith ye shall be able to quench all the fiery darts of the wicked."

God has given us the Word of God, the sword of the Spirit. This is the armor that the believer is to put on in this great contest in which he is fighting for his life against a vicious enemy that wants to harm him.

Paul urged believers to put on the whole armor of God, not just part of it, because believers need total protection. It is a life-and-death struggle to withstand the devil's wiles. He is such a powerful enemy that the only chance of survival we have is to put on the whole armor of God. I rejoice that when I fail to get it all done, the Lord is more gracious than I can think. I can run to Him for safety: "For Satan trembles when he sees the weakest saint upon his knees." When we get on our knees and look up into the face of the Lord Jesus Christ, we are safe in Him.

Stand Therefore

The believer must stand firm with a clear idea of God, Christ, and Calvary. He must keep it clear in his message that Christ Jesus died for sinners and rose from the dead. He must speak firmly on the truth that Christ is now in the presence of God that He is praying for us and praise His name—He will return! These things have been revealed, and they all come together. The believer should affirm them as they are. To be sure, Satan wants to interfere with the communication of the gospel. He will oppose any presentation of it.

Paul reminded the Christians at Ephesus there was an active enemy opposing their testimony that they must withstand. Believers must stand firmly on the position they have taken in the conflict. All the parts of the armor of God are described as protection to be used with one exception: the sword of the Spirit. This is the only offensive weapon provided, but it is adequate as it is the Word of God. The one activity that is to be performed constantly is praying especially for one another and for those who minister the gospel.

Shield of Faith

It is true that we are saved by faith; that is wonderfully, gloriously true. Souls can accept Jesus Christ as their Savior and never doubt their destiny. God will see them through "He which hath begun a good work in you will (complete) it" (Philippians 1:6).

The famous scripture "The just shall live by faith" includes both these ideas. When we say "the just," we do not mean naturally good people because we know no one is good, not one. When we use the word *just*, we mean "justified." The believer is justified by faith in Jesus Christ. Justified souls will live day in and day out by faith.

As believers go through their days, they are faced again and again with challenging issues that prompt them to look to God for help and believe in Him. Paul spoke of believers receiving "the gift of faith." In 1 Corinthians chapters 12 and 14, we read that one of the gifts of the Spirit is faith. Did the believers not have faith when they became believers? They certainly did! But is seems possible that a good many people miss a greater blessing here because they think all was taken care of when they accepted Christ.

Sword of the Spirit

In Ephesians, Paul recognized that God had arranged for believers to be guided and become more mature in Christ Jesus. To this end, God arranged for believers to be filled with the Holy Spirit for their daily living. Paul understood that even with this background, there would be spiritual conflict.

Believers have an enemy—a vicious, active, cunning, capable adversary. Paul said that because of this, believers should put on the whole armor of God and take up the Word of God, the sword.

The helmet protects the head because the brain determines what is true and false. Any false, biased, or one-sided ideas will be wrong. We need salvation to protect our heads, our thinking.

Salvation is the work of God through Jesus Christ. When we call to mind what God has done through Jesus Christ, when we understand the relationship we have with Christ Jesus, we will have faith and our minds will be protected from error. Everything that comes to mind can be checked by the revelation in Christ.

After we come to know Him, when any thoughts come, we can consider them in the presence of Christ. If it is acceptable to Him, we will accept it. If not, out it goes. The gospel is a message to be believed. In the gospel, all people are the creatures of God made by Him and responsible to Him for their conduct. The gospel is for those who need help, and that means everyone as all have done wrong and are doing wrong. Some do not know how to do right. They need help, and the gospel provides that.

The gospel is grounded in certain events in the life of Jesus Christ. The gospel brings to mind that God was in Christ to reconcile the world to Himself, that Jesus was the Son of God and came to the world to give His life as a ransom for many. Christ died at Calvary's cross for sinners. God accepted that death as a substitute sacrifice for sinners, and based on it, He will forgive anyone who accepts Christ Jesus as Savior and Lord.

Christ Jesus died, was buried, and rose again on the third day. He was seen, and He ascended into heaven in full view of them all. He is now in the presence of God praying for us, and He is coming again. This is the gospel.

Praying Always

With everything that is in the Bible in hand, what are we to do? We are to pray and pray always! Believers are told to pray always because they will have repeated opportunities to deny themselves and do God's will. No one can see and obey the will of God in his or her own strength or wisdom. Believers need the blessing of God.

Paul told us to pray because we constantly need the grace of God He will give us freely when asked. The government provides soldiers to give us protection for our homes, but conditions in our spiritual lives are different. When we are saved, we are filled with the Spirit, who will live in us forever and provide ammunition for the spiritual warfare we face every day.

We Christians need to understand that we are dead in Christ since we are crucified with Him. We may be living, but we are not our own. Our business is Christ's business as well. He is the commander in chief of God's armed forces.

What The Bible Says

> Finally, my brethren, be strong in the Lord, and in the power of his might. Put on the whole armor of God, that ye may be able to stand against the wiles of the devil. For we wrestle not against flesh and blood, but against principalities, against powers, against the rulers of darkness of this world, against spiritual wickedness in high places. Wherefore take unto you the whole armor of God, that ye may be able to withstand in the evil day, and having done all, to stand. Stand therefore, having your loins girt about with truth, and having on the breast plate of righteousness; And your feet shod with the preparation of the gospel of peace; Above all, taking the shield of faith, wherewith ye shall be able to quench all the fiery darts of the wicked. And take the helmet of salvation, and the sword of the Spirit, which is the word of God: Praying always with all prayer and supplication in the Spirit, and watching thereunto with all perseverance and supplication for all saints. (Ephesians 6:10–18)

> For I am a man under authority, having soldiers under me: and I say to this man, Go, and he goeth; and to another, Come, and he cometh; and to my servant, Do this, and he doeth it. (Matthew 8:9)

And when the angel which spake unto Cornelius was departed, he called two of his household servants, and a devout soldier of them that waited on him continually. (Acts 10:7)

Thou therefore endure hardness as a good soldier of Jesus Christ. No man that warreth entangleth himself with the affairs of this life; that he may please him who hath chosen him to be a soldier. (2 Timothy 2:3–4)

The night is far spent, the day is at hand: let us therefore cast off the works of darkness, and let us put on the armor of light. (Romans 13:12)

By the word of truth, by the power of God, by the armor of righteousness on the right hand and on the left. (2 Corinthians 6:7)

But let us, who are of the day, be sober, putting on the breastplate of faith and love; and for an helmet, the hope of salvation. (1 Thessalonians 5:8)

And righteousness shall be the girdle of his lions, and faithfulness the girdle of his reins. (Isaiah 11:5)

He hath clothed me with the garments of salvation, he hath covered me with the robe of righteousness, as a bridegroom decketh himself with ornaments, and as bride adorneth herself with her jewels. (Isaiah 61:10)

For though we walk in the flesh, we do not war after the flesh: (For the weapons of our warfare are not carnal, but mighty through God to the pulling down of strong holds). (2 Corinthians 10:3–4)

This charge I commit unto thee, son Timothy, according to the prophecies which went before on thee, that thou by them mightest war a good warfare. (1 Timothy 1:18)

Dearly beloved, I beseech you as strangers and pilgrims, abstain from fleshly lusts. which war against the soul; Having your conversation honest among the Gentiles: that, whereas, they speak against you as evildoers, they may by your good works, which they shall behold, glorify God in the day of visitation. (1 Peter 2:11–12)

And thus shall ye eat it; with your loins girded, your shoes on your feet, and your staff in your hand; and ye shall eat it in haste: it is the Lord's Passover. (Exodus 12:11)

Stand Up for Jesus
Stand up, stand up for Jesus,
Ye soldiers of the cross,
Lift up his royal banner,
It must not suffer loss,
From victory unto victory
His army he shall lead
Till every foe is vanquished,
And Christ is Lord indeed.
(George Duffield, 1818–1888)

On We March
The Lord's command to go into the world
and preach the gospel unto all,
Is just as true today as when his first
disciples heard this mighty call;
So let us gird ourselves and go to battle
'gainst the powers of sin and wrong,
Join the fight for the right, in his
everlasting might, and sing our marching song.
On we march with the blood and the fire,
To the ends of the earth we will go;
And the Savior's love will be the
theme of our song
Because we love him so.
(Charles Mehling 1889–1969)

The Voice of Jesus
We're God's Army and we fight
Wherever wrong is found;
A lowly cot or stately home May be our battle ground.
We own no man as enemy,
Sin is our challenged foe;
We follow Jesus, Son of God,
As to the war we go.
(Charles Wesley 1707–1788)

We have been called to be soldiers of the cross. The battle is the Lord's from what the songs say. Jesus will help us fight the foe. We are fighting for what is right and opposing what is wrong—sin. The devil is the foe. He must be driven out of our lives. Jesus is our commander in chief. Although foes surround us, we will press through the throng. This indeed is a fierce battle, but victory will come. The war will go on until the world is possessed.

Many people of faith have bravely fought till death and are now wearing the crown of life. I want to be a soldier like those martyrs. It is time to put on the armor of God and rush to conquer, never to yield. The enemy must know that wherever we are, we are fighting for God almighty. We must take a stand for God because He will give us the victor's crown one day. We will go home to reign in heaven's bright and sunny regions.

In this war, we will continue to fight against the forces of sin. Satan's power must be overthrown. We fight not against sinners but against sin. Jesus died for us and rose to live forever more. He pardons those who call on His name, and He turns them into His soldiers. We storm the forts of darkness and bring them down. The devil's kingdom must be destroyed wherever it is, but we can only do so if we put on the whole armor of God in Christ Jesus. Our position in this war and the promises of victory are all prepared for us in Christ according to God's divine and eternal plan.

What The Bible Says

> For the weapons of our warfare are not carnal, but mighty through God to the pulling down of strongholds. (2 Corinthians 10:4)

Finally, my brethren, be strong in the Lord, and in the power of his might. Put on the whole armor of God that ye may be able to stand against the wiles of the devil. For we wrestle not against flesh and blood, but against principalities, against powers, against the rulers of the darkness of this world, against spiritual wickedness in high places. Wherefore take unto you the whole armor of God that ye may be able to withstand in the evil day, and having done all, to stand. Stand therefore, having your loins girt about with truth, and having on the breastplate of righteousness; And your feet shod with the preparation of the gospel of peace; Above all, taking the shield of faith, wherewith ye shall be able to quench all the fiery darts of the wicked. And take the helmet of salvation, and the sword of the Spirit, which is the word of God: Praying always with all prayer and supplication in the Spirit, and watching thereunto with all perseverance and supplication for all saints. (Ephesians 6:10–18)

He hath also prepared for him the instruments of death; he ordaineth his arrows against the persecutors. (Psalm 7:13)

Submit yourselves to God. Resist the devil, and he will flee from you. (James 4:7)

Ye are of God, little children, and have overcome them; because greater is he that is in you, than he who is in the world. (1 John 4:4)

For though we walk in the flesh, we do not war after the flesh: (For the weapons of our warfare are not carnal, but mighty through God to the pulling down of strongholds;) Casting down imaginations, and every high thing that exalteth itself against the knowledge of God, and bringing into captivity every thought to the obedience of Christ. (2 Corinthians 10:3–5)

Be sober, be vigilant; because your adversary the devil, as a roaring lion, walketh about, seeking whom he may devour:. Whom resist stedfast in the faith, knowing that the same afflictions are accomplished in your brethren that are in the world. (1 Peter 5:8–9)

No weapon that is formed against thee shall prosper; and every tongue that shall rise against thee in judgment thou shalt condemn. This is the heritage of the servants of the LORD, and their righteousness is of me, saith the Lord. (Isaiah 54:17)

Nay, in all these things we are more than conquerors through him that loved us. (Romans 8:37)

But thanks be to God, which giveth us the victory through our Lord Jesus Christ. (1 Corinthians 15:57)

Not by might nor by power, but by my Spirit, says the LORD of hosts. (Zechariah 4:6)

But the Lord is faithful, who shall establish you, and keep you from evil. (2 Thessalonians 3:3)

Behold, I given unto you power to tread on serpents and scorpions, and over all the power of the enemy: and nothing shall by any means hurt you. (Luke 10:19)

The thief cometh not, but for to steal, and to kill, and to destroy: I am come that they might have life and have it more abundantly. (John 10:10)

Verily I say unto you, whatsoever ye shall bind on earth shall be bound in heaven: and whatsoever ye shall loose on earth will be loosed in heaven. Again, I say unto you, that if two of you shall agree on earth as touching anything that they shall ask, it shall be done for them of my Father which is in heaven. (Matthew 18:18–19)

The LORD shall cause thine enemies that rise up against thee to be smitten before thy face: they shall come out against thee one way, and flee before thee seven ways. (Deuteronomy 28:7)

These things I have spoken unto you, that in me ye might have peace. In the world ye shall have tribulation: but be of good cheer; I have overcome the world. (John 16:33)

There hath no temptation taken you but such as is common to man: but God is faithful, who will not suffer you to be tempted above that ye are able; but will with the temptation also make a way to escape, that ye may be able to bear it. (1 Corinthians 10:13)

And ye shall know the truth, and the truth shall make you free. (John 8:32)

Be not overcome of evil, but overcome evil with good. (Romans 12:21)

And they overcame him by the blood of the Lamb, and by the word of their testimony; and they loved not their lives unto the death. (Revelation 12:11)

Fight the good fight of faith, lay hold on eternal life, whereunto thou art also called, and hast professed a good profession before many witnesses. (1 Timothy 6:12)

For this purpose the Son of God was manifested, that he might destroy the works of the devil. (1 John 3:8)

But they that wait upon the LORD shall renew their strength; they shall mount up with wings as eagles; they shall run, and not be weary; and they shall walk, and not faint. (Isaiah 40:31)

One man of you shall chase a thousand: for the LORD your God, he it is that fighteth for you, as he hath promised you. (Joshua 23:10)

Ye shall not fear them: for the LORD your God he shall fight for you. (Deuteronomy 3:22)

What shall we then say to these things? If God be for us, who can be against us? (Romans 8:31)

Through thee will we push down our enemies: through thy name will we tread them under that rise up against us. (Psalm 44:5)

Have not I commanded thee? Be strong and of a good courage; be not afraid, neither be thou dismayed: for the LORD thy God is with thee whithersoever thou goest. (Joshua 1:9)

For thou hast girded me with strength unto the battle: thou hast subdued under me those that rose up against me. (Psalm 18:39)

He that dwelleth in the secret place of the most High shall abide under the shadow of the Almighty. I will say of the LORD, He is my refuge and my fortress: my God; in him will I trust. Surely he shall deliver thee from the snare of the fowler, and from the noisome pestilence. He shall cover thee with his feathers, and under his wings shalt thou trust: his truth shall be thy shield and buckler. (Psalm 91:1–4)

Thus saith the LORD unto you, Be not afraid nor dismayed by reason of this great multitude; for the battle is not yours, but God's. (2 Chronicles 20:15)

They come from a far country, from the end of heaven, even the LORD, and the weapons of his indignation, to destroy the whole land. (Isaiah 13:5)

The LORD hath opened his armory, and hath brought forth the weapons of his indignation: for this is the work of the Lord GOD of hosts in the land of the Chaldeans. (Jeremiah 50:25)

And, behold, six men came from the way of the higher gate, which lieth toward the north, and every man a slaughter weapon in his hand; and one man among them was clothed with linen, with a writer's inkhorn by his side: and they went in, and stood beside the brazen altar. (Ezekiel 9:2)

Draw out also the spear, and stop the way against them that persecute me: say unto my soul, I am thy salvation. (Psalm 35:3)

The sun and moon stood still in their habitation: at the light of thine arrows they went, and at the shining of thy glittering spear. (Habakkuk 3:11)

And Moses said unto the people, Fear ye not, standstill, and see the salvation of the LORD, which he will shew to you today: For the Egyptians, ye have seen today shall see them again no more forever. The LORD shall fight for you and ye shall hold you peace. (Exodus 14:13–14)

And the LORD said unto Moses, Stretch out thine hand over the sea, and that that waters may come again upon the Egyptians, upon their chariots, and upon their horsemen. And Moses stretched forth his hand over the sea … the Egyptians fled against it; and the LORD overthrew the Egyptians in the midst of the sea. (Exodus 14:26–27)

For the LORD your God dried up the waters of Jordan from before you, until ye were passed over, as the LORD your God did to the Red sea, which he dried up from before us, until we were gone over. (Joshua 4:23)

The Lord said unto Joshua; stretch out the spear that is in thy hand toward Ai; for I will give it into thine hand. (Joshua 8:18)

And the LORD said unto Joshua, see, I have given into thine hand Jericho, and the king thereof, and the mighty men of velour. (Joshua 6:2)

And he answered, Fear not: for they that are with us are more than they be with them. And Elisha prayed, and said, LORD, I pray thee, open his eyes, that he may see. And the LORD opened the eyes of the young man; and he saw: and behold, the mountain was full of horses and chariots of fire round about Elisha. (2 Kings 6:16–17)

Though an host should encamp against me, my heart shall not fear: though war should rise against me, in this will I be confident. (Psalm 27:3)

And all the inhabitants of the earth are reputed as nothing: and he doeth according to his will in the army of heaven, and among the inhabitants of the earth: and none can stay his hand, or say unto him, What doest thou? (Daniel 4:35)

All nations before him are as nothing; and they are counted to him less than nothing, and vanity. (Isaiah 40:17)

And the armies which were in heaven followed him upon white horses, clothed in fine linen, white and clean. And out of his mouth goeth a sharp sword, that with it he should smite the nations: and he shall rule them with a rod of iron: and he treadeth the winepress of the fierceness and wrath of Almighty God. And he hath on his vesture and on his thigh a name written, KING OF KINGS, AND LORD OF LORDS. (Revelation 19:14–16)

Is there any number of his armies? and upon whom doth not his light? (Job 25:3)

This day will the LORD deliver thee into mine hand; and I will smite thee, and take thine head from thee; and I will give the carcasses of the host of the Philistines this day unto the fowls of the air, and to the wild beasts of the earth; that all the earth may know that there is a God in Israel. (1 Samuel 17:46)

But thou hast saved us from our enemies, and hast put them to shame that hated us. (Psalm 44:7)

He shall cover thee with his feathers, and under his wings shalt thou trust: his truth shall be thy shield and buckler. (Psalm 91:4)

Thou shalt not be afraid for the terror by night; nor the arrow that flieth by day, A thousand shall fall at thy side and ten thousand at thy right hand; but it shall not come nigh to thee. (Psalm 91:5, 7)

He teacheth my hands to war, so that a bow of steel is broken by mine arms. (Psalm 18:34; 2 Samuel 22:35)

Though an host should encamp against me, my heart shall not fear: though war should rise against me, in this will I be confident. (Psalm 27:3)

He maketh wars to cease unto the end of the earth; he breaketh the bow, and cutteth the spear in sunder; he burneth the chariot in the fire. (Psalm 46:9)

Blessed be the LORD my strength, which teacheth my hands to war, and my fingers to fight. (Psalm 144:1)

It is he that giveth salvation unto kings: who delivereth David his servant from the hurtful sword. (Psalm 144:10)

Every purpose is established by counsel: and with good advice make war. (Proverbs 20:18, 24:6)

When thou goest out to battle against thine enemies, and seest horses, and chariots, and a people more than thou, be not afraid of them: for the LORD thy God is with thee, which brought thee up out of the land of Egypt. (Deuteronomy 20:1)

Wherefore it is said in the book of the wars of the LORD, What he did in the Red Sea, and in the brooks of Arnon, and at the stream of the brooks at goeth down to the dwelling of Ar, and lieth upon the border of Moab. (Numbers 21:14–15)

Principles

- God can fight the wars of His children and His nations today.
- God can destroy our enemies when we put our faith in Him.
- God's armies are greater than any human army.
- God's weapons are more destructive than humanity's weapons.
- God's power was demonstrated in the victories of Israel.
- God's ways of fighting are different from ours.
- God's weapons of war are always reliable, but humanity's weapons are not.
- We are soldiers of the cross.
- Jesus Christ is our commander in chief.
- We need spiritual armor for this war.
- The devil is our enemy in this war.
- We are more than conquerors through Jesus Christ.
- We must wear our armor every day and everywhere.
- We must be aware of the wiles of the devil.

CHAPTER 23

The Constitution and the Bible: Amendment 3—Quartering of Soldiers

No soldier shall, in time of peace be quartered in any house, without the consent of the Owner, or in time of war, but in a manner to be prescribed by law.

Since the time of founding, Americans' homes have been their most important physical possession. The colonists took to heart eighteenth-century British prime minister William Pitt's sentiment: "Every man's home is his castle." The Third Amendment addressed the Framers' particular grievance with the Quartering Act of 1774, a policy that forced the colonists to provide accommodations for British troops in their homes at night while these same soldiers terrorized their towns by day. This constant invasion of the colonists' privacy by the British soldiers was condemned in the Declaration of Independence and was ultimately outlawed by the Third Amendment.

The Third Amendment Today

> America was born during a time of martial law. Government troops stationed themselves in homes and trespassed on property without regard for the rights of owners.
>
> People often question whether the Third Amendment is germane to our lives today. Although it is generally true that Americans' homes have been safe from soldiers since the Revolutionary War and the military may not threaten

private property *per se*, the Third Amendment is still critically relevant. The right to keep the government out of our homes is an important safeguard against government abuse, and it also reinforces the principle that civilian authority is superior to the military. History clearly shows that citizens of martial states and of military dictatorships are rarely free. Subordinating the military to elected leaders is vital to a democracy.

We must remember that governments have a tendency to seek more and more control, especially in the wake of catastrophes and natural disasters. Many see the federal government's response to tragic events such as 9/11 and Hurricane Katrina as evidence that the United States is approaching a police state that wouldn't hesitate to declare martial law. With the increased military presence, we must be particularly vigilant about protecting the rights afforded by the Third Amendment, as well as the rest of the Bill of Rights.

The Third Amendment reinforces the principle that civilian-elected officials are superior to the military by prohibiting the military from entering any citizen's home without "the consent of the owner." Today's military may not as of yet technically threaten private property. However, with the police increasingly posing as military forces—complete with weapons, uniforms, assault vehicles, etc.—a good case could be made for the fact that SWAT team raids, which break down the barrier between public and private property, have done away with this critical safeguard. Indeed, the increasing militarization of the police, the use of sophisticated weaponry against Americans and the government's increasing tendency to employ military personnel domestically have eviscerated the Third Amendment. At all levels (federal, local and state), through the use of fusion centers, information sharing with the national intelligence agencies, and monetary grants for weapons and training from the Pentagon, the local

> police and the military have for all intents and purposes joined forces. In the process, the police have become a "standing" or permanent army, one composed of full-time professional soldiers who do not disband, which is exactly what the Founders feared. (https://www.rutherford.org/issues/amendment_iii_the_quartering_amendment)

While the Constitution prohibits soldiers from using private residences for accommodation, Romans 8:10–20 reads,

> And if Christ be in you, the body is dead because of sin; but the Spirit is life because of righteousness. But if the Spirit of him that raised up Jesus from the dead dwell in you, he that raised up Christ from the dead shall also quicken your mortal bodies by his Spirit that dwelleth in you. Therefore, brethren, we are debtors, not to the flesh, to live after the flesh. For if ye live after the flesh, ye shall die: but if ye through the Spirit do mortify the deeds of the body, ye shall live.
>
> For as many as are led by the Spirit of God, they are the sons of God. For ye have not received the spirit of bondage again to fear; but ye have received the Spirit of adoption, whereby we cry, Abba, Father. The Spirit itself beareth witness with our spirit, that we are the children of God: And if children, then heirs; heirs of God, and joint-heirs with Christ; if so be that we suffer with him, that we may be also glorified together. For I reckon that the sufferings of this present time are not worthy to be compared with the glory which shall be revealed in us. For the earnest expectation of the creature waiteth for the manifestation of the sons of God For the creature was made subject to vanity, not willingly, but by reason of him who hath subjected the same in hope.

What The Bible Says

> At that day ye shall know that I am in my Father, and ye in me, and I in you. (John 14:20)

I in them, and thou in me, that they may be made perfect in one; and that the world may know that thou hast sent me, and hast loved them, as thou hast loved me. (John 17:23)

And if Christ be in you, the body is dead because of sin; but the Spirit is life because of righteousness. (Romans 8:10)

I am crucified with Christ: nevertheless I live; yet not I, but Christ liveth in me: and the life which I now live in the flesh I live by the faith of the Son of God, who loved me, and gave himself for me. (Galatians 2:20)

That Christ may dwell in your hearts by faith; that ye, being rooted and grounded in love. (Ephesians 3:17)

To whom God would make known what is the riches of the glory of this mystery among the Gentiles; which is Christ in you, the hope of glory. (Colossians 1:27)

And he that keepeth his commandments dwelleth in him, and he in him. And hereby we know that he abideth in us, by the Spirit which he hath given us. (1 John 3:24)

Behold, I stand at the door, and knock: if any man hear my voice, and open the door, I will come in to him, and will sup with him, and he with me. (Revelation 3:20)

That good thing which was committed unto thee keep by the Holy Ghost which dwelleth in us. (2 Timothy 1:14)

In whom ye also are builded together for an habitation of God through the Spirit. (Ephesians 2:22)

That Christ may dwell in your hearts by faith; that ye, being rooted and grounded in love. (Ephesians 3:17)

To whom God would make known what is the riches of the glory of this mystery among the Gentiles; which is Christ in you, the hope of glory. (Colossians 1:27)

But Christ as a son over his own house; whose house are we, if we hold fast the confidence and the rejoicing of the hope firm unto the end. (Hebrews 3:6)

Jesus answered and said unto him, If a man love me, he will keep my words: and my Father will love him, and we will come unto him, and make our abode with him. (John 14:23)

Know ye not that ye are the temple of God, and that the Spirit of God dwelleth in you. (1 Corinthians 3:16)

In 2 Corinthians 13:5, the apostle Paul asked the Corinthian believers a question: "*Or do you not realize about yourselves that Jesus Christ is in you?*" We might find this phrase, "Jesus Christ is in you" surprising, or perhaps we just read over it without thinking too much about its significance. But what does this phrase mean? And what is its importance for our Christian lives today?

In saying, "Jesus Christ is in you," Paul wasn't speaking poetically or metaphorically. He truly meant that Jesus Christ is literally, practically dwelling within the believers. Many other verses in the Word of God confirm the fact that the Lord Jesus Christ actually dwells in His believers.

We too, like the Corinthians, need to *realize* this fact about ourselves. Christ is not merely outside of us, a Helper in our time of need, but He dwells in us, living in and with us all the time. (https://blog.biblesforamerica.org/8-verses-showing-jesus-lives/)

How Can Christ Be in Us?

Christ is the holy God incarnated as a man, and we are fallen sinners. So how can Christ live in us? To accomplish His desire to dwell within mankind, God took some tremendous steps. First, God Himself became a man named Jesus Christ. This man, Jesus, lived a genuine human life on this earth, yet without sin. In His living, His actions, and His speaking, He fully expressed God.

After living and experiencing everything of human life for thirty-three and a half years, Jesus died on the cross for our sins. Through His redemptive death, we can be forgiven of our sins and brought back to God. But this is not all. After three days He rose in victory from the dead, and in resurrection He became the life-giving Spirit. As the Spirit, He is available to everyone and will enter anyone who believes into Him. Thus, when we pray to receive the Lord Jesus, God actually comes to live within us today.

"And if Christ be in you, the body is dead because of sin; but the Spirit is life because of righteousness" (Romans 8:10).

We human beings were created by God with a body on the outside and a soul and spirit on the inside. Our spirit is our deepest part, created to contact and receive the Spirit of God. When we received Jesus as our Savior, He cleansed us of our sins and He came into our spirit as life. Thus, because Christ is in us, our "spirit is life because of righteousness."

"For God, who commanded the light to shine out of darkness, hath shined in our hearts, to give the light of the knowledge of the glory of God in the face of Jesus Christ. But we have this treasure in earthen vessels, that the excellency of the power may be of God, and not of us" (2 Corinthians 4:6–7).

The apostle Paul describes the believers as earthen vessels that contain "this treasure." What is this treasure? It is Jesus Christ, in whose face we see the glory of God. Christ lives in us earthen vessels as a precious treasure, revealing to us the glory of God from within.

"*But when it pleased God … to reveal His Son in me …*" (Galatians 1:15–16). We might think this verse should read, "It pleased God … to reveal His Son *to* me." But in the original language of the New Testament, Greek, the verse reads "to reveal His Son *in* me." God's plan is to reveal His Son in us, from within, rather than to us, from without. Or, to put it another way, God reveals Christ to us from within us. To those who have Christ in us, God is pleased to reveal in us more of the wonderful Person of Christ.

"*I am crucified with Christ: nevertheless I live; yet not I, but Christ liveth in me …*" (Galatians 2:20).

Here, Paul did not say "I live in a Christ-like way," or, "I glorify Christ through my behavior." No, he said, "Christ … lives in me," clearly telling us that Christ lives in His believers. The Christian life is not a matter of behaving like Christ, but of allowing Christ Himself to live in and through us.

"*My little children, of whom I travail in birth again until Christ be formed in you*" (Galatians 4:19).

Paul viewed the believers in Galatia as his spiritual children. He had labored to help them receive Christ at their salvation, and in this verse, he continues to labor on them so that the Christ they received would be fully formed in them. Christ lives in us from the time we are saved, but He wants to be *formed* in us in a definite way. Day by day, we need to give Him the opportunity to be formed in us. As we do, Christ will be able to express Himself more fully through us in our daily life.

"*That Christ may may dwell in your hearts by faith* ..." (Ephesians 3:17).

When we believed into Christ, He came to live in our spirit, the deepest part of our being. But Christ also wants to make His home in the rest of our inward being: our hearts and our souls. By living in our spirit, Christ is the new source of our new life. But our soul—our mind, emotion, and will—can still choose to ignore Him as our new source and go on just as before. In this case, Christ is in us, but He's limited in us, kept only in our spirit. So He cannot be *expressed* through us very much. The Lord Jesus wants to make His home not only in our spirit, but also in all the parts of our soul.

"...*Christ in you, the hope of glory*" (Colossians 1:27).

This verse shows that Christ is in us in a particular way: as our hope of glory. When we believed in Him, Christ came to live in our spirit. Now, He is making His home in our hearts. In the future, when He returns, He will even spread to our body outwardly so that God's glory can shine through us in a full way. The Christ who lives in us is our hope of such glory.

"*When He shall comes to be glorified in His saints, and to be admired in all that believe (because our testimony among you was believed) in that day.*" - 2 Thessalonians 1:10

Christ's second coming will surely be a marvel. But according to this verse, the most marvelous thing will not be the outward display of His coming; it will be His glory revealed from within His believers. The Christ in us, who lives in us and is being formed in us, will be revealed *from within us*, and even our bodies will be transformed to match Him.

What a glory to God, a marvel to man, and a shame to the devil, that people on this earth would choose to receive Christ and allow Him to grow in them and express Himself through them throughout their lives! (https://blog.biblesforamerica.org/8-verses-showing-jesus-lives/)

Principles

- Christ lives in us all the time.
- Christ is being formed in us.
- Our bodies are being transformed to match Him.
- Christ is making His home in us.
- God has come to live with us.
- Lord Jesus Christ actually dwells in His believers.
- We are crucified with Christ.

CHAPTER 24

The Constitution and The Bible: Amendment 4—The Right to Privacy

The right of the people to be secure in their persons, houses, papers, and effects, against unreasonable searches and seizures, shall not be violated, and no Warrants shall issue, but upon probable cause, supported by Oath or affirmation, and particularly describing the place to be searched, and the persons or things to be seized.

> The Fourth Amendment (Amendment IV) to the United States Constitution is part of the Bill of Rights that prohibits unreasonable searches and seizures. It requires "reasonable" governmental searches and seizures to be conducted only upon issuance of a warrant, judicially sanctioned by probable cause, supported by oath or affirmation, particularly describing the place to be searched and the persons or things to be seized. Under the Fourth Amendment, search and seizure (including arrest) should be limited in scope according to specific information supplied to the issuing court, usually by a law enforcement officer who has sworn by it. Fourth Amendment case law deals with three issues: what government activities constitute "search" and "seizure"; what constitutes probable cause for these actions; and how violations of Fourth Amendment rights should be addressed. Early court decisions limited the amendment's scope to a law enforcement officer's physical intrusion onto private property, but with *Katz v. United States* (1967), the Supreme Court held that its

> protections, such as the warrant requirement, extend to the privacy of individuals as well as physical locations. Law enforcement officers need a warrant for most search and seizure activities, but the Court has defined a series of exceptions for consent searches, motor vehicle searches, evidence in plain view, exigent circumstances, border searches, and other situations.
>
> The exclusionary rule is one way the amendment is enforced. Established in *Weeks v. United States* (1914), this rule holds that evidence obtained through a Fourth Amendment violation is generally inadmissible at criminal trials. Evidence discovered as a later result of an illegal search may also be inadmissible as "fruit of the poisonous tree," unless it inevitably would have been discovered by legal means.
>
> The Fourth Amendment was adopted in response to the abuse of the writ of assistance, a type of general search warrant issued by the British government, and a major source of tension in pre-Revolutionary America. The Fourth Amendment was introduced in Congress in 1789 by James Madison, along with the other amendments in the Bill of Rights, in response to Anti-Federalist objections to the new Constitution. Congress submitted the amendment to the states on September 28, 1789. By December 15, 1791, the necessary three-fourths of the states had ratified it. On March 1, 1792, Secretary of State Thomas Jefferson announced the adoption of the amendment. (https://pastdaily.com/2018/04/24/1956-fourth-amendment-past-daily-reference-room/)

The right to privacy prevents the government from intruding unnecessarily in our lives. We feel threatened when people invade our privacy. The Bible is a kingdom of light in which God knows all that is taking place in the lives of His subjects. The Bible says God sent His Son, Jesus Christ, into the world so He might shed light on a dark world. The Lord's light exposes the works of the devil and demands repentance in our lives.

When we are born again, Jesus Christ takes residence in our lives in the form of the Holy Spirit and is constantly training us to be soldiers of His cross. The goal is for us to conform to His image ultimately so we can accomplish greater exploits than He did on earth for the Kingdom. We have to abandon the works of darkness if we are going to live successful Christian lives. Our goal is bring light to darkness and save souls that are lost in darkness for Jesus Christ, our Lord and Savior. Nothing is hidden from the sight of God.

Today, Jesus sits at the right hand of the Father, where He is ever making intercession on our behalf. The Holy Spirit is our light who works to show us the way, what Jesus is expecting from us in our new lives. As Christians, our lives are an open book to God, so we need to walk worthy of our calling. "Be ye holy, for I am holy." We lose our right to privacy when we respond to His calling, but walking in His light is a Christian's greatest joy.

Our daily lives should in no way deny Jesus Christ His rightful place in them. He is our assurance for salvation. He promised us the Holy Spirit, who is to teach, counsel, comfort, and convict us of sin and lead us into all truth. Naturally, the presence of the Holy Spirit in our lives means that everything we do is scrutinized and weighed by the Holy Spirit. Nothing is outside His sight. We cannot afford to exercise our constitutional rights to the detriment of our relationship with Jesus Christ. We cannot expect any neutral decisions on our part as soldiers of the cross.

The Bible says we live for Christ. This implies that our right to live independent of Christ has been lost. As children of God, we have lost ownership of ourselves. In Christ, we live, move, and have our being. All our actions as His soldiers are monitored by the Holy Spirit to teach us His Word, give us His commands, show us the way to salvation, and deliver us from error. The omnipresent, omnipotent, and omniscient God is with us all the time day and night, in times of peace and in times of war, in good times and in bad times.

We are sealed with the Holy Spirit on our day of salvation as a guarantee for our eternal life. We cannot ignore the fact that He is omniscient. This means that whatever we do must be pleasing in His sight. We are under His microscopic eye all the time.

What The Bible Says

> I am crucified with Christ: nevertheless I live; yet not I, but Christ liveth in me: and the life which I now live in the

flesh I live by the faith of the Son of God, who loved me, and gave himself for me. (Galatians 2:20)

I am in them, and thou in me, that they may be made perfect in one. (John 17:23)

For to this end Christ both died, and rose, and revived, that he might be Lord both of the dead and living. (Romans 14:9)

The night is far spent, the day is at hand: let us therefore cast off the works of darkness, and let us put on the armor of light. (Romans 13:12)

For the word of God is quick, and powerful, and sharper than any two-edged sword, piercing even to the dividing asunder of soul and spirit, and of the joints and marrow, and is a discerner of the thoughts and intents of the heart. (Hebrews 4:12)

But if we walk in the light, as he is in the light, we have fellowship one with another, and the blood of Jesus Christ his Son cleanseth us from all sin. (1 John 1:7)

God is light, and in him is no darkness at all. (1 John 1:5)

Let your light so shine before men, that they may see your good works, and glorify your Father which is in heaven. (Matthew 5:16)

I am the light of the world: he that followeth me shall not walk in darkness, but shall have the light of life. (John 8:12)

The LORD shall be unto thee everlasting light, and thy God thy glory. (Isaiah 60:19)

That was the true Light, which lighteth every man that cometh into the world. (John 1:9)

I am come a light into the world, that whosoever believeth on me should not abide in darkness. (John 12:46)

The Jesus said unto them, Yet a little while is the light with you … for he that walketh in darkness knoweth not whither he goeth. (John 12:35)

The Lord is my light. (Psalms 27:1, 36:9, 119:105, 43:3, 36:9)

Let us walk in the light of the Lord. (Isaiah 2:5)

The people which sat in darkness saw great light; and to them which sat in the region and shadow of death light is sprung up. (Matthew 4:16)

Ye are all children of light. (1 Thessalonians 5:5)

Know ye not that your bodies are members of Christ? (1 Corinthians 6:15, 12:27; Ephesians 5:30)

What? know ye not that your body is the temple of the Holy Ghost which is in you, which ye have of God, and ye are not your own? (1 Corinthians 6:19)

This I say then, Walk in the Spirit, and ye shall not fulfill the lust of the flesh. (Galatians 5:16)

But the fruit of the Spirit is love, joy, peace, longsuffering, gentleness, goodness, faith, Meekness, temperance: against such there is no law. (Galatians 6:22–23)

In whom ye also trusted, after that ye heard the word of truth, the gospel of your salvation: in whom also after that ye believed, ye were sealed with that holy Spirit of promise. (Ephesians 1:13)

Who hath also sealed us, and given the earnest of the Spirit in your hearts. (2 Corinthians 1:22)

And we are his witnesses of these things; and so is also the Holy Ghost, whom God hath given to them that obey him. (Acts 5:32)

Now the God of hope fill you with all joy and peace in believing, that ye may abound in hope, through the power of the Holy Ghost. (Romans 15:13)

I indeed baptize you with water unto repentance. but he that cometh after me is mightier than I, whose shoes I am not worthy to bear: he shall baptize you with the Holy Ghost, and with fire. (Matthew 3:11)

Jesus answered, Verily, verily, I say unto thee, Except a man be born of water and of the Spirit, he cannot enter into the Kingdom. (John 3:5)

But ye shall receive power, after that the Holy Ghost is come upon you: and ye shall be witnesses unto me both in Jerusalem, and in all Judaea, and in Samaria, and unto the uttermost part of the earth. (Acts 1:8)

And they were all filled with the Holy Ghost, and began to speak with other tongues, as the Spirit gave them utterance. (Acts 2:4)

While Peter yet spake these words, the Holy Ghost fell on all them which heard the word. (Acts 10:44)

Who, when they were come down, prayed for them, that they might receive the Holy Ghost. (Acts 8:15)

And the disciples were filled with joy, and with the Holy Ghost. (Acts 13:52)

And when Paul had laid his hands upon them, the Holy Ghost came on them; and they spake with tongues, and prophesied. (Acts 19:6)

Then Peter said unto them, Repent, and be baptized every one of you in the name of Jesus Christ for the remission of sins, and ye shall receive the gift of the Holy Ghost. (Acts 2:38)

For man looketh on the outward appearance, but the LORD looketh on the heart. (1 Samuel 16:7)

For the Lord searcheth all hearts, and understandeth all the imaginations of the thoughts. (1 Chronicles 28:9)

Then hear thou from heaven thy dwelling place, and forgive, and render unto every man according unto all his ways, whose heart thou knowest; (for thou only knowest the hearts of the children of men). (2 Chronicles 6:30)

O Lord, thou hast searched me, and known me … and art acquainted with ways. (Psalm 139:1, 3)

The eyes of the Lord are in every place, beholding the evil and the good. (Proverbs 15:3)

For I know their works and their thoughts. (Isaiah 66:18)

But thou, O LORD, Knowest me: thou hast seen me, and tried mine heart toward thee. (Jeremiah 12:3)

I the LORD search the heart, I try the reins, even to give every man according to his ways, and according to the fruit of his doings. (Jeremiah 17:10)

For I know the things that come into your mind, every one of them. (Ezekiel 11:5)

Known unto God are all his works from the beginning of the world. (Acts 15:18)

O the depth of the riches both of the wisdom and knowledge of God! how unsearchable are his judgements, and his ways past finding out! (Romans 11:33)

And again, The Lord knoweth the thoughts of the wise, that they are vain. (1 Corinthians 3:20)

In whom are hid all the treasures of wisdom and knowledge. (Colossians 2:3)

I know thy works, and thy labor, and thy patience, and how thou canst not bear which are evil. (Revelation 2:2)

And grieve not the holy Spirit of God, whereby ye are sealed unto the day of redemption. (Ephesians 4:30)

Principles

- Jesus Christ now lives in us.
- We have no right to privacy with God.
- We live in the light of Jesus Christ.
- All our activities are now exposed to His scrutiny.
- We must live holy lives since we live for Christ.
- We cannot hide anything from God.
- We are no longer our own.

CHAPTER 25

The Constitution and The Bible: Amendments 5–8—Rights of Defendants before the Courts

Amendment 5: Capital Offenses

No person shall be held to answer for a capital, or otherwise infamous crime, unless on a presentment of a Grand Jury except in arising in the land or naval force, or in the Militia, when in actual service in time of war or public danger; nor shall any person be subject for the same offence to be twice put in jeopardy of life or limb, not shall be compelled in any criminal case to be a witness against himself, not be deprived of life, liberty, without due process of law; nor shall private property be taken for public use without just compensation.

Amendment 6: The Right to a Speedy and Public Trial

In all criminal prosecutions, the accused shall enjoy the right to a speedy and public trial, by an impartial jury of the State and district wherein the crime shall have been committed.

Amendment 7: The Right to a Trial by Jury

In Suits at common law, where the value in controversy shall exceed twenty dollars, the right of trial Jury shall be preserved, and no fact tried by a Jury shall be otherwise re-examined in any court of the United States, than according to the rules of common law.

Amendment 8: No Excessive Bail or Cruel and Unusual Punishment

Excessive bail shall not be required, nor excessive fine imposed, nor cruel and unusual punishments inflicted.

Amendments 5 and 14: Due Process

National government [Fifth) and the state government (Fourteenth) shall not deprive any person of life, liberty, or property without due process of law.

Summary of Defendants' Rights

Limits of Conduct of Police and Prosecutors

- No coerced confessions or illegal interrogation.
- No entrapment.
- Upon questioning, suspect must be informed of rights.

Defendants' Pretrial Rights

- writ of habeas corpus (article 1, section 9)
- prompt arraignment (Amendment 6)
- legal counsel (Amendment 6)
- reasonable bail (Amendment 8)
- defendant must be informed of charges (Amendment 6)
- right to remain silent (Amendment 6)

Defendants' Trial Rights

- speedy and public trial before a jury (Amendment 6)
- impartial jury selected from cross section of community (Amendments 6 and 7)

- trial atmosphere free of prejudice, fear, and outside interference.
- no compulsory self-incrimination (Amendment 5)
- adequate counsel (Amendment 6)
- no cruel or unusual punishment (Amendment 8)
- the right to appeal convictions
- no double jeopardy (Amendment 5)

Due Process

Procedural due process refers to the methods by which a law is enforced; substantive due process requires that laws and regulations be fair and reasonable with limits on what that power may be used to do no matter how it is used. It focuses on the content of the law.

Congress or any state legislature may prescribe the death penalty, also known as capital punishment, for murder and other capital crimes. The United States Supreme Court said this about the death penalty in "*Gregg v. Georgia*", 1976. Landmark Cases: Historic Supreme Court Decisions, Volume 2".

> The imposition of the death penalty for the crime of murder has a long history of acceptance both in the United States and in England … It is apparent from the text of the Constitution itself that the existence of capital punishment was accepted by the Framers. At the time the Eighth Amendment was ratified, capital punishment was a common sanction in every State. Indeed, the First Congress of the United States enacted legislation providing death as the penalty for specified crimes. The Fifth Amendment, adopted at the same time as the Eighth, contemplated the continued existence of the capital sanction by imposing certain limits on the prosecution of capital cases.

Bible and Capital Punishment

In the Old Testament, the death penalty was legal. God commanded people to be executed for murder, adultery, homosexuality, sorcery, kidnapping, and other crimes.

God instituted the death penalty, and Christians are to never to fight it. Scripture makes it clear that the government has the authority to determine when it is to be used.

Most of the time in the United States, murder does not result in the death penalty, but when it does, we are not to rejoice or oppose it unless the person is innocent.

At the end of the day, all sin results in being sentenced to eternity in hell.

The only way we can escape the wrath of God is by accepting Christ as our Lord and Savior.

What The Bible Says

> He that smiteth a man, he shall be surely put to death. (Exodus 21:12)

> And if he smite him with an instrument of iron, so that he die, he is a murderer: the murderer shall surely be put to death. And if he smite him with throwing a stone, wherewith he may die, and he die, he is a murderer: the murderer shall surely be put to death. (Numbers 35:16–17)

> But if any man hate his neighbor, and lie in wait for him, and rise up against him, and smite him mortally that he die, and fleeth into one of these cities: Then the elders of his city shall send and fetch him thence, and deliver him into the hand of the avenger of blood, that he may die. (Deuteronomy 19:11–12)

> But if a man come presumptuously upon his neighbor, to slay him with guile; thou shalt take him from mine altar, that he may die. And he that smiteth his father, or his mother, shall be surely put to death. And he that stealeth a man, and selleth him, or if he be found in his hand, he shall surely be put to death. And he that curseth his father, or his mother, shall surely be put to death. (Exodus 21:14–17)

> Cursed be he that smiteth his neighbor secretly. And all the people shall say, Amen. (Deuteronomy 27:24)

> Whoso killeth any person, the murderer shall be put to death by the mouth of witnesses: but one witness shall not testify against any person to cause him to die. Moreover ye shall take no satisfaction for the life of a murderer, which is guilty of death: but he shall be surely put to death. And ye shall take no satisfaction for him that is fled to the city of his refuge, that he should come again to dwell in the land, until the death of the priest. (Numbers 35:30–32)

> Whoso sheddeth man's blood, by man shall his blood be shed: for in the image of God made he man. (Genesis 9:6)

> Whosoever lieth with a beast shall surely be put to death. (Exodus 22:19)

The crime of not repenting and putting your trust in Christ for salvation is punishable by eternity in hell.

> In flaming fire taking vengeance on them that know not God, and that obey not the gospel of our Lord Jesus Christ: Who shall be punished with everlasting destruction from the presence of the Lord, and from the glory of his power. (2 Thessalonians 1:8–9)

> He that believeth on the Son hath everlasting life: and he that believeth not the Son shall not see life; but the wrath of God abideth on him. (John 3:36)

> But the fearful, and unbelieving, and the abominable, and murderers, and whoremongers, and sorcerers, and idolaters, and all liars, shall have their part in the lake which burneth with fire and brimstone: which is the second death. (Revelation 21:8)

> And there shall in no wise enter into it anything that defileth, neither whatsoever worketh abomination, or maketh a lie: but they which are written in the Lamb's book of life. (Revelation 21:27)

Due Process in the Bible

We can escape the death penalty in the Bible. God's government provides for due process for us in that we are given an opportunity to hear the gospel and repent before we are condemned. God has made full provision for us to come to the knowledge of His plan of salvation. Furthermore, we have been given an advocate, Jesus Christ, who is always interceding for us in heaven.

We must adopt God's provision for our restoration into fellowship with Him if we are to escape eternal separation from Him. We know that the Word is perfect for its purpose: it is fully and admirably fitted to produce the most practical effect on those who are brought to understand it.

We must believe in the finished work of Jesus Christ on the cross. He fulfilled the due-process requirements of the law on behalf of all humanity, but only those who are born again can qualify to meet the due-process dictates of the law.

What The Bible Says

> But as many as received him, to them gave he power to become the sons of God, even to them that believe on his name. (John 1:12)

> For God so loved the world, that he gave his only begotten Son, that whosoever believeth in him should not perish, but have everlasting life. (John 3:16)

> The same came for a witness, to bear witness of the Light, that all men through him might believe. (John 1:7)

> He that believeth on him is not condemned: but he that believeth not is condemned already, because he hath not believed in the name of the only begotten Son of God. (John 3:18)

He that believeth on the Son hath everlasting life: and he that believeth not the Son shall not see life; but the wrath of God abideth on him. (John 3:36)

Verily, verily, I say unto you, He that heareth my word, and believeth on him that sent me, hath everlasting life, and shall not come into condemnation; but is passed from death unto life. (John 5:24)

Jesus answered and said unto them, This is the work of God, that ye believe on him whom he hath sent. (John 6:29)

Jesus said unto her, I am the resurrection, and the life: he that believeth in me, though he were dead, yet shall he live. (John 11:25)

Jesus cried and said, He that believeth on me, believeth not on me, but on him that sent me. (John 12:44)

To him give all the prophets witness, that through his name whosoever believeth, him shall receive remission of sins. (Acts 10:43)

And by him all that believe are justified from all things, from which ye could not be justified by the law of Moses. (Acts 13:39)

And when the Gentiles heard this, they were glad, and glorified the word of the Lord: and as many as were ordained to eternal life believed. (Acts 13:48)

For I am not ashamed of the gospel of Christ: for it is the power of God unto salvation to every one that believeth; to the Jew first, and also to the Greek. (Romans 1:16)

That if thou shalt confess with thy mouth the Lord Jesus, and shalt believe in thine heart that God hath raised him from the dead, thou shalt be saved. (Romans 10:9)

> And this is his commandment, That we should believe on the name of his Son Jesus Christ, and love one another, as he gave us commandment. (1 John 3:23)

> These things have I written unto you that believe on the name of the Son of God; that ye may know that ye have eternal life, and that ye may believe on the name of the Son of God. (1 John 5:13)

> For we which have believed, do enter into rest, as he said … (Hebrews 4:3)

Guarantees under the Constitution

Under the Constitution, people are presumed innocent until proven guilty. Those who are arrested are granted basic rights covered by Amendments 5–8. We have attempted to create a judicial system that demands proof of accusation, avoids double jeopardy, provides for speedy trial, access to legal advice for those who cannot afford a lawyer, trial by jury in some cases, and imposition of reasonable fines.

The Bible and Sinners

Under the Constitution, we are innocent until proven guilty, but in the Bible, we are all sinners and are all guilty. We must repent.

The Constitution provides for legal representation in courts; in the Bible, Jesus Christ is our legal representative before the law of God.

Sin Is Crime

The Bible views sin as a crime that emanated from Adam's fall. In God's mind, all have sinned and come short of His glory and must repent to receive eternal life. The alternative is eternal spiritual and physical death. Our sin nature must be transformed through the blood of Jesus by our acceptance of His lordship. "But God commendeth his love toward us, in that, while we were yet sinners, Christ died for us" (Romans 5:8).

All Sin Is Punishable by Death

> For the wages of sin [is] death; but the gift of God [is] eternal life through Jesus Christ our Lord. (Romans 6:23)

> Wherefore, as by one man sin entered into the world, and death by sin; and so death passed upon all men, for that all have sinned. (Romans 5:12)

> But your iniquities have separated between you and your God, and your sins have hid his face from you, that he will not hear. (Isaiah 59:2)

> The soul that sinneth, it shall die. The son shall not bear the iniquity of the father, neither shall the father bear the iniquity of the son: the righteousness of the righteous shall be upon him, and the wickedness of the wicked shall be upon him. (Ezekiel 18:20)

> For all have sinned, and come short of the glory of God. (Romans 3:23)

Eternal Life Is Guaranteed in the Bible

Only sin can separate us from God, who provided for the removal of our sins by the blood of Jesus. We can have eternal life with God in His kingdom if we repent. Eternal death is not our portion after we become children of God.

What The Bible Says

> For God so loved the world, that he gave his only begotten Son, that whosoever believeth in him should not perish, but have everlasting life. (John 3:16)

> And I give unto them eternal life; and they shall never perish, neither shall any man pluck them out of my hand. My Father, which gave them me, is greater than all; and no

man is able to pluck them out of my Father's hand. I and my Father are one. (John 10:28–30)

But the God of all grace, who hath called us unto his eternal glory by Christ Jesus, after that ye have suffered a while, make you perfect, establish, strengthen, settle you. (1 Peter 5:10)

For the wages of sin is death; but the gift of God is eternal life through Jesus Christ our Lord. (Romans 6:23)

He that believeth on the Son hath everlasting life: and he that believeth not the Son shall not see life; but the wrath of God abideth on him. (John 3:36)

Principles

- We are guilty of sin from the time of our birth.
- The penalty of sin is death.
- We are declared innocent once we are born again.
- We receive the gift of eternal life once we are declared innocent.
- All who are saved by the blood of Jesus Christ will not suffer eternal punishment.
- No earthly judge has control over our eternal life in God's kingdom.
- It is time to repent and avoid capital punishment.

CHAPTER 26

Amendment 16 (Ratified February 3, 1913)

Power to Tax: The Constitution and The Bible

> The Congress shall have power to lay and collect taxes on incomes, from whatever source derived, without apportionment among the several States, and without regard to any census or enumeration.

> Christians know that everything we have ultimately belongs to God. We are stewards and are called on to invest our money and other resources into things with eternal value. We are called on to provide for our families (1 Timothy 5:8) and to give generously (2 Corinthians 9:6–8). It is also wise to save (Proverbs 6:6–8) and perfectly acceptable to spend money on ourselves and thank God for His good gifts (James 1:17; Colossians 3:17). Paying taxes is the duty of citizens, and Christians are called to be good citizens. But Christians are ultimately citizens of heaven (Philippians 3:20). Reducing our tax burden in this life should have as its goal investing in God's kingdom for eternity. (https://www.gotquestions.org/taxes-Bible.html)

Let's be honest. Even Christians hate the corruptness of the IRS, but no matter how corrupt the tax system is we still have to pay our income taxes and other taxes. The whole "they're always ripping me off" statement is never an excuse to cheat on your tax returns. We are to have nothing to do with anything illegal and we are to submit to our authorities. Even Jesus paid taxes. If you cheat on your returns you are lying, stealing, and disobeying God and He will never be mocked. Don't be envious of people who lie on their tax returns. Christians are not to follow the world. Any covetous thought must be brought to the Lord immediately in prayer. God will provide for your needs. You must not try to milk the system. Never forget that fraud is a crime. (https://biblereasons.com/paying-taxes/)

What The Bible Says

Let every soul be subject unto the higher powers. For there is no power but of God: the powers that be are ordained of God. Whosoever therefore resisteth the power, resisteth the ordinance of God: and they that resist shall receive to themselves damnation. For rulers are not a terror to good works, but to the evil. Wilt thou then not be afraid of the power? do that which is good, and thou shalt have praise of the same: For he is the minister of God to thee for good. But if thou do that which is evil, be afraid; for he beareth not the sword in vain: for he is the minister of God, a revenger to execute wrath upon him that doeth evil. Wherefore ye must needs be subject, not only for wrath, but also for conscience sake. For this cause pay ye tribute also: for they are God's ministers, attending continually upon this very thing. Render therefore to all their dues: tribute to whom tribute is due; custom to whom custom; fear to whom fear; honor to whom honor. (Romans 13:1–7)

Put them in mind to be subject to principalities and powers, to obey magistrates, to be ready to every good work, To speak evil of no man, to be no brawlers, but gentle, shewing all meekness unto all men. (Titus 3:1–2)

Submit yourselves to every ordinance of man for the Lord's sake: whether it be to the king, as supreme; Or unto governors, as unto them that are sent by him for the punishment of evildoers, and for the praise of them that do well. For so is the will of God, that with well doing ye may put to silence the ignorance of foolish men: As free, and not using your liberty for a cloke of maliciousness, but as the servants of God. (1 Peter 2:13–16)

Withhold not good from them to whom it is due, when it is in the power of thine hand to do it. (Proverbs 3:27)

Caesar

And the chief priests and the scribes the same hour sought to lay hands on him; and they feared the people: for they perceived that he had spoken this parable against them. And they watched him, and sent forth spies, which should feign themselves just men, that they might take hold of his words, that so they might deliver him unto the power and authority of the governor. And they asked him, saying, Master, we know that thou sayest and teachest rightly, neither acceptest thou the person of any, but teachest the way of God truly: Is it lawful for us to give tribute unto Caesar, or no? But he perceived their craftiness, and said unto them, Why tempt ye me? Shew me a penny. Whose image and superscription hath it? They answered and said, Caesar's. And he said unto them, Render therefore unto Caesar the things which be Caesar's, and unto God the things which be God's. And they could not take hold of his words before the people: and they marveled at his answer, and held their peace. (Luke 20:19–26)

He answereth and saith unto them, He that hath two coats, let him impart to him that hath none; and he that hath meat, let him do likewise. Then came also publicans to be baptized, and said unto him, Master, what shall we do? And he said unto them, Exact no more than that which is appointed you. And the soldiers likewise demanded of him, saying, And what shall we do? And he said unto them, Do violence to no man, neither accuse any falsely; and be content with your wages. And as the people were

> in expectation, and all men mused in their hearts of John, whether he were the Christ, or not; John answered, saying unto them all, I indeed baptize you with water; but one mightier than I cometh, the latchet of whose shoes I am not worthy to unloose: <u>he shall baptize you with the Holy Ghost and with fire</u>. (Luke 3:11–16)

> And when they were come, they say unto him, Master, we know that thou art true, and carest for no man: for thou regardest not the person of men, but teachest the way of God in truth: Is it lawful to give tribute to Caesar, or not? Shall we give, or shall we not give? But he, knowing their hypocrisy, said unto them, Why tempt ye me? bring me a penny, that I may see it. And they brought it. And he saith unto them, Whose is this image and superscription? And they said unto him, Caesar's. And Jesus answering said unto them, Render to Caesar the things that are Caesar's, and to God the things that are God's. And they marveled at him. (Mark 12:14–17)

Tax collectors (publicans) were corrupt people, and just like today, they were not too popular.

> For John came neither eating nor drinking, and they say, He hath a devil. The Son of man came eating and drinking, and they say, Behold a man gluttonous, and a winebibber, a friend of publicans and sinners. But wisdom is justified of her children. Then began he to upbraid the cities wherein most of his mighty works were done, because they repented not. (Matthew 11:18–20)

> But what think ye? A certain man had two sons; and he came to the first, and said, Son, go work to day in my vineyard. He answered and said, I will not: but afterward he repented, and went. And he came to the second, and said likewise. And he answered and said, I go, sir: and went not. Whether of them twain did the will of his father? They say unto him, The first. Jesus saith unto them, Verily I say unto you, That

the publicans and the harlots go into the Bible before you. For John came unto you in the way of righteousness, and ye believed him not: but the publicans and the harlots believed him: and ye, when ye had seen it, repented not afterward, that ye might believe him. (Matthew 21:28–32)

And when Jesus came to the place, he looked up, and saw him, and said unto him, Zacchaeus, make haste, and come down; for to day I must abide at thy house. And he made haste, and came down, and received him joyfully. And when they saw it, they all murmured, saying, That he was gone to be guest with a man that is a sinner. And Zacchaeus stood, and said unto the Lord: Behold, Lord, the half of my goods I give to the poor; and if I have taken anything from any man by false accusation, I restore him fourfold. (Luke 19:5–8)

Reminders

For nothing is secret, that shall not be made manifest; neither any thing hid, that shall not be known and come abroad. (Luke 19:5–8)

Ye shall not steal, neither deal falsely, neither lie one to another. (Leviticus 19:11)

Let not thine heart envy sinners: but be thou in the fear of the LORD all the day long. For surely there is an end; and thine expectation shall not be cut off. Hear thou, my son, and be wise, and guide thine heart in the way. (Proverbs 23:17–19)

Examples

And there was a great cry of the people and of their wives against their brethren the Jews. For there were that said, We, our sons, and our daughters, are many: therefore we take up corn for them, that we may eat, and live. Some also there were that said, We have mortgaged our lands,

> vineyards, and houses, that we might buy corn, because of the dearth. There were also that said, We have borrowed money for the king's tribute, and that upon our lands and vineyards. (Nehemiah 5:1–4)

> And all the men of Israel, when they saw the man, fled from him, and were sore afraid. And the men of Israel said, Have ye seen this man that is come up? surely to defy Israel is he come up: and it shall be, that the man who killeth him, the king will enrich him with great riches, and will give him his daughter, and make his father's house free in Israel. (1 Samuel 17:24–25)

Bonus

> Let no man despise thy youth; but be thou an example of the believers, in word, in conversation, in charity, in spirit, in faith, in purity. (1 Timothy 4:12)

> Tell us therefore, What thinkest thou? Is it lawful to give tribute unto Caesar, or not? But Jesus perceived their wickedness, and said, Why tempt ye me, ye hypocrites? Shew me the tribute money. And they brought unto him a penny. And he saith unto them, Whose is this image and superscription? They say unto him, Caesar's. Then saith he unto them, Render therefore unto Caesar the things which are Caesar's; and unto God the things that are God's. (Matthew 22:17–21)

> For this cause pay ye tribute also: for they are God's ministers, attending continually upon this very thing. Render therefore to all their dues: tribute to whom tribute is due; custom to whom custom; fear to whom fear; honor to whom honor. (Romans 13:6–7)

It seems there is an endless amount of the types of taxes to which citizens and participants in the local and global economy are subjected. Taxes are unpopular, and sometimes the government agencies in charge of collecting those taxes are thought of with disgust, whether they are corrupt or not. This is nothing new. Tax collectors were not thought highly of in Bible times either (Matthew 11:19, 21:31–32; Luke 3:12–13).

> As much as we hate taxes, as much as any tax system can be corrupt and unfair, as much as we believe there are far better things our money could go toward—The Bible commands, yes, commands us to pay our taxes. Romans 13:1–7 makes it clear that we are to submit ourselves to the government. The only instance in which we are allowed to disobey the government is when it tells us to do something The Bible forbids. The Bible does not forbid paying taxes. In fact, The Bible encourages us to pay taxes. Therefore, we must submit to God and His Word—and pay our taxes.
>
> Generally speaking, taxes are intended to enable the beneficial running of society. Depending on one's priorities, tax revenue is not always put to the best use. The most frequent objection to paying taxes is that the money is being misused by the government or even used for evil purposes by the government. That, however, is not our concern. When Jesus said, "Give to Caesar …," the Roman government was by no means a righteous government. When Paul instructed us to pay taxes, Nero, one of the most evil Roman emperors in history, was the head of the government. We are to pay our taxes even when the government is not God-honoring.
>
> We are free to take every legal tax deduction available. We do not have to pay the maximum amount of taxes possible. If the government allows you a tax break, you are free to take it. If there is a legal way you can shelter some of your money from being taxed, you are free to shelter it. Illegal and/or dishonest methods of evading taxes must be rejected. Romans 13:2 reminds us, "Whosoever therefore resisteth the power, resisteth the ordinance of God: and they that resist shall receive to themselves damnation." (https://www.gotquestions.org/taxes-Bible.html

Principles

- We must pay our taxes to the government.
- We must pay taxes regularly and the correct amount.
- We can save taxes only where it is legal.
- We must pay even when we disagree with the government and its policies.
- Paying taxes is part of our duty as stewards of God's wealth.

CHAPTER 27

The Constitution and The Bible: Amendment 18 (Repealed by Amendment 21

Section 1

> After one year from the ratification of this article the manufacture, sale, or transportation of intoxicating liquors within, the importation thereof into, or the exportation thereof from the United States and all territory subject to the jurisdiction thereof for beverage purposes is hereby prohibited.

Alcohol Abuse in the US

Alcohol has been a major problem in our world for time immemorial. It appears we are fighting a losing war, but we cannot give up. While we have come up with professional tools to fight alcoholism, we know that God has addressed this issue in The Bible. We have made laws to curb the abuse of alcohol but have failed to control its consumption and abuse resulting in destruction of families and individual lives.

One in eight American adults is an alcoholic according to a study by Christopher Ingraham that was published in JAMA Psychiatry.

> [It] finds that the rate of alcohol use disorder, what's colloquially known as "alcoholism," rose by a shocking 49 percent in the first decade of the 2000s. One in eight American adults, or 12.7 percent of the U.S. population, now meets diagnostic criteria for alcohol use disorder,

according to the study. The study's authors characterize the findings as a serious and overlooked public health crisis, noting that alcoholism is a significant driver of mortality from a cornucopia of ailments: "fetal alcohol spectrum disorders, hypertension, cardiovascular diseases, stroke, liver cirrhosis, several types of cancer and infections, pancreatitis, type 2 diabetes, and various injuries." Indeed, the study's findings are bolstered by the fact that deaths from a number of these conditions, particularly alcohol-related cirrhosis and hypertension, have risen concurrently over the study period. The Centers for Disease Control and Prevention estimates that 88,000 people a year die of alcohol-related causes, more than twice the annual death toll of opiate overdose.

How did the study's authors judge who counts as "an alcoholic"?

The study's data comes from the National Epidemiologic Survey on Alcohol and Related Conditions (NESARC), a nationally representative survey administered by the National Institutes of Health. Survey respondents were considered to have alcohol use disorder if they met widely used diagnostic criteria for either alcohol abuse or dependence.

For a diagnosis of alcohol abuse, an individual must have exhibited at least one of the following characteristics in the past year (bulleted text is quoted directly from the National Institutes of Health):

- Recurrent use of alcohol resulting in a failure to fulfill major role obligations at work, school, or home (e.g., repeated absences or poor work performance related to alcohol use; alcohol-related absences, suspensions, or expulsions from school; neglect of children or household).

- Recurrent alcohol use in situations in which it is physically hazardous (e.g., driving an automobile or operating a machine when impaired by alcohol use).
- Recurrent alcohol-related legal problems (e.g., arrests for alcohol-related disorderly conduct).
- Continued alcohol use despite having persistent or recurrent social or interpersonal problems caused or exacerbated by the effects of alcohol. (https://www.washingtonpost.com/news/wonk/wp/2017/08/11/study-one-in-eight-american-adults-are-alcoholics/?noredirect=on&utm_term=.7600a5a2d707)

These would include arguments with spouses about the consequences of intoxication.

For a diagnosis of alcohol dependence, an individual must experience at least three of the following seven symptoms (again, bulleted text is quoted directly from the National Institutes of Health):

- Need for markedly increased amounts of alcohol to achieve intoxication or desired effect; or markedly diminished effect with continued use of the same amount of alcohol.
- The characteristic withdrawal syndrome for alcohol; or drinking (or using a closely related substance) to relieve or avoid withdrawal symptoms.
- Drinking in larger amounts or over a longer period than intended.
- Persistent desire or one or more unsuccessful efforts to cut down or control drinking.
- Important social, occupational, or recreational activities given up or reduced because of drinking.
- A great deal of time spent in activities necessary to obtain, to use, or to recover from the effects of drinking.
- Continued drinking despite knowledge of having a persistent or recurrent physical or psychological

problem that is likely to be caused or exacerbated by drinking.

"The Surgeon General's Call to Action To Prevent and Reduce Underage Drinking" Office of the Surgeon General (US); National Institute on Alcohol Abuse and Alcoholism (US); Substance Abuse and Mental Health Services Administration (US). (2007)

Meeting either of those criteria—abuse or dependence—would lead to an individual being characterized as having an alcohol use disorder (alcoholism). The study found that rates of alcoholism were higher among men (16.7 percent), Native Americans (16.6 percent), people below the poverty threshold (14.3 percent), and people living in the Midwest (14.8 percent). Stunningly, nearly 1 in 4 adults under age 30 (23.4 percent) met the diagnostic criteria for alcoholism.

Some caveats

While the study's findings are alarming, a different federal survey, the National Survey on Drug Use and Health (NSDUH), has shown that alcohol use disorder rates are lower and falling, rather than rising, since 2002. Grant says she's not sure what's behind the discrepancies between the two federal surveys, but it's difficult to square the declining NSDUH numbers with the rising mortality rates seen in alcohol-driven conditions like cirrhosis and hypertension. A surveys found that the disparities are probably caused by how each survey asks about alcohol disorders: It found that the NESARC questionnaire used in the current study is a "more sensitive instrument" that leads to a "more thorough probing" of the criteria for alcohol use disorder. If the more sensitive data used in the current study is indeed more accurate, there's one final caveat to note: The study's data go only through 2013. If the observed trend continues, the true rate of alcoholism today would be even higher. ("One in eight American adults is an alcoholic study," Christopher Ingraham, https://www.washingtonpost.com/people/christopher-ingraham/)

For years, well-meaning, sincere Christians have debated the subject of drinking. Let me be clear by saying there isn't a single verse in The Bible that says a Christian cannot have a drink; although The Bible clearly warns about the destructive and addictive nature of alcohol (Proverbs 20:1; 21:17; 23:29–35; Ephesians 5:18) and is very clear that drunkenness is always wrong (Romans 13:13; Galatians 5:19--21; 1 Peter 4:3; Habakkuk 2:15; 1 Corinthians 5:11).

The Bible is also clear that mature Christians should avoid causing others to stumble by drinking (Romans 14:21), and that leaders ought to avoid drinking alcohol (Proverbs 31:4–7) and cannot be given to drunkenness (1 Timothy 3:3, 8 Titus 1:7.) (https://www.fahanchurch.org/canachristiandrinkalcohol.htm)

What The Bible Says about Alcohol

And be not drunk with wine, wherein is excess; but be filled with the Spirit. (Ephesians 5:18)

Be sober, be vigilant; because your adversary the devil, as a roaring lion, walketh about, seeking whom he may devour. (1 Peter 5:8)

Who hath woe? who hath sorrow? who hath contentions? who hath babbling? who hath wounds without cause? who hath redness of eyes? They that tarry long at the wine; they that go to seek mixed wine. Look not thou upon the wine when it is red, when it giveth his color in the cup, when it moveth itself aright. At the last it biteth like a serpent, and stingeth like an adder. Thine eyes shall behold strange women, and thine heart shall utter perverse things. (Proverbs 23:29–35)

Nor thieves, nor covetous, nor drunkards, nor revilers, nor extortioners, shall inherit the Bible. (1 Corinthians 6:10)

Wine is a mocker, strong drink is raging: and whosoever is deceived thereby is not wise. (Proverbs 20:1)

Envyings, murders, drunkenness, revellings, and such like: of the which I tell you before, as I have also told you in time past, that they which do such things shall not inherit the Kingdom. (Galatians 5:21)

Woe unto them that are mighty to drink wine, and men of strength to mingle strong drink. (Isaiah 5:22)

Let us walk honestly, as in the day; not in rioting and drunkenness, not in chambering and wantonness, not in strife and envying. (Romans 13:13)

If any man defile the temple of God, him shall God destroy; for the temple of God is holy, which temple ye are. (1 Corinthians 3:17)

Woe unto them that rise up early in the morning, that they may follow strong drink; that continue until night, till wine inflame them! (Isaiah 5:11)

What? know ye not that your body is the temple of the Holy Ghost which is in you, which ye have of God, and ye are not your own? For ye are bought with a price: therefore glorify God in your body, and in your spirit, which are God's. (1 Corinthians 6:19–20)

But now I have written unto you not to keep company, if any man that is called a brother be a fornicator, or covetous, or an idolator, or a railer, or a drunkard, or an extortioner; with such an one no not to eat. (1 Corinthians 5:11)

Know ye not that the unrighteous shall not inherit the Kingdom? Be not deceived: neither fornicators, nor idolaters, nor adulterers, nor effeminate, nor abusers of themselves with mankind, Nor thieves, nor covetous, nor drunkards, nor revilers, nor extortioners, shall inherit the Kingdom. (1 Corinthians 6:9–10)

And take heed to yourselves, lest at any time your hearts be overcharged with surfeiting, and drunkenness, and cares of this life, and so that day come upon you unawares. (Luke 21:34)

It is good neither to eat flesh, nor to drink wine, nor any thing whereby thy brother stumbleth, or is offended, or is made weak. (Romans 14:21)

But they also have erred through wine, and through strong drink are out of the way; the priest and the prophet have erred through strong drink, they are swallowed up of wine, they are out of the way through strong drink; they err in vision, they stumble in judgment. (Isaiah 28:7)

Woe to the crown of pride, to the drunkards of Ephraim, whose glorious beauty is a fading flower, which are on the head of the fat valleys of them that are overcome with wine! (Isaiah 28:1)

Drink no longer water, but use a little wine for thy stomach's sake and thine often infirmities. (1 Timothy 5:23)

Deacons likewise must be dignified, not double-tongued, not addicted to much wine, not greedy for dishonest gain. (1 Timothy 3:8)

The Son of man is come eating and drinking; and ye say, Behold a gluttonous man, and a winebibber, a friend of publicans and sinners! (Luke 7:34)

He that loveth pleasure shall be a poor man: he that loveth wine and oil shall not be rich. (Proverbs 21:17)

The aged women likewise, that they be in behavior as becometh holiness, not false accusers, not given to much wine, teachers of good things. (Titus 2:3)

It is not for kings, O Lemuel, it is not for kings to drink wine; nor for princes strong drink. (Proverbs 31:4)

He shall separate himself from wine and strong drink, and shall drink no vinegar of wine, or vinegar of strong drink, neither shall he drink any liquor of grapes, nor eat moist grapes, or dried. (Numbers 6:3)

And be not conformed to this world: but be ye transformed by the renewing of your mind, that ye may prove what is that good, and acceptable, and perfect, will of God. (Romans 12:2)

But he said unto me, Behold, thou shalt conceive, and bear a son; and now drink no wine nor strong drink, neither eat any unclean thing: for the child shall be a Nazarite to God from the womb to the day of his death. (Judges 13:7)

And went to him, and bound up his wounds, pouring in oil and wine, and set him on his own beast, and brought him to an inn, and took care of him. (Luke 10:34)

For he shall be great in the sight of the Lord, and shall drink neither wine nor strong drink; and he shall be filled with the Holy Ghost, even from his mother's womb. (Luke 1:15)

And he drank of the wine, and was drunken; and he was uncovered within his tent. (Genesis 9:21)

Whoredom and wine and new wine take away the heart. (Hosea 4:11)

But Daniel purposed in his heart that he would not defile himself with the portion of the king's meat, nor with the wine which he drank: therefore he requested of the prince of the eunuchs that he might not defile himself. (Daniel 1:8)

The words of king Lemuel, the prophecy that his mother taught him. What, my son? and what, the son of my womb? and what, the son of my vows? Give not thy strength unto women, nor thy ways to that which destroyeth kings. It is not for kings, O Lemuel, it is not for kings to drink wine; nor for princes strong drink: Lest they drink, and forget the law, and pervert the judgment of any of the afflicted. (Proverbs 31:1–31)

The words of king Lemuel, the prophecy that his mother taught him. What, my son? and what, the son of my womb? and what, the son of my vows? Give not thy strength unto women, nor thy ways to that which destroyeth kings. It is not for kings, O Lemuel, it is not for kings to drink wine; nor for princes strong drink: Lest they drink, and forget the law, and pervert the judgment of any of the afflicted. Give strong drink unto him that is ready to perish, and wine unto those that be of heavy hearts. (Proverbs 31:1–6)

The merciful man doeth good to his own soul: but he that is cruel troubleth his own flesh. (Proverbs 11:17)

And the LORD spake unto Moses, saying, Speak unto the children of Israel, and say unto them, When either man or woman shall separate themselves to vow a vow of a Nazarite, to separate themselves unto the LORD: He shall separate himself from wine and strong drink, and shall drink no vinegar of wine, or vinegar of strong drink, neither shall he drink any liquor of grapes, nor eat moist grapes, or dried. All the days of his separation shall he eat nothing that is made of the vine tree, from the kernels even to the husk. All the days of the vow of his separation there shall no razor come upon his head: until the days be fulfilled, in the which he separateth himself unto the LORD, he shall be holy, and shall let the locks of the hair of his head grow. (Numbers 6:1–27)

Principles

- Alcohol is not good for our relationship with God and others.
- Alcohol destroys families.
- Alcohol is not good for leaders.
- Alcohol causes us to lose good judgment.
- Alcohol may cause us to stumble in our walk with God.

CHAPTER 28

Homosexuality: The Constitution and The Bible

Every society has homosexuals regardless of geographical location. This is an issue we must understand socially, physically, and spiritually. Every family is affected by this issue in one way or another; we cannot ignore it. God has a lot to say about homosexuality and the Constitution as well. In his article "The Gay Rights Controversy," published by Exploring Constitutional Law, Doug Linder (2018) wrote this.

> Two Supreme Court decisions involving gay rights, one decade apart, have left a lot of people wondering just where the law now stands with respect to the right to engage in homosexual conduct. The Court first considered the matter in the 1986 case of Bowers v Hardwick, a challenge to a Georgia law authorizing criminal penalties for persons found guilty of sodomy. Although the Georgia law applied both to heterosexual and homosexual sodomy, the Supreme Court chose to consider only the constitutionality of applying the law to homosexual sodomy. Charges were later dropped.) In Bowers, the Court ruled 5 to 4 that the Due Process Clause "right of privacy" recognized in cases such Griswold and Roe does not prevent the criminalization of homosexual conduct between consenting adults. One of the five members of the majority, Justice Powell, later described his vote in the case as a mistake. (Interestingly, Powell's concurring opinion suggests that were Georgia to have imprisoned Hardwick for his conduct, that might be cruel and unusual punishment.) In 1999, the Georgia Supreme Court struck

down the statute first challenged in Bowers as a violation of the Georgia Constitution.

In 1996, the Supreme Court again considered gay rights issues in Romer v Evans, a challenge to a provision in the Colorado Constitution (adopted by a 54% to 46% vote) that prohibited the state or its subdivisions from adopting any laws that gave preferred or protected status to homosexuals. (The provision, Amendment 2, effectively repealed anti-discrimination laws in Boulder, Aspen, and Denver.) By a 6 to 3 vote, the Court found the Colorado provision to lack a rational basis, and therefore to violate the equal protection rights of homosexuals. Justice Kennedy's opinion concluded Amendment 2 was "born of animosity" toward gays.

The Supreme Court in 2003 considered a challenge to a Texas law that criminalized homosexual sodomy, but not heterosexual sodomy. The case, Lawrence v Texas, raised both substantive due process and equal protection issues. Voting 5 to 4, the Court overruled its earlier decision in Bowers v Hardwick and found that the state lacked a legitimate interest in regulating the private sexual conduct of consenting adults. Justice O'Connor added a sixth vote to overturn the conviction, but rested her decision solely on the Equal Protection Clause.

In 2013, in United States v Windsor, the Court invalidated a provision of the Defence of Marriage Act (DOMA) on the grounds that it violated the equal protection principles embodied in the Due Process Clause of the Fifth Amendment. In a 5 to 4 decision by Justice Kennedy, the Court said, "careful consideration" had to be given to "discriminations of unusual character." That, coupled with the deference that the federal government owes states with respect to how they define marriage, led to striking down the federal law that did not recognize same-sex marriage for federal purposes (e.g. joint filing of a tax return) even when a couple was lawfully married under state law.

In 2015, facing a circuit split, the Supreme Court resolved the question of whether state bans on gay marriage violated the Equal Protection and/or Due Process Clause of the 14th Amendment. In Obergefell v Hodges, a five-member Court majority concluded that the bans did indeed violate both 14 Amendment provisions. Writing for the Court, Justice Kennedy said the Framers of the Constitution "did not presume to know the extent of freedom in all of its dimensions, and so they entrusted future generations a charter protecting the right of all persons to enjoy liberty as me we learn its meaning." With "new insights" into liberty's meaning, "The Court now holds that same sex couples may exercise the fundamental right to marry." (http://law2.umkc.edu/faculty/projects/ftrials/conlaw/gayrights.htm)

What The Bible Says about Homosexuality

God's timeless Word reveals His plan for humanity and His intentions for marriage and sexuality. While scripture teaches that homosexual acts are sinful, these Bible verses aren't about condemning homosexuals, gays, lesbians, or transgender people. Rather, read God's loving warning and offer of grace for those who have strayed from His will for sex. We live in a fallen world with a fallen nature, but in Christ, we can be new creations.

> There is one lawgiver, who is able to save and to destroy: who art thou that judgest another? (James 4:12)

> Let brotherly love continue. Be not forgetful to entertain strangers: for thereby some have entertained angels unawares. Remember them that are in bonds, as bound with them; and them which suffer adversity, as being yourselves also in the body. Marriage is honorable in all, and the bed undefiled: but whoremongers and adulterers

God will judge. Let your conversation be without covetousness; and be content with such things as ye have: for he hath said, I will never leave thee, nor forsake thee. (Hebrews 13:1–5)

So when they continued asking him, he lifted up himself, and said unto them, He that is without sin among you, let him first cast a stone at her. And again he stooped down, and wrote on the ground. And they which heard it, being convicted by their own conscience, went out one by one, beginning at the eldest, even unto the last: and Jesus was left alone, and the woman standing in the midst. When Jesus had lifted up himself, and saw none but the woman, he said unto her, Woman, where are those thine accusers? hath no man condemned thee? She said, No man, Lord. And Jesus said unto her, Neither do I condemn thee: go, and sin no more. (John 8:7–11)

For this cause God gave them up unto vile affections: for even their women did change the natural use into that which is against nature: And likewise also the men, leaving the natural use of the woman, burned in their lust one toward another; men with men working that which is unseemly, and receiving in themselves that recompense of their error which was meet. And even as they did not like to retain God in their knowledge, God gave them over to a reprobate mind, to do those things which are not convenient. (Romans 1:26–28)

For all the law is fulfilled in one word, even in this; Thou shalt love thy neighbor as thyself. (Galatians 5:14)

I will therefore put you in remembrance, though ye once knew this, how that the Lord, having saved the people out of the land of Egypt, afterward destroyed them that believed not. And the angels which kept not their first estate, but left their own habitation, he hath reserved in everlasting chains under darkness unto the judgment of the great day. Even as Sodom and Gomorrah, and the cities about them in like manner, giving themselves over to fornication, and going after strange flesh, are set forth for an example, suffering the vengeance of eternal fire. Likewise also these filthy dreamers defile the flesh, despise dominion, and speak evil of dignities. (Jude 1:5–8)

But we know that the law is good, if a man use it lawfully; Knowing this, that the law is not made for a righteous man, but for the lawless and disobedient, for the ungodly and for sinners, for unholy and profane, for murderers of fathers and murderers of mothers, for manslayers, For whoremongers, for them that defile themselves with mankind, for menstealers, for liars, for perjured persons, and if there be any other thing that is contrary to sound doctrine; According to the glorious gospel of the blessed God, which was committed to my trust. (1 Timothy 1:8–11)

But from the beginning of the creation God made them male and female. For this cause shall a man leave his father and mother, and cleave to his wife; And they twain shall be one flesh: so then they are no more twain, but one flesh. What therefore God hath joined together, let not man put asunder. (Mark 10:6–9)

Nevertheless, to avoid fornication, let every man have his own wife, and let every woman have her own husband. (1 Corinthians 7:2)

Owe no man any thing, but to love one another: for he that loveth another hath fulfilled the law. For this, Thou shalt not commit adultery, Thou shalt not kill, Thou shalt not steal, Thou shalt not bear false witness, Thou shalt not covet; and if there be any other commandment, it is briefly comprehended in this saying, namely, Thou shalt love thy neighbor as thyself. Love worketh no ill to his neighbor: therefore love is the fulfilling of the law. (Romans 13:8–10)

> Know ye not that the unrighteous shall not inherit the Kingdom? Be not deceived: neither fornicators, nor idolaters, nor adulterers, nor effeminate, nor abusers of themselves with mankind, Nor thieves, nor covetous, nor drunkards, nor revilers, nor extortioners, shall inherit the Kingdom. And such were some of you: but ye are washed, but ye are sanctified, but ye are justified in the name of the Lord Jesus, and by the Spirit of our God. (1 Corinthians 6:9–11)

> Thou shalt not lie with mankind, as with womankind: it is abomination. (Leviticus 18:22)

> But he that is joined unto the Lord is one spirit. Flee fornication. Every sin that a man doeth is without the body; but he that committeth fornication sinneth against his own body. What? know ye not that your body is the temple of the Holy Ghost which is in you, which ye have of God, and ye are not your own? For ye are bought with a price: therefore glorify God in your body, and in your spirit, which are God's. (1 Corinthians 6:17–20)

> If a man also lie with mankind, as he lieth with a woman, both of them have committed an abomination: they shall surely be put to death; their blood shall be upon them. (Leviticus 20:13)

Principles

- We are sinners who must repent; we need a savior.
- Homosexuality is sin before God.
- Homosexuals can be saved by the grace of our Lord Jesus Christ
- Christ is available to save all sinners including homosexuals.
- Homosexuals can be freed from the sin of homosexuality once they are saved.
- God loves homosexuals just as all sinners but hates sin.

CHAPTER 29

Living and Exercising Our Rights as Christians

As we draw to the end of our discourse, the question remains: How do I exercise my rights are a Christian citizen? Andrew L. Seidel, a constitutional attorney and director of strategic response at the Freedom From Religion Foundation shares some interesting thoughts for the reader on this discourse.

"When Virginia ratified 10 of the 12 proposed amendments to the Constitution on December 15, 1791, it became the 10th state to do so and gifted America with an enduring legacy, the Bill of Rights. We celebrate that heritage today. But for President Trump and many religious Americans, those rights are not secured by the Constitution or "We the People." Instead, they are a gift from God. Trump is marking Bill of Rights Day and Human Rights Week with a proclamation that invoked our "God-given rights" three times. Trump has made similar claims many times, but so have other presidents, including President Obama. Roy Moore's entire career is based on his idea that "Our rights are given by God." He even argues that religious liberty "comes from God, not from the Constitution." Premising our rights on some supernatural benevolence is dangerous." (Andrew L. Seidel, December 15, 2017 "The Bill of Rights, Thomas Jefferson, and the danger of 'God-given rights' (https://religionnews.com/2017/12/15/the-bill-of-rights-thomas-jefferson-and-the-danger-of-god-given-rights/)

Bill Bright, the late director of Campus Crusade for Christ, expressed his ideas for the Christian in America when he wrote the following.

> Citizenship in a free country is a blessing from God. Our great system of self-government assures every Christian a voice in the affairs of the nation, and enables us to bring a heavenly perspective to the earthly realm. God wants us

to do His will in government, just as in the church and in the home. But too often we have disobeyed our Lord. We have ceased to be the "salt of the earth" and the "light of the world," as Christ has commanded us. As a result, the moral fiber of America is rotting away—and our priceless freedom is in grave jeopardy. Atheism is penetrating every area of our national life. America is faced with the greatest crisis in its history. We are in danger of losing our nation by default, and with it our individual freedoms and possibly our very lives. If that should happen, our opportunity to help fulfill the Great Commission throughout the United States and the world will also be lost. And hundreds of millions will never have an opportunity to receive our Savior. British statesman Edmund Burke said, "All that is necessary for the triumph of evil is for good men to do nothing." It has been reliably estimated that more than half of the people of the United States profess faith in Jesus Christ. By following the simple guidelines contained in this booklet, even a small percentage of us can be used by God to set this nation on a new course of righteousness for His glory. Charles Finney, who helped introduce half a million Americans to Christ, wrote in 1835:

The time has come that Christians must vote for honest men and take consistent ground in politics, or the Lord will curse them … God cannot sustain this free and blessed country, which we love and pray for, unless the Church will take right ground. Politics are a part of religion in such a country as this, and Christians must do their duty to the country as part of their duty to God … God will bless or curse this nation according to the course Christians take in politics.

Your Christian Citizen Checklist

Mark Twain understood the importance of a Christian's responsibility as a citizen. He wrote: "A Christian's first duty is to God. It then follows, as a matter of course, that it is his duty to carry his Christian code of morals to the polls and vote them ... If Christians should vote their duty to God at the polls, they would carry every election, and do it with ease ... it would bring about a moral revolution that would be incalculably beneficent. It would save the country."

- With so much at stake in our nation, honestly answer these questions about your role:
- Do I pray faithfully for a spiritual revival to sweep America?
- Am I registered to vote? Do I encourage other Christians to register?
- Am I making a serious effort, along with my Christian friends, to become informed about the candidates and issues?
- Am I actively involved in helping to select and elect godly candidates to office?

God's Plan for a Nation's Leadership

To protect His people, God warns against ungodly leaders. The rule of the wicked is a direct violation of His will. "The wicked shall not rule the godly, lest the godly be forced to do wrong" (Psalm 125:3). Instead, God's plan is for us to have leaders who know Him and will rule according to His Word. "He that ruleth over men must be just, ruling in the fear of God." (2 Samuel 23:3).

John Jay, first Chief Justice of the US Supreme Court, was one of the three men most responsible for drafting the Constitution. In 1816, he wrote:

"Providence has given to our people the choice of their rulers, and it is the duty—as well as the privilege and interest—of our Christian nation to select and prefer Christians for their rulers."

> Voting for and supporting moral candidates who support moral public policies is the mini- mum required of Christian citizens in a system of self-government. Godly people must vote for godly rulers. Christian lawyer Michael Whitehead put it this way: "If America is to be saved, saved Americans must lead the way." (http://voteundergod.com/files/Your_Five%20Duties_as_a_Christian_Citizen.pdf)

Knowing Your Government, Its Laws, and the Scope of Your Citizenship

Francis J Beckwith wrote,

> Scripture seems to teach that we have an obligation to understand the nature of our government and its laws and employ that knowledge so that the gospel is not disadvantaged by the state. According to Paul, Christians ought to obey generally applicable laws because they receive their authority from God. Thus, to disobey such laws is tantamount to disobeying God. Paul writes:
>
> Obey the rulers who have authority over you. Only God can give authority to anyone, and he puts these rulers in their places of power. People who oppose the authorities are opposing what God has done, and they will be punished. Rulers are a threat to evil people, not to good people. There is no need to be afraid of the authorities. Just do right, and they will praise you for it. After all, they are God's servants, and it is their duty to help you.
>
> In order to comply with Paul's instructions, one must be conversant with the laws of one's government and the rules and regulations that one is required to obey. The Apostle also rejects a consequentialist justification for this obedience. That is, he says that we should obey the law, not merely because we will be punished if we don't obey it, but rather, because "it is the right thing to do" *even if* we know that we won't be punished if we disobey.

Peter's Exhortation

The same Peter who courageously stood up for the gospel in the Book of Acts tells us in his first epistle that in this world we are "aliens and exiles," and that we ought to "having [our] conversation honest among the Gentiles [i.e., unbelievers], that, whereas they speak against [us] as evildoers, they may be [our] good works, which they shall behold, glorify God in the day of visitation." (1 Peter 2:11–12). Peter goes on to write:

Submit yourselves to every ordinance of man for the Lord's sake: whether it be to the king, as supreme; Or unto governors, as unto them that are sent by him for the punishment of evildoers, and for the praise of them that do well. For so is the will of God, that with well doing ye may put to silence the ignorance of foolish men: As free, and not using your liberty for a cloke of maliciousness, but as the servants of God. Honor all men. Love the brotherhood. Fear God. Honor the king. (1 Peter 2:13–17)

So, the Christian must use his freedom wisely and be honorable to his unbelieving neighbors as well as accept and respect the rule of law and the authorities put in place to protect it, all for the sake of the common good. In a liberal democracy, such as the United States, the Christian citizen has unprecedented access to the levers of power in comparison to his predecessors in the ancient and medieval worlds. Thus, Peter's instructions, as well as the example set by the apostles in Acts, may have more practical application in our modern age than at any time in the 1500 years following the establishment of the first-century church. (https://www.equip.org/article/the-christian-citizen/)

What Legal Rights Do Christians Have?

The magazine *Trustworthy Word*, which was born out of a desire to equip churches with handouts as a resource for biblical teaching on various topics, gives crucial advice to Christians in the following text.

Know Your Rights as a Christian in America

Christians have certain religious rights and freedoms in America. It is important for Christians know their rights and freedoms are so that they can practice, share, and model their faith wherever they are allowed. They need to recognize and respect limits set within their workplace but not be intimidated into silence or disobedience to God's command to "be my witnesses" (Acts 1:8).

Below are links to and quotes from help documents by the American Center for Law & Justice

Bibles and Bible studies in the workplace:
(http://media.aclj.org/pdf/Bibles-and-Bible-Studies-in-the-Workplace.pdf) [29]

"In sum, the First Amendment does not require the censorship of private religious speech in the workplace. It protects such religious expression from government censorship. The ACLJ strongly encourages individuals to meet for voluntary Bible study during nonworking hours."

Religious Expression in the workplace:
(http://media.aclj.org/pdf/2-Religious-Expression-in-the-Workplace-Formatted.pdf) [35]

"Furthermore, employers can even hold regular devotional or prayer meetings for employees so long as attendance is not required. ... Moreover, active participation of management in these meetings does not make them discriminatory. ... To ensure that employees understand that devotional meetings are voluntary, notice of the meetings should state that they are not mandatory and it is a good idea to hold these meetings before the work day begins, during breaks, or after work."

"In sum, prayer is not illegal, unauthorized, inappropriate, nor improper—and as long as employees pray before or after work hours, or during official breaks, there should be no problem at all. In addition, employers are required to provide reasonable accommodation to employees' religious beliefs."

Sharing Your Faith and Witnessing:
(http://media.aclj.org/pdf/Sharing-Your-Faith-Witnessing.pdf).[32]

"The streets and sidewalks of the United States are an open forum for evangelism. The Constitution guarantees the right to preach the Gospel in public places."

"When you give away religious tracts in public places—streets, sidewalks, and parks—you are engaged in a form of speech and publication protected by the United States Constitution and civil rights laws. When you speak with someone about the Gospel while in a public place, you enjoy constitutional protection."

"Giving away free Gospel tracts and talking to people about salvation are not the same thing as soliciting. The Supreme Court has held that there is a difference between soliciting and leafleting. … As long as you are giving away your literature for free, and not asking for donations, you are engaging in the most protected form of speech."

"If I am witnessing on the public sidewalk in front of a business, am I "loitering," and can I be required to move away from the business? No! "Loitering" is the criminal offense of remaining in a certain place (such as a public street) for no apparent reason."

Sharing Your Faith and Witnessing in School:
(http://media.aclj.org/pdf/Sharing-Your-Faith-Witnessing-at-School.pdf) [34]

"Students' First Amendment rights include the right to distribute Gospel tracts during non-instructional time, the right to wear shirts with overtly Christian messages and symbols, and the right to pray and discuss matters of religion with others. Further, schools may not prevent students from bringing their Bibles to school."

Student Free Speech Rights:
(http://media.aclj.org/pdf/Student-Free-Speech-Rights.pdf) [30]

"The fact is, however, from the moment they step onto the public school campus to the moment they graduate, public school students enjoy substantial rights to free speech, free press, assembly and religion. ... students have the right to discuss religious beliefs, and even share religious materials, with their peers between classes, at break, at lunch, and before and after school. The Supreme Court has also clearly established the right of students to organize and participate in Bible clubs."

Student Rights at Graduation and School Events:
(http://media.aclj.org/pdf/1-Student-Rights-at-Graduation,-School-Events.pdf)

"Are valedictorians and salutatorians permitted to make religious remarks as a part of their speeches Yes, although such remarks must be "non-proselytizing" and "non-sectarian" in some jurisdictions."

Teacher and Administrator Rights and Responsibilities (http://media.aclj.org/pdf/1-Teacher,-Administrator-Rights-&-Responsibilities.pdf)[1]

"Moreover, the Establishment Clause does not prohibit all religious instruction in public schools. "The Bible may constitutionally be used in an appropriate study of history, civilization, ethics, comparative religion, or the like." … In fact, the Supreme Court has recognized that "it might well be said that one's education is not complete without a study of comparative religion or the history of religion and its relationship to the advancement of civilization."

"Thus, teachers can teach about and/or distribute material with religious content for educational purposes. In addition, teachers may discuss religious matters with their students on an individual basis if the student initiates the topic, the student is not compelled or forced to discuss the topic, and the student is not compelled to accept the teacher's views."

"Thus, teachers have "the right to discuss alternate theories of the creation of life and could independently research such topics." … However, teachers have a responsibility to teach the curriculum in the manner designated by their superiors. … Furthermore, teachers may not refuse to teach a subject with which he or she disagrees when that subject is specifically prescribed by the curriculum the teacher has been hired to teach."

So they called them and charged them not to speak or teach at all in the name of Jesus. But Peter and John answered them, "Whether it be right in the sight of God to hearken unto you more than unto God, judge ye. For we cannot but speak the things which we have seen and heard." (Acts 4:18–20) (http://www.trustworthyword.com/what-legal-rights-do-christians-have/)

Christians should be guided by the Bible, the Word of God, or His Covenant with them in exercising their rights so they can live peaceably in their pursuit of life, liberty, and happiness under human authority and still express full respect for the principles espoused by the Bible.

It is my prayer that reader will find comfort in knowing that their allegiance to God cannot be compromised by the dictates of temporary earthly demands of humankind through constitutionally designed rights and privileges. Christians are accountable to a higher power, that is God who demands total obedience to His Constitution, The Bible.. Life is eternal, and God comes first in our earthly existence, social, economic and political decisions and choices. In **Joshua 1:8** King James Version (**KJV**). God says, "This book of the law shall not depart out of thy mouth; but thou shalt meditate therein day and night, that thou mayest observe to do according to all that is written therein: for then thou shalt make thy way prosperous, and then thou shalt have good success."

APPENDIX 1

US Constitution

Preamble

We the People of the United States, in Order to form a more perfect Union, establish Justice, insure domestic Tranquillity, provide for the common defence, promote the general Welfare, and secure the Blessings of Liberty to ourselves and our Posterity, do ordain and establish this Constitution for the United States of America.

Article I

Section 1

All legislative Powers herein granted shall be vested in a Congress of the United States, which shall consist of a Senate and House of Representatives.

Section 2

The House of Representatives shall be composed of Members chosen every second Year by the People of the several States, and the Electors in each State shall have the Qualifications requisite for Electors of the most numerous Branch of the State Legislature.

No Person shall be a Representative who shall not have attained to the Age of twenty five Years, and been seven Years a Citizen of the United States, and who shall not, when elected, be an Inhabitant of that State in which he shall be chosen.

Representatives and direct Taxes shall be apportioned among the several States which may be included within this Union, according to their respective Numbers, which shall be determined by adding to the whole Number of free Persons, including those bound to Service for a Term of Years, and excluding Indians not taxed, three fifths of all other Persons. (Note: changed by section 2 of the Fourteenth Amendment.) The actual Enumeration shall be made within three Years after the first Meeting of the Congress of the United States, and within every subsequent Term of ten Years, in such Manner as they shall by Law direct. The Number of Representatives shall not exceed one for every thirty Thousand, but each State shall have at Least one Representative; and until such enumeration shall be made, the State of New Hampshire shall be entitled to choose three, Massachusetts eight, Rhode-Island and Providence Plantations one, Connecticut five, New-York six, New Jersey four, Pennsylvania eight, Delaware one, Maryland six, Virginia ten, North Carolina five, South Carolina five, and Georgia three.

When vacancies happen in the Representation from any State, the Executive Authority thereof shall issue Writs of Election to fill such Vacancies.

The House of Representatives shall choose their Speaker and other Officers; and shall have the sole Power of Impeachment.

Section 3

The Senate of the United States shall be composed of two Senators from each State, chosen by the Legislature thereof (Note: changed by the Seventeenth Amendment.) for six Years; and each Senator shall have one Vote.

Immediately after they shall be assembled in Consequence of the first Election, they shall be divided as equally as may be into three Classes. The Seats of the Senators of the first Class shall be vacated at the Expiration of the second Year, of the second Class at the Expiration of the fourth Year, and of the third Class at the Expiration of the sixth Year, so that one third may be chosen every second Year; and if Vacancies happen by Resignation, or otherwise, during the Recess of the Legislature of any State, the Executive thereof may make temporary Appointments until the next Meeting of the Legislature, which shall then fill such Vacancies. (Note: changed by the Seventeenth Amendment.)

No Person shall be a Senator who shall not have attained to the Age of thirty Years, and been nine Years a Citizen of the United States, and who shall not, when elected, be an Inhabitant of that State for which he shall be chosen.

The Vice President of the United States shall be President of the Senate, but shall have no Vote, unless they are equally divided.

The Senate shall choose their other Officers, and also a President pro tempore, in the Absence of the Vice President, or when he shall exercise the Office of President of the United States.

The Senate shall have the sole Power to try all Impeachments. When sitting for that Purpose, they shall be on Oath or Affirmation. When the President of the United States is tried, the Chief Justice shall preside: And no Person shall be convicted without the Concurrence of two thirds of the Members present.

Judgment in Cases of Impeachment shall not extend further than to removal from Office, and disqualification to hold and enjoy any Office of honor, Trust or Profit under the United States: but the Party convicted shall nevertheless be liable and subject to Indictment, Trial, Judgment and Punishment, according to Law.

Section 4

The Times, Places and Manner of holding Elections for Senators and Representatives, shall be prescribed in each State by the Legislature thereof; but the Congress may at any time by Law make or alter such Regulations, except as to the Places of choosing Senators.

The Congress shall assemble at least once in every Year, and such Meeting shall be on the first Monday in December (Changed by section 2 of the Twentieth Amendment.) unless they shall by Law appoint a different Day.

Section 5

Each House shall be the Judge of the Elections, Returns and Qualifications of its own Members, and a Majority of each shall constitute a Quorum to do Business; but a smaller Number may adjourn from day to day, and may be authorized to compel the Attendance of absent Members, in such Manner, and under such Penalties as each House may provide.

Each House may determine the Rules of its Proceedings, punish its

Members for disorderly Behavior, and, with the Concurrence of two thirds, expel a Member.

Each House shall keep a Journal of its Proceedings, and from time to time publish the same, excepting such Parts as may in their Judgment require Secrecy; and the Yeas and Nays of the Members of either House on any question shall, at the Desire of one fifth of those Present, be entered on the Journal.

Neither House, during the Session of Congress, shall, without the Consent of the other, adjourn for more than three days, nor to any other Place than that in which the two Houses shall be sitting.

Section 6

The Senators and Representatives shall receive a Compensation for their Services, to be ascertained by Law, and paid out of the Treasury of the United States. They shall in all Cases, except Treason, Felony and Breach of the Peace, be privileged from Arrest during their Attendance at the Session of their respective Houses, and in going to and returning from the same; and for any Speech or Debate in either House, they shall not be questioned in any other Place.

No Senator or Representative shall, during the Time for which he was elected, be appointed to any civil Office under the Authority of the United States, which shall have been created, or the Emoluments whereof shall have been increased during such time; and no Person holding any Office under the United States, shall be a Member of either House during his Continuance in Office.

Section 7

All Bills for raising Revenue shall originate in the House of Representatives; but the Senate may propose or concur with Amendments as on other Bills.

Every Bill which shall have passed the House of Representatives and the Senate, shall, before it become a Law, be presented to the President of the United States; If he approve he shall sign it, but if not he shall return it, with his Objections to that House in which it shall have originated, who shall enter the Objections at large on their Journal, and proceed to reconsider it. If after such Reconsideration two thirds of that House shall agree to pass the Bill, it shall be sent, together with the Objections, to the other House, by which it shall likewise be reconsidered, and if approved by two thirds of that House, it shall become a Law. But in all such Cases the Votes of both Houses shall be determined by yeas and Nays, and the Names of the Persons voting for and against the Bill shall be entered on the Journal of each House respectively. If any Bill shall not be returned by the President within ten Days (Sundays excepted) after it shall have been presented to him, the Same shall be a Law, in like Manner as if he had signed it, unless the Congress by their Adjournment prevent its Return, in which Case it shall not be a Law.

Every Order, Resolution, or Vote to which the Concurrence of the Senate and House of Representatives may be necessary (except on a question of Adjournment) shall be presented to the President of the United States; and before the Same shall take Effect, shall be approved by him, or being disapproved by him, shall be passed by two thirds of the Senate and House of Representatives, according to the Rules and Limitations prescribed in the Case of a Bill.

Section 8

The Congress shall have Power To lay and collect Taxes, Duties, Imposts and Excises, to pay the Debts and provide for the common Defence and general Welfare of the United States; but all Duties, Imposts and Excises shall be uniform throughout the United States;

To borrow Money on the credit of the United States;

To regulate Commerce with foreign Nations, and among the several States, and with the Indian Tribes;

To establish an uniform Rule of Naturalization, and uniform Laws on the subject of Bankruptcies throughout the United States;

To coin Money, regulate the Value thereof, and of foreign Coin, and fix the Standard of Weights and Measures;

To provide for the Punishment of counterfeiting the Securities and current Coin of the United States;

To establish Post Offices and post Roads;

To promote the Progress of Science and useful Arts, by securing for limited Times to Authors and Inventors the exclusive Right to their respective Writings and Discoveries;

To constitute Tribunals inferior to the supreme Court;

To define and punish Piracies and Felonies committed on the high Seas, and Offences against the Law of Nations;

To declare War, grant Letters of Marque and Reprisal, and make Rules concerning Captures on Land and Water;

To raise and support Armies, but no Appropriation of Money to that Use shall be for a longer Term than two Years;

To provide and maintain a Navy;

To make Rules for the Government and Regulation of the land and naval Forces;

To provide for calling forth the Militia to execute the Laws of the Union, suppress Insurrections and repel Invasions;

To provide for organizing, arming, and disciplining, the Militia, and for governing such Part of them as may be employed in the Service of the United States, reserving to the States respectively, the Appointment of the Officers, and the Authority of training the Militia according to the discipline prescribed by Congress;

To exercise exclusive Legislation in all Cases whatsoever, over such District (not exceeding ten Miles square) as may, by Cession of particular States, and the Acceptance of Congress, become the Seat of the Government of the United States, and to exercise like Authority over all Places purchased by the Consent of the Legislature of the State in which the Same shall be, for the Erection of Forts, Magazines, Arsenals, dock-Yards, and other needful Buildings;—And

To make all Laws which shall be necessary and proper for carrying into Execution the foregoing Powers, and all other Powers vested by this Constitution in the Government of the United States, or in any Department or Officer thereof.

Section 9

The Migration or Importation of such Persons as any of the States now existing shall think proper to admit, shall not be prohibited by the Congress prior to the Year one thousand eight hundred and eight, but a Tax or duty may be imposed on such Importation, not exceeding ten dollars for each Person.

The Privilege of the Writ of Habeas Corpus shall not be suspended, unless when in Cases of Rebellion or Invasion the public Safety may require it.

No Bill of Attainder or ex post facto Law shall be passed.

No Capitation, or other direct, Tax shall be laid, unless in Proportion to the Census or Enumeration herein before directed to be taken. (Note: see the Sixteenth Amendment.)

No Tax or Duty shall be laid on Articles exported from any State.

No Preference shall be given by any Regulation of Commerce or Revenue to the Ports of one State over those of another: nor shall Vessels bound to, or from, one State, be obliged to enter, clear, or pay Duties in another.

No Money shall be drawn from the Treasury, but in Consequence of Appropriations made by Law; and a regular Statement and Account of the Receipts and Expenditures of all public Money shall be published from time to time.

No Title of Nobility shall be granted by the United States: And no Person holding any Office of Profit or Trust under them, shall, without the Consent of the Congress, accept of any present, Emolument, Office, or Title, of any kind whatever, from any King, Prince, or foreign State.

Section 10

No State shall enter into any Treaty, Alliance, or Confederation; grant Letters of Marque and Reprisal; coin Money; emit Bills of Credit; make any Thing but gold and silver Coin a Tender in Payment of Debts; pass any Bill of Attainder, ex post facto Law, or Law impairing the Obligation of Contracts, or grant any Title of Nobility.

No State shall, without the Consent of the Congress, lay any Imposts or Duties on Imports or Exports, except what may be absolutely necessary for executing it's inspection Laws: and the net Produce of all Duties and Imposts, laid by any State on Imports or Exports, shall be for the Use of the Treasury of the United States; and all such Laws shall be subject to the Revision and Control of the Congress.

No State shall, without the Consent of Congress, lay any Duty of Tonnage, keep Troops, or Ships of War in time of Peace, enter into any Agreement or Compact with another State, or with a foreign Power, or engage in War, unless actually invaded, or in such imminent Danger as will not admit of delay.

Article II

Section 1

The executive Power shall be vested in a President of the United States of America. He shall hold his Office during the Term of four Years, and, together with the Vice President, chosen for the same Term, be elected, as follows

Each State shall appoint, in such Manner as the Legislature thereof may direct, a Number of Electors, equal to the whole Number of Senators and Representatives to which the State may be entitled in the Congress: but no Senator or Representative, or Person holding an Office of Trust or Profit under the United States, shall be appointed an Elector.

The Electors shall meet in their respective States, and vote by Ballot for two Persons, of whom one at least shall not be an Inhabitant of the same State with themselves. And they shall make a List of all the Persons voted for, and of the Number of Votes for each; which List they shall sign and certify, and transmit sealed to the Seat of the Government of the United States, directed to the President of the Senate. The President of the Senate shall, in the Presence of the Senate and House of Representatives, open all the Certificates, and the Votes shall then be counted. The Person having the greatest Number of Votes shall be the President, if such Number be a Majority of the whole Number of Electors appointed; and if there be more than one who have such Majority, and have an equal Number of Votes, then the House of Representatives shall immediately choose by Ballot one of them for President; and if no Person have a Majority, then from the five highest on the List the said House shall in like Manner choose the President. But in choosing the President, the Votes shall be taken by States, the Representation from each State having one Vote; a quorum for this Purpose shall consist of a Member or Members from two thirds of the States, and a Majority of all the States shall be necessary to a Choice. In every Case, after the Choice of the President, the Person having the greatest Number of Votes of the Electors shall be the Vice President. But if there should remain two or more who have equal Votes, the Senate shall choose from them by Ballot the Vice President. (Note: changed by the Twelfth Amendment.)

The Congress may determine the Time of choosing the Electors, and the Day on which they shall give their Votes; which Day shall be the same throughout the United States.

No Person except a natural born Citizen, or a Citizen of the United States, at the time of the Adoption of this Constitution, shall be eligible to the Office of President; neither shall any Person be eligible to that Office who shall not have attained to the Age of thirty five Years, and been fourteen Years a Resident within the United States.

In Case of the Removal of the President from Office, or of his Death, Resignation, or Inability to discharge the Powers and Duties of the said Office, the Same shall devolve on the Vice President, and the Congress may by Law provide for the Case of Removal, Death, Resignation or Inability, both of the President and Vice President, declaring what Officer shall then act as President, and such Officer shall act accordingly, until the Disability be removed, or a President shall be elected. (Note: changed by the Twenty-Fifth Amendment.)

The President shall, at stated Times, receive for his Services, a Compensation, which shall neither be increased nor diminished during the Period for which he shall have been elected, and he shall not receive within that Period any other Emolument from the United States, or any of them.

Before he enter on the Execution of his Office, he shall take the following Oath or Affirmation:—"I do solemnly swear (or affirm) that I will faithfully execute the Office of President of the United States, and will to the best of my Ability, preserve, protect and defend the Constitution of the United States."

Section 2

The President shall be Commander in Chief of the Army and Navy of the United States, and of the Militia of the several States, when called into the actual Service of the United States; he may require the Opinion, in writing, of the principal Officer in each of the executive Departments, upon any Subject relating to the Duties of their respective Offices, and he shall have Power to grant Reprieves and Pardons for Offences against the United States, except in Cases of Impeachment.

He shall have Power, by and with the Advice and Consent of the Senate, to make Treaties, provided two thirds of the Senators present concur; and he shall nominate, and by and with the Advice and Consent of the Senate, shall appoint Ambassadors, other public Ministers and Consuls, Judges of the supreme Court, and all other Officers of the United States, whose Appointments are not herein otherwise provided for, and which shall be established by Law: but the Congress may by Law vest the Appointment of such inferior Officers, as they think proper, in the President alone, in the Courts of Law, or in the Heads of Departments.

The President shall have Power to fill up all Vacancies that may happen during the Recess of the Senate, by granting Commissions which shall expire at the End of their next Session.

Section 3

He shall from time to time give to the Congress Information of the State of the Union, and recommend to their Consideration such Measures as he shall judge necessary and expedient; he may, on extraordinary Occasions, convene both Houses, or either of them, and in Case of Disagreement between them, with Respect to the Time of Adjournment, he may adjourn them to such Time as he shall think proper; he shall receive Ambassadors and other public Ministers; he shall take Care that the Laws be faithfully executed, and shall Commission all the Officers of the United States.

Section 4

The President, Vice President and all civil Officers of the United States, shall be removed from Office on Impeachment for, and Conviction of, Treason, Bribery, or other high Crimes and Misdemeanors.

Article III

Section 1

The judicial Power of the United States shall be vested in one supreme Court and in such inferior Courts as the Congress may from time to time ordain and establish. The Judges, both of the supreme and inferior Courts, shall hold their Offices during good Behavior, and shall, at stated Times, receive for their Services, a Compensation, which shall not be diminished during their Continuance in Office.

Section 2

The judicial Power shall extend to all Cases, in Law and Equity, arising under this Constitution, the Laws of the United States, and Treaties made, or which shall be made, under their Authority;—to all Cases affecting Ambassadors, other public Ministers and Consuls;—to all Cases of admiralty and maritime Jurisdiction;—to Controversies to which the United States shall be a Party;—to Controversies between two or more States;—between a State and Citizens of another State; (Note: changed by the Eleventh Amendment.)—between Citizens of different States, —between Citizens of the same State claiming Lands under Grants of different States, and between a State, or the Citizens thereof, and foreign States, Citizens or Subjects. (Note: changed by the Eleventh Amendment.)

In all Cases affecting Ambassadors, other public Ministers and Consuls, and those in which a State shall be Party, the supreme Court shall have original Jurisdiction. In all the other Cases before mentioned, the supreme Court shall have appellate Jurisdiction, both as to Law and Fact, with such Exceptions, and under such Regulations as the Congress shall make.

The Trial of all Crimes, except in Cases of Impeachment, shall be by Jury; and such Trial shall be held in the State where the said Crimes shall have been committed; but when not committed within any State, the Trial shall be at such Place or Places as the Congress may by Law have directed.

Section 3

Treason against the United States shall consist only in levying War against them, or in adhering to their Enemies, giving them Aid and Comfort. No Person shall be convicted of Treason unless on the Testimony of two Witnesses to the same overt Act, or on Confession in open Court.

The Congress shall have Power to declare the Punishment of Treason, but no Attainder of Treason shall work Corruption of Blood, or Forfeiture except during the Life of the Person attainted.

Article IV

Section 1

Full Faith and Credit shall be given in each State to the public Acts, Records, and judicial Proceedings of every other State. And the Congress may by general Laws prescribe the Manner in which such Acts, Records and Proceedings shall be proved, and the Effect thereof.

Section 2

The Citizens of each State shall be entitled to all Privileges and Immunities of Citizens in the several States.

A Person charged in any State with Treason, Felony, or other Crime, who shall flee from Justice, and be found in another State, shall on Demand of the executive Authority of the State from which he fled, be delivered up, to be removed to the State having Jurisdiction of the Crime.

No Person held to Service or Labor in one State, under the Laws thereof, escaping into another, shall, in Consequence of any Law or Regulation therein, be discharged from such Service or Labor, but shall be delivered up on Claim of the Party to whom such Service or Labor may be due. (Note: changed by the Thirteenth Amendment.)

Section 3

New States may be admitted by the Congress into this Union; but no new State shall be formed or erected within the Jurisdiction of any other State; nor any State be formed by the Junction of two or more States, or Parts of States, without the Consent of the Legislatures of the States concerned as well as of the Congress.

The Congress shall have Power to dispose of and make all needful Rules and Regulations respecting the Territory or other Property belonging to the United States; and nothing in this Constitution shall be so construed as to Prejudice any Claims of the United States, or of any particular State.

Section 4

The United States shall guarantee to every State in this Union a Republican Form of Government, and shall protect each of them against Invasion; and on Application of the Legislature, or of the Executive (when the Legislature cannot be convened) against domestic Violence.

Article V

The Congress, whenever two thirds of both Houses shall deem it necessary, shall propose Amendments to this Constitution, or, on the Application of the Legislatures of two thirds of the several States, shall call a Convention for proposing Amendments, which, in either Case, shall be valid to all Intents and Purposes, as Part of this Constitution, when ratified by the Legislatures of three fourths of the several States, or by Conventions in three fourths thereof, as the one or the other Mode of Ratification may be proposed by the Congress; Provided that no Amendment which may be made prior to the Year One thousand eight hundred and eight shall in any Manner affect the first and fourth Clauses in the Ninth Section of the first Article; and that no State, without its Consent, shall be deprived of its equal Suffrage in the Senate.

Article VI

All Debts contracted and Engagements entered into, before the Adoption of this Constitution, shall be as valid against the United States under this Constitution, as under the Confederation.

This Constitution, and the Laws of the United States which shall be made in Pursuance thereof; and all Treaties made, or which shall be made, under the Authority of the United States, shall be the supreme Law of the Land; and the Judges in every State shall be bound thereby, any Thing in the Constitution or Laws of any State to the Contrary notwithstanding.

The Senators and Representatives before mentioned, and the Members of the several State Legislatures, and all executive and judicial Officers, both of the United States and of the several States, shall be bound by Oath or Affirmation, to support this Constitution; but no religious Test shall ever be required as a Qualification to any Office or public Trust under the United States.

Article VII

The ratification of the conventions of nine states shall be sufficient for the establishment of this Constitution between the states so ratifying the same.

Bill of Rights: Amendments I–X

Amendment I

Congress shall make no law respecting an establishment of religion, or prohibiting the free exercise thereof; or abridging the freedom of speech, or of the press; or the right of the people peaceably to assemble, and to petition the Government for a redress of grievances.

Amendment II

A well regulated Militia, being necessary to the security of a free State, the right of the people to keep and bear Arms, shall not be infringed.

Amendment III

No Soldier shall, in time of peace be quartered in any house, without the consent of the Owner, nor in time of war, but in a manner to be prescribed by law.

Amendment IV

The right of the people to be secure in their persons, houses, papers, and effects, against unreasonable searches and seizures, shall not be violated, and no Warrants shall issue, but upon probable cause, supported by Oath or affirmation, and particularly describing the place to be searched, and the persons or things to be seized.

Amendment V

No person shall be held to answer for a capital, or otherwise infamous crime, unless on a presentment or indictment of a Grand Jury, except in cases arising in the land or naval forces, or in the Militia, when in actual service in time of War or public danger; nor shall any person be subject for the same offense to be twice put in jeopardy of life or limb; nor shall be compelled in any criminal case to be a witness against himself, nor be deprived of life, liberty, or property, without due process of law; nor shall private property be taken for public use, without just compensation.

Amendment VI

In all criminal prosecutions, the accused shall enjoy the right to a speedy and public trial, by an impartial jury of the State and district wherein the crime shall have been committed, which district shall have been previously ascertained by law, and to be informed of the nature and cause of the accusation; to be confronted with the witnesses against him; to have compulsory process for obtaining witnesses in his favor, and to have the Assistance of Counsel for his defence.

Amendment VII

In Suits at common law, where the value in controversy shall exceed twenty dollars, the right of trial by jury shall be preserved, and no fact tried by a jury, shall be otherwise re-examined in any Court of the United States, than according to the rules of the common law.

Amendment VIII

Excessive bail shall not be required, nor excessive fines imposed, nor cruel and unusual punishments inflicted.

Amendment IX

The enumeration in the Constitution, of certain rights, shall not be construed to deny or disparage others retained by the people.

Amendment X

The powers not delegated to the United States by the Constitution, nor prohibited by it to the States, are reserved to the States respectively, or to the people.

Amendment XI

(Passed by Congress March 4, 1794. Ratified February 7, 1795; Article III, section 2, of the Constitution was modified by amendment 11.)

The Judicial power of the United States shall not be construed to extend to any suit in law or equity, commenced or prosecuted against one of the United States by Citizens of another State, or by Citizens or Subjects of any Foreign State.

Amendment XII

(Passed by Congress December 9, 1803. Ratified June 15, 1804. (Note: A portion of Article II, section 1 of the Constitution was superseded by the 12th amendment.)

The Electors shall meet in their respective states and vote by ballot for President and Vice-President, one of whom, at least, shall not be an inhabitant of the same state with themselves; they shall name in their ballots the person voted for as President, and in distinct ballots the person voted for as Vice-President, and they shall make distinct lists of all persons voted for as President, and of all persons voted for as Vice-President, and of the number of votes for each, which lists they shall sign and certify, and transmit sealed to the seat of the government of the United States, directed to the President of the Senate;—the President of the Senate shall, in the presence of the Senate and House of Representatives, open all the certificates and the votes shall then be counted;—The person having the greatest number of votes for President, shall be the President, if such number be a majority of the whole number of Electors appointed; and if no person have such majority, then from the persons having the highest numbers not exceeding three on the list of those voted for as President, the House of Representatives shall choose immediately, by ballot, the President. But in choosing the President, the votes shall be taken by states, the representation from each state having one vote; a quorum for this purpose shall consist of a member or members from two-thirds of the states and a majority of all the states shall be necessary to a choice. [And if the House of Representatives shall not choose a President whenever the right of choice shall devolve upon them, before the fourth day of March next following, then the Vice-President shall act as President, as in case of the death or other constitutional disability of the President. —]* The person having the greatest number of votes as Vice-President, shall be the Vice-President, if such number be a majority of the whole number of Electors appointed, and if no person have a majority, then from the two highest numbers on the list, the Senate shall choose the Vice-President; a quorum for the purpose shall consist of two-thirds of the whole number of Senators, and a majority of the whole number shall be necessary to a choice. But no person constitutionally ineligible to the office of President shall be eligible to that of Vice-President of the United States. (*Superseded by section 3 of the 20th amendment.)

Amendment XIII

(Passed by Congress January 31, 1865. Ratified December 6, 1865. A portion of Article IV, section 2, of the Constitution was superseded by the 13th amendment.)

Section 1

Neither slavery nor involuntary servitude, except as a punishment for crime whereof the party shall have been duly convicted, shall exist within the United States, or any place subject to their jurisdiction.

Section 2

Congress shall have power to enforce this article by appropriate legislation.

Amendment XIV

Passed by Congress June 13, 1866. Ratified July 9, 1868. Article I, section 2, of the Constitution was modified by section 2 of the 14th amendment.

Section 1

All persons born or naturalized in the United States, and subject to the jurisdiction thereof, are citizens of the United States and of the State wherein they reside. No State shall make or enforce any law which shall abridge the privileges or immunities of citizens of the United States; nor shall any State deprive any person of life, liberty, or property, without due process of law; nor deny to any person within its jurisdiction the equal protection of the laws.

Section 2

Representatives shall be apportioned among the several States according to their respective numbers, counting the whole number of persons in each State, excluding Indians not taxed. But when the right to vote at any election for the choice of electors for President and Vice-President of the United States, Representatives in Congress, the Executive and Judicial officers of a State, or the members of the Legislature thereof, is denied to any of the male inhabitants of such State, being twenty-one years of age,* and citizens of the United States, or in any way abridged, except for participation in rebellion, or other crime, the basis of representation therein shall be reduced in the proportion which the number of such male citizens shall bear to the whole number of male citizens twenty-one years of age in such State.

Section 3

No person shall be a Senator or Representative in Congress, or elector of President and Vice-President, or hold any office, civil or military, under the United States, or under any State, who, having previously taken an oath, as a member of Congress, or as an officer of the United States, or as a member of any State legislature, or as an executive or judicial officer of any State, to support the Constitution of the United States, shall have engaged in insurrection or rebellion against the same, or given aid or comfort to the enemies thereof. But Congress may by a vote of two-thirds of each House, remove such disability.

Section 4

The validity of the public debt of the United States, authorized by law, including debts incurred for payment of pensions and bounties for services in suppressing insurrection or rebellion, shall not be questioned. But neither the United States nor any State shall assume or pay any debt or obligation incurred in aid of insurrection or rebellion against the United

States, or any claim for the loss or emancipation of any slave; but all such debts, obligations and claims shall be held illegal and void.

Section 5

The Congress shall have the power to enforce, by appropriate legislation, the provisions of this article. (*Changed by section 1 of the 26th amendment.)

Amendment XV

(Passed by Congress February 26, 1869. Ratified February 3, 1870.)

Section 1

The right of citizens of the United States to vote shall not be denied or abridged by the United States or by any State on account of race, color, or previous condition of servitude—

Amendment XVI

(Passed by Congress July 2, 1909. Ratified February 3, 1913. Article I, section 9, of the Constitution was modified by amendment 16.)
The Congress shall have power to lay and collect taxes on incomes, from whatever source derived, without apportionment among the several States, and without regard to any census or enumeration.

AMENDMENT XVII

(Passed by Congress May 13, 1912. Ratified April 8, 1913. Article I, section 3, of the Constitution was modified by the 17th amendment.)

The Senate of the United States shall be composed of two Senators from each State, elected by the people thereof, for six years; and each Senator shall have one vote. The electors in each State shall have the qualifications requisite for electors of the most numerous branch of the State legislatures.

When vacancies happen in the representation of any State in the Senate, the executive authority of such State shall issue writs of election to fill such vacancies: Provided, That the legislature of any State may empower the executive thereof to make temporary appointments until the people fill the vacancies by election as the legislature may direct.

This amendment shall not be so construed as to affect the election or term of any Senator chosen before it becomes valid as part of the Constitution.

Amendment XVIII

(Passed by Congress December 18, 1917. Ratified January 16, 1919. Repealed by amendment 21.)

Section 1

After one year from the ratification of this article the manufacture, sale, or transportation of intoxicating liquors within, the importation thereof into, or the exportation thereof from the United States and all territory subject to the jurisdiction thereof for beverage purposes is hereby prohibited.

Section 2

The Congress and the several States shall have concurrent power to enforce this article by appropriate legislation.

Section 3

This article shall be inoperative unless it shall have been ratified as an amendment to the Constitution by the legislatures of the several States, as provided in the Constitution, within seven years from the date of the submission hereof to the States by the Congress.

Amendment XIX

(Passed by Congress June 4, 1919. Ratified August 18, 1920.)

The right of citizens of the United States to vote shall not be denied or abridged by the United States or by any State on account of sex.

Congress shall have power to enforce this article by appropriate legislation.

Amendment XX

(Passed by Congress March 2, 1932. Ratified January 23, 1933. Article I, section 4, of the Constitution was modified by section 2 of this amendment. In addition, a portion of the 12th amendment was superseded by section 3.)

Section 1

The terms of the President and the Vice President shall end at noon on the 20th day of January, and the terms of Senators and Representatives at noon on the 3d day of January, of the years in which such terms would have ended if this article had not been ratified; and the terms of their successors shall then begin.

Section 2

The Congress shall assemble at least once in every year, and such meeting shall begin at noon on the 3d day of January, unless they shall by law appoint a different day.

Section 3

If, at the time fixed for the beginning of the term of the President, the President elect shall have died, the Vice President elect shall become President. If a President shall not have been chosen before the time fixed for the beginning of his term, or if the President elect shall have failed to qualify, then the Vice President elect shall act as President until a President shall have qualified; and the Congress may by law provide for the case wherein neither a President elect nor a Vice President elect shall have qualified, declaring who shall then act as President, or the manner in which one who is to act shall be selected, and such person shall act accordingly until a President or Vice President shall have qualified.

Section 4

The Congress may by law provide for the case of the death of any of the persons from whom the House of Representatives may choose a President whenever the right of choice shall have devolved upon them, and for the case of the death of any of the persons from whom the Senate may choose a Vice President whenever the right of choice shall have devolved upon them.

Section 5

Sections 1 and 2 shall take effect on the 15th day of October following the ratification of this article.

Section 6

This article shall be inoperative unless it shall have been ratified as an amendment to the Constitution by the legislatures of three-fourths of the several States within seven years from the date of its submission.

Amendment XXI

(Passed by Congress February 20, 1933. Ratified December 5, 1933.)

Section 1

The eighteenth article of amendment to the Constitution of the United States is hereby repealed.

Section 2

The transportation or importation into any State, Territory, or possession of the United States for delivery or use therein of intoxicating liquors, in violation of the laws thereof, is hereby prohibited.

Section 3

This article shall be inoperative unless it shall have been ratified as an amendment to the Constitution by conventions in the several States, as provided in the Constitution, within seven years from the date of the submission hereof to the States by the Congress.

Amendment XXII

Passed by Congress March 21, 1947. Ratified February 27, 1951.

Section 1

No person shall be elected to the office of the President more than twice, and no person who has held the office of President, or acted as President, for more than two years of a term to which some other person was elected President shall be elected to the office of the President more than once. But this Article shall not apply to any person holding the office of President when this Article was proposed by the Congress, and shall not prevent any person who may be holding the office of President, or acting as President, during the term within which this Article becomes operative from holding the office of President or acting as President during the remainder of such term.

Section 2

This article shall be inoperative unless it shall have been ratified as an amendment to the Constitution by the legislatures of three-fourths of the several States within seven years from the date of its submission to the States by the Congress.

Amendment XXIII

(Passed by Congress June 16, 1960. Ratified March 29, 1961.)

Section 1

The District constituting the seat of Government of the United States shall appoint in such manner as the Congress may direct:

A number of electors of President and Vice President equal to the whole number of Senators and Representatives in Congress to which the District would be entitled if it were a State, but in no event more than the least populous State; they shall be in addition to those appointed by the States, but they shall be considered, for the purposes of the election of President and Vice President, to be electors appointed by a State; and they shall meet in the District and perform such duties as provided by the twelfth article of amendment.

Section 2

The Congress shall have power to enforce this article by appropriate legislation.

Amendment XXIV

(Passed by Congress August 27, 1962. Ratified January 23, 1964.)

Section 1

The right of citizens of the United States to vote in any primary or other election for President or Vice President, for electors for President or Vice President, or for Senator or Representative in Congress, shall not be denied or abridged by the United States or any State by reason of failure to pay any poll tax or other tax.

Section 2

The Congress shall have power to enforce this article by appropriate legislation.

Amendment XXV

(Passed by Congress July 6, 1965. Ratified February 10, 1967. Article II, section 1, of the Constitution was affected by the 25th amendment.)

Section 1

In case of the removal of the President from office or of his death or resignation, the Vice President shall become President.

Section 2

Whenever there is a vacancy in the office of the Vice President, the President shall nominate a Vice President who shall take office upon confirmation by a majority vote of both Houses of Congress.

Section 3

Whenever the President transmits to the President pro tempore of the Senate and the Speaker of the House of Representatives his written declaration that he is unable to discharge the powers and duties of his office, and until he transmits to them a written declaration to the contrary, such powers and duties shall be discharged by the Vice President as Acting President.

Section 4

Whenever the Vice President and a majority of either the principal officers of the executive departments or of such other body as Congress may by law provide, transmit to the President pro tempore of the Senate and the Speaker of the House of Representatives their written declaration that the President is unable to discharge the powers and duties of his office, the Vice President shall immediately assume the powers and duties of the office as Acting President.

Thereafter, when the President transmits to the President pro tempore of the Senate and the Speaker of the House of Representatives his written declaration that no inability exists, he shall resume the powers and duties of his office unless the Vice President and a majority of either the principal officers of the executive department or of such other body as Congress may by law provide, transmit within four days to the President pro tempore of the Senate and the Speaker of the House of Representatives their written declaration that the President is unable to discharge the powers and duties of his office. Thereupon Congress shall decide the issue, assembling within forty-eight hours for that purpose if not in session. If the Congress, within twenty-one days after receipt of the latter written declaration, or, if Congress is not in session, within twenty-one days after Congress is required to assemble, determines by two-thirds vote of both Houses that the President is unable to discharge the powers and duties of his office, the

Vice President shall continue to discharge the same as Acting President; otherwise, the President shall resume the powers and duties of his office.

Amendment XXVI

Passed by Congress March 23, 1971. Ratified July 1, 1971. Amendment 14, section 2, of the Constitution was modified by section 1 of the 26th amendment.

Section 1

The right of citizens of the United States, who are eighteen years of age or older, to vote shall not be denied or abridged by the United States or by any State on account of age.

Section 2

The Congress shall have power to enforce this article by appropriate legislation.

Amendment XXVII

(Originally proposed September 25, 1789. Ratified May 7, 1992.).

No law, varying the compensation for the services of the Senators and Representatives, shall take effect, until an election of Representatives shall have intervened.

APPENDIX 2

Summary of the Amendments to the Constitution

List of amendments to the United States Constitution, From Wikipedia, the free encyclopedia

No.	Subject
1st	Prohibits Congress from making any law respecting an establishment of religion, impeding the free exercise of religion, abridging the freedom of speech, infringing on the freedom of the press, interfering with the right to peaceably assemble or prohibiting the petitioning for a governmental redress of grievances.
2nd	A well regulated Militia, being necessary to the security of a free State, the right of the people to keep and bear Arms, shall not be infringed.
3rd	Places restrictions on the quartering of soldiers in private homes without the owner's consent, prohibiting it during peacetime.
4th	Prohibits unreasonable searches and seizures and sets out requirements for search warrants based on probable cause as determined by a neutral judge or magistrate.
5th	Sets out rules for indictment by grand jury and eminent domain, protects the right to due process, and prohibits self-incrimination and double jeopardy.
6th	Protects the right to a fair and speedy public trial by jury, including the rights to be notified of the accusations, to confront the accuser, to obtain witnesses and to retain counsel.

No.	Subject
7th	Provides for the right to trial by jury in certain civil cases, according to common law.
8th	Prohibits excessive fines and excessive bail, as well as cruel and unusual punishment.
9th	Protects rights not enumerated in the Constitution.
10th	Reinforces the principle of federalism by stating that the federal government possesses only those powers delegated to it by the states or the people through the Constitution.
11th	Makes states immune from suits from out-of-state citizens and foreigners not living within the state borders; lays the foundation for sovereign immunity.
12th	Revises presidential election procedures by having the President and Vice President elected together as opposed to the Vice President being the runner up.
13th	Abolishes slavery, and involuntary servitude, except as punishment for a crime.
14th	Defines citizenship, contains the Privileges or Immunities Clause, the Due Process Clause, the Equal Protection Clause, and deals with post–Civil War issues.
15th	Prohibits the denial of the right to vote based on race, color or previous condition of servitude.
16th	Permits Congress to levy an income tax without apportioning it among the states or basing it on the United States Census.
17th	Establishes the direct election of United States Senators by popular vote.
18th	Prohibited the manufacturing or sale of alcohol within the United States. (Repealed December 5, 1933, via 21st Amendment.)
19th	Prohibits the denial of the right to vote based on sex.
20th	Changes the date on which the terms of the President and Vice President (January 20) and Senators and Representatives (January 3) end and begin.

No.	Subject
21st	Repeals the 18th Amendment and makes it a federal offense to transport or import intoxicating liquors into US states and territories where such transport or importation is prohibited by the laws of those states and territories.
22nd	Limits the number of times that a person can be elected president: a person cannot be elected president more than twice, and a person who has served more than two years of a term to which someone else was elected cannot be elected more than once.
23rd	Grants the District of Columbia electors (the number of electors being equal to the least populous state) in the Electoral College.
24th	Prohibits the revocation of voting rights due to the non-payment of a poll tax or any other tax.
25th	Addresses succession to the Presidency and establishes procedures both for filling a vacancy in the office of the Vice President, as well as responding to Presidential disabilities.
26th	Prohibits the denial of the right of US citizens, eighteen years of age or older, to vote on account of age.
27th	Delays laws affecting Congressional salary from taking effect until after the next election of representatives.

NOTES

Abraham Lincoln, Speech, March30, 1863 "Proclamation Appointing A National Fast day" Washington D, C. http://www.abrahamlincolnonline.org/lincoln/speeches/fast.htm

"America's Changing Religious Landscape." Pew Research Center: Religion & Public Life. 5/12/2015.

"American Religious Identification Survey." CUNY Graduate Center. 2001; archived from the original on 7/9/2011; retrieved 6/17/2007.

Andrew L. Seidel, December 15, 2017 "The Bill of Rights, Thomas Jefferson, and the danger of 'God-given rights" (https://religionnews.com/2017/12/15/the-bill-of-rights-thomas-jefferson-and-the-danger-of-god-given-rights/)

"'No ones' on the Rise." Pew Research Center: Religion & Public Life. October 9, 2012.

The Doctrine of the Trinity - www.biblestudytools.com/bible-study/topical-studies/the-doctrine-of-the-trinity-11626770.html

Benjamin Franklin, (The writings of Benjamin Franklin, Boston and |London 1722-1726) https://www.beliefnet.com/resourcelib/docs/44/letter_from_benjamin_franklin_to_ezra_stiles_1.html

Bercovitch, Sacvan and Cyrus R. K. Patell. 1997. *The Cambridge History of American Literature: 1590–1820.* Cambridge University Press; https://books.google.com/books?id=s3j5JV–SEOMC&pg=PA196 196–97].

Barry, John M. 2012. "Roger Williams and the Creation of the American Soul." Smithsonian.

Bill Bright, 2002, "Your Five Duties As a Christian Citizen" Campus Crusade for Christ www.amazon.com › Christian Books & Bibles › Christian Living

Charles Hodge 1972) "The Church Is Everywhere Represented As One." Jonathan Lockwood Huie: *www.funny-quotes-life.com/quote/church-everywhere-represented-one...*

Finke, Roger, and Rodney Stark. 2005. *The Churching of America, 1776–2005.* Rutgers University Press, 22–23. Online at Google Books.

"U.S. on the History of "In God We Trust." United States Department of the Treasury; retrieved 4/22/2009.

Hall, Kermit, ed. 2005. *The Oxford Companion to the Supreme Court of the United States.* Archived 3/4/ 2016 at the Wayback Machine, 303–4.

Hamburger, Philip. 2004. *Separation of Church and State*; archived 6/24/2016 at the Wayback Machine; 287–334, 342.

Hall, Kermit, ed. 2005. *The Oxford Companion to the Supreme Court of the United States*; archived 3/4/2016 at the Wayback Machine, 262–63.

Hamilton, Neil A. 2002. *Rebels And Renegades: A Chronology of Social And Political Dissent In The United States.* Taylor & Francis, 11.

"*Gregg v. Georgia*", 1976. Landmark Cases: Historic Supreme Court Decisions, Volume 2"

John MacArthur, Truth Matters (Nashville, Tenn.: Thomas Nelson Publishers, 2004) 7-8. 33

Littlejohn, Bradford. 2012. "What does it mean to be a Christian Citizen?" The DAVENANT Institute.

Max Lucado, "*God Is with You Every Day*" 2015, 365-day Devotional, Grace for the Moment)

Land, Richard. "Citizen Christian: Their Rights and Responsibilities" September 2012.

Newport, Frank. 2015. "Percentage of Christians in U.S. Drifting Down, but Still High." Gallup; retrieved 3/5/2017.

US Public Health Service Commissioned Corps and the National Oceanic and Atmospheric Administration Commissioned Officer Corps.

"Quick Facts and Figures."Sss.gov. retrieved 10/17/2017.

"Wayback Machine" (PDF). Web.archive.org. archived from the original (PDF) on 9/5/2015; retrieved 10/18 2017.

Carl, Jonathan and Caleb Phelps. "What legal rights do Christians have?" Trustworthy WORD- www.trustworthyword.com/

"15 Fascinating Facts You Never Learned About America." Reader's Digest." rd.com.

"Let's Sea The 10 Biggest Navies In The World." TheRichest.com. 1/27/2014;

The Rutherford Institute:"Amendment III: The Quartering Amendment."

www.rutherford.org/constitutional_corner/amendment_iii_the_quartering_amendment

Beckwith, Francis J. 2011. "The Christian Citizen"; article ID: JAF4343, *Christian Research Journal*, vol. 34, no. 3 (2011).

Grudem, Systematic Theology, 1994, 255. (Grand Rapids: Zondervan and Leicester, England: InterVarsity). https://archive.org/details/SystematicTheologyAnIntroductionToBiblicalDoctrineGrudemWayne1994

...

ESV Study Bible. Wheaton, IL: Crossway Bibles, 2008. (Logos Bible Software edition) Center for Foreign Journalists. https://www.logos.com/product/5253/esv-study-bible

Pastor Michael Haley, *Daily Devotional, A Prescription For Peace, Part 3*, April 20, 2018. https://www.linkedin.com/in/pastor-mike-haley-a5864479

https://www.crosswalk.com/devotionals/daily-hope-with-rick-warren/...

http://media.aclj.org/pdf/Bibles-and-Bible-Studies-in-the-Workplace.pdf.

http://media.aclj.org/pdf/Student-Free-Speech-Rights.pdf.

http://media.aclj.org/pdf/1-Student-Rights-at-Graduation,-School-Events.pdf.

http://media.aclj.org/pdf/Sharing-Your-Faith-Witnessing.pdf.

http://media.aclj.org/pdf/1-Teacher,-Administrator-Rights-&-Responsibilities.pdf.

http://media.aclj.org/pdf/Sharing-Your-Faith-Witnessing-at-School.pdf.

http://media.aclj.org/pdf/2-Religious-Expression-in-the-Workplace-Formatted.pdf.

Perman, Matt. "What is the Doctrine of Trinity?" https://www.desiringgod.org/articles/what-is-the-doctrine-of-the-trinity.

Bancuk, Lisa A. "Right to Assemble"; https://www.learningtogive.org/resources/rightassemble.

National Center for Constitutional Studies, "Why Should We Study the Constitution?" Posted on 7/15/2014; https://nccsid.wordpress.com/2014/07/15/why-should-we-study-the-constitution/.

"Biblical Reasons to read The Bible." http://biblereasons.com/reasons-to-read-the-bible/

Trinity Bible Verses. https://overviewbible.com/trinity-bible-verses/.

Bible Gateway. www.biblegateway.com.

Faith Gateway. Devotionals Daily newsletter@e.faithgateway.com, 5/15/2018.

Ingraham, Christopher. "Alcoholism is on the rise." *The Washington Post,* August 2017.

Linder, Doug. 2018. "The Gay Rights Controversy" in *Exploring Constitutional Conflicts* law2.umkc.edu/faculty/projects/ftrials/conlaw/gayrights.htm

ABOUT THE AUTHOR

Morgan Chawawa is a lecturer at Botswana Open University. He teaches undergraduate and graduate courses on contemporary public administrative systems, organization behavior, and leadership. He worked at the University of Zimbabwe, Zimbabwe Open University, BA ISAGO University, and Botho University, Botswana.

He worked for the government of Zimbabwe as a district administrator and town clerk. His research and consulting activities focus on politics and community development issues. He has worked as a visiting scholar at Sunway University, Malaysia. He taught a political science course, "Introduction to the US Constitution," at Perimeter College, formerly DeKalb College, Atlanta, Georgia, USA and participated in the review of the textbook *Government by the People* in 1994, published by McGraw Hill.

He received a Bachelor of Science in urban government administration and a master's degree in public administration from Georgia State University in Atlanta. He is an ABD in political science at the same university.

He received a Doctor of Ministry from Immanuel Theological College in Georgia, and was an Adjunct Professor with the Baptist Theological College of South Africa and Rhema Bible College, Zimbabwe.

He is a born-again Christian. This was born out of his desire to establish the application of his faith to the US Constitution as a lecturer in Introduction to American Government courses and his having an African background. Having been baptized into Christianity, he developed a passion and hunger to live faithfully for God and find out whether Christians face conflict or compromise in living under God's Covenant, The Bible, and under the demands of the US Constitution as citizens of the United States.

CPSIA information can be obtained
at www.ICGtesting.com
Printed in the USA
BVHW081030150819
555975BV00001B/28/P

9 781973 653820